FORTY-NINER

FORTY-NINER

*The Extraordinary
Gold Rush Odyssey of
Joseph Goldsborough Bruff*

Ken Lizzio

THE COUNTRYMAN PRESS
A division of W. W. Norton & Company
Independent Publishers Since 1923

For information about permission to reproduce selections
from this book, write to Permissions, The Countryman Press,
500 Fifth Avenue, New York, NY 10110

For information about special discounts for bulk purchases,
please contact W. W. Norton Special Sales at
specialsales@wwnorton.com or 800-233-4830

Manufacturing by LSC Communications, Harrisonburg
Book design by Lovedog Studio
Production manager: Devon Zahn

The Countryman Press
www.countrymanpress.com

A division of W. W. Norton & Company, Inc.
500 Fifth Avenue, New York, NY 10110
www.wwnorton.com

978-1-68268-050-6

10 9 8 7 6 5 4 3 2 1

Hurrah for a trip o'er the plains,
No matter for clouds and rains,
'Go ahead' is the order that rules!

—*J. Goldsborough Bruff*

At our house at Burlington, we had a nice yard,
and plum trees, and peaches, and gooseberries:
and we could go a little ways, and get all them
things. Oh, how I miss em!

—*Billy, 6-year-old emigrant boy*

I wish California had sunk into the ocean
before I had ever heard of it.

—*James Wilkins, California 49er*

CONTENTS

PREFACE

I FIRST DISCOVERED THE REMARKABLE STORY OF Joseph Goldsborough Bruff, or J. Goldsborough Bruff as he preferred to sign himself, in Theodora Kroeber's *Ishi in Two Worlds*. Bruff never met Ishi, the celebrated "last wild Indian in North America," having left California a decade before Ishi was born. Their connection lay in the fact that on his way to the California gold fields in the winter of 1849, Bruff became marooned in the High Sierras in the territory of Ishi's forebears, the Yahi.

That year Bruff was one of nearly 90,000 individuals, American as well as foreign, who caught the gold fever and hastened over land and sea to California. Over the next four years, at least another 300,000 would make the journey in search of adventure, fortune, and a better life. Yet it was the first wave of Americans who went overland in 1849—some 35,000 of them—that came to define the California Gold Rush. The "49ers" were among the very first Americans to see and experience the American frontier with its primitive Indians and other natural curiosities such as the shaggy buffalo and the antelope. The tallgrass prairie, vast deserts, and soaring mountains described by early explorers promised landscapes unlike anything to be found in the East. For Bruff and countless other emigrants, the journey was expected to be an adventure every bit as exciting as the quest for gold.

Like dozens of other emigrants that year, Bruff kept a journal of his experiences along the emigrant trail and in the gold fields. That his journal is regarded as one of the most detailed and comprehensive that came out of the Gold Rush era makes it puzzling why his extraordinary story has never been told in its entirety, as Kroeber herself wondered.

By any measure, J.G. Bruff was an extraordinary man. A sailor, mapmaker, artist, writer of light verse, amateur geologist, Bruff could seemingly do anything and was interested in everything. He belonged to the Metropolitan Mechanics Institute and the Washington Monument Association. He served as Recording Secretary of the National Art Association before which he presented two papers and was a member of the National Institution for the Promotion of Science.

With such an open and inquisitive mind, Bruff's journal makes the perfect guide for life on the Gold Rush trail. With a keen eye for detail, each day he recorded meteorological data, the flora, fauna, and minerals of each region, and his experiences on the trail and in the gold fields. Over the course of the journey, with quill and inkpot, he made entries each day in a neat hand, an extraordinary accomplishment considering the arduous conditions of the trail, particularly the frigid Sierra winter. He made entries in his journal every day, testimony to his strength of will and character. He also drew more than 300 sketches of landscapes and aspects of life on the trail, many of which were the very first scenes of the American frontier such as the northern California coastline and the Klamath Indians.

As "Captain" of the Washington, DC, Gold Mining Company,

Bruff also ably led a large party of men across the dangerous and unfamiliar American frontier. His insistence on leading his party in the manner of a military expedition was unusual, but it proved key to the group's success. Day after day he resolved problems along the trail demonstrating wisdom, fairness, and above all concern for the welfare of his men and other travelers on the trail. At the end of each day, while the other men were resting from the day's exhausting march, the indefatigable Bruff was laying out the next day's trip and making entries and sketches in his journal by the light of the campfire. He reveled in his military role, however artificial, precisely because the real thing had tragically been denied him by life's circumstances.

As commander of the expedition, Bruff enforced a strict discipline that enabled him to keep a very diverse and at times fractious group of men together all the way to California. For this accomplishment—and this is what makes his story unique—he was repaid in the rudest of specie by his men: abandonment. Some of the men who resented being treated as subordinates left Bruff to starve in the High Sierras. Even the men who respected and supported Bruff showed little concern for his welfare that winter, so anxious were they to get to the gold fields. Such was the wanton selfishness that the Gold Rush inspired in almost everyone.

Bruff responded to the betrayal by his men in the same way he responded to that impossible and solitary winter in the Sierras: with stoicism, optimism, and generosity. Even as he struggled with hunger and his own failing health, he never stopped assisting hundreds of gold seekers worse off than himself. Whether they knew it or not, many of them owed their lives to the extraordinary man from Washington. Yet time and again, the very people he had helped selfishly disregarded his own pleas for assistance in getting off the mountain.

Bruff told his wife he would be gone for eight months and did not return for more than two years. During all that time, he faithfully recorded an entry in his journal every day on the trail, come hell or high water. Indeed, that many of those days were hell testified to a tragic truth about the Gold Rush: For many, if not most emigrants, the Gold Rush was a bust. Some never made it to California, having turned back or perished along the way from disease, accident, Indian attack, even suicide. If they were lucky enough to have made it to California, they usually had little luck in finding gold. Most returned to their previous lives disappointed, dispirited, and poorer for the experience.

Not Bruff, however. Even though he, too, failed to find gold, he turned his arduous journey into a trove of information and illustrations of the great American West that became a priceless treasure to those who followed him. In the end, it became the gold he mined.

FORTY-NINER

Bruff's Journey 1849

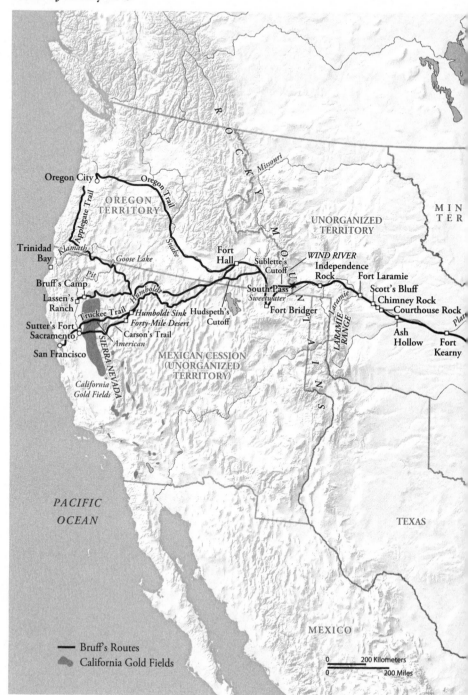

Oregon City

OREGON TERRITORY

Oregon Trail

Trinidad Bay

Klamath

Goose Lake

Snake

Fort Hall

Sublette's Cutoff

Bruff's Camp

Pit

Humboldt

WIND RIVER

Independence Rock

Fort Laramie

Lassen's Ranch

South Pass

Scott's Bluff

Chimney Rock

Courthouse Rock

Humboldt Sink

Sweetwater

Hudspeth's Cutoff

Truckee Trail

Forty-Mile Desert

Fort Bridger

Sutter's Fort

Carson's Trail

Sacramento

American

San Francisco

SIERRA NEVADA

Ash Hollow

Fort Kearny

Platt

California Gold Fields

MEXICAN CESSION (UNORGANIZED TERRITORY)

UNORGANIZED TERRITORY

MIN TER

R O C K Y

Missouri

M O U N T A I N S

LARAMIE RANGE

PACIFIC OCEAN

TEXAS

MEXICO

— Bruff's Routes

California Gold Fields

| 0 | | 200 Kilometers |
| 0 | | 200 Miles |

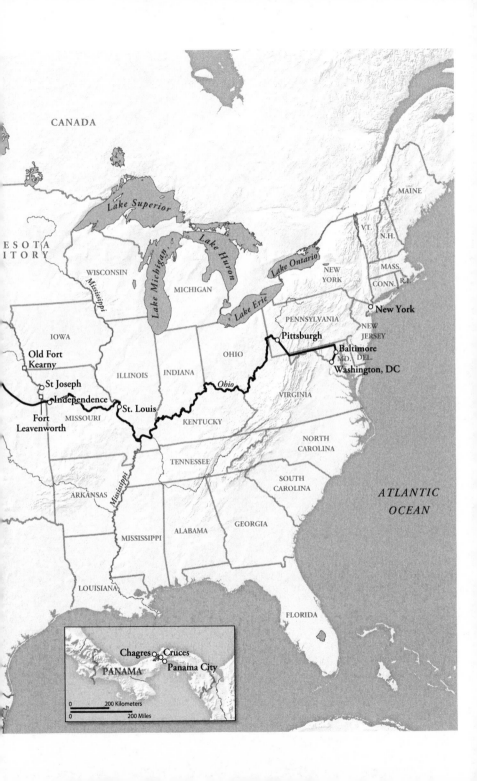

Chapter One

"SOME KIND OF METTLE . . ."

JAMES WILSON MARSHALL SPENT MOST OF HIS LIFE trying to stay one step ahead of misfortune. Born in Hopewell Township, New Jersey, the only male of four children had hoped to follow in his father's footsteps as a carpenter and wagonmaker. But when James was in his early twenties, his father died leaving him with a mountain of debt. Like many bereft men of his day, Marshall headed west, taking up a homestead claim in Missouri. Fate intervened again when a bout of malaria rendered him feverish and too weak to farm. On the advice of his doctor, in 1844 he left Missouri for Oregon's fertile Willamette Valley. Marshall found the Northwest's soggy climate disagreeable and after a few months headed to California. After a stint in the army during the Mexican War, Marshall tried his hand at ranching but failed at that, too.

Penniless and down on his luck, he landed at John Sutter's fort on the American River. Sutter was planning to build a sawmill and sent Marshall to look for a suitable site. After a month exploring the western slope of the Sierra Nevada, Marshall returned in late summer of 1847 with a proposal to build the mill 40 miles upriver from Sutter's Fort at a place known as Coloma. Sutter offered Marshall a share in the mill in return for his supervision of the mill's construction. Work began in September 1847 and within five months was nearly complete, save for one final task—deepening the millrace that was too shallow to power the wheel.

On the cold, sunny morning of January 24, 1848, Marshall went down to the American River to examine the race. As he approached the water, something glittering in the riverbed caught his eye. He picked up the object, round and about half the size of a pea, and examined it closely. He then walked down to the tail end of the race where he picked up a few more of the shiny objects from a shallow pool. When he returned to his cabin for breakfast, he called to the men to gather around. Emptying his pockets, Marshall showed them what he had found. "Boys," he exclaimed, "I believe I have found a gold mine!"

Marshall and his men weren't entirely sure it was gold, though. One of the men at the mill that day had later entered in his diary, "Monday 24th. This day, some kind of mettle was found in the tail race that looks like goald [sic], first discovered by James Martial, the Boss of the Mill." Convinced of his unremitting bad luck, Marshall had thought the find a fluke in any case. Surely a single nugget of the precious metal did not suggest a mother lode. But after finding more shiny nuggets in the river in the ensuing days, Marshall took his stones to Sutter, who essayed them. Not only was it gold, but 23 carat gold—very high quality. Concerned the news would ignite an influx of gold seekers into the valley, Sutter asked Marshall and his men to keep news of the gold a secret for six weeks until work on a flour mill could be completed. In return the men could work the streams on his property for the yellow metal in their spare time.

Sutter needn't have worried. When rumors of the gold reached

San Francisco in February, no one paid any attention. Nor was anyone stirred to action when, on March 15, the weekly *Californian* ran an article announcing gold found "in considerable quantities" in the American River. To Californians it seemed old news. Gold had already been found in southern California as early as 1842 by a ranchero named Francisco Lopez. One day, while culling a wild onion from the ground, he noticed some yellow flakes caught among its roots. The discovery touched off a minor rush that—because of the trifling deposits—played out in a few short months.

Nevertheless, in April the *Californian Star* sent its hard-nosed editor, Edward Kemble, to Sutter's to get at the bottom of the gold rumors. When Kemble arrived, just as he had expected, no one was at work in the rivers. After briefly speaking with Marshall and panning for gold himself along the river, Kemble pronounced the entire affair "a sham, as superb a take-in as ever was got up to guzzle the gullible." With a stroke of his pen, Kemble had bungled the story of the decade, if not the century.

Enter a Mormon and opportunist named Sam Brannan. Ever since he had been sworn to secrecy at Sutter's Mill, Brannan had been quietly calculating how to turn the news to his advantage. Brannan had arrived in California in 1846 from New York with a group of Latter-day Saints. Although he purported to be looking for a safe haven for the persecuted Mormons outside the United States, Brannan was more interested in the region's financial possibilities. Having just opened a general store at Sutter's Mill, Brannan concluded surer money was to be made "mining the miners" rather than the gold itself. He quietly stocked his store with all the shovels, pans, and pickaxes he could find and waited. In mid-May, the period of sworn secrecy having passed, he bought a bottle of gold in Sacramento for $12 and headed for San Francisco's Montgomery Street. Brandishing his bottle of gold in one hand and waving his hat with the other, Brannan bellowed, "Gold, gold from the American River!"

Nothing about California's sleepy past hinted at what was about to happen. The Spanish, who were eager to find gold ever since they set foot in California in the early sixteenth century, never found much to like about the region's wooded canyons and hilly grasslands. When they finally mounted an exploratory expedition in 1530, it went in the wrong direction. Acting on reports of a city made of gold and silver, the Seven Cities of Cibola, Spanish conquistador Francisco Vázquez de Coronado found only mud huts in New Mexico. Some of the Indians who told him of the fabled city were deliberately trying to lead the unwanted Coronado to his death in the desert. A year later he resumed his search, going as far as the prairies of Kansas. Having found gold and silver in Mexico and Peru and with more pressing needs at home, Spain abandoned the costly search for El Dorado in 1603. Thereafter, it used California as a dumping ground for criminals, drunkards, and other undesirables.

Spain renewed its interest in the province in the late eighteenth century but only out of fear of Russian expansion south of Alaska. To boost its presence, the Spanish hurriedly built presidios throughout the region and dispatched Franciscan missionaries to convert the Indians—not to bring them closer to God but to the Spanish. But Spain never penetrated into the interior and was content to ply the coastal waters instead. Had the Spanish bothered to explore California's interior, they might have found gold far earlier, a discovery that would have completely altered the region's future.

After Mexico achieved independence in 1821, it continued Spain's policy of exporting convicts to California. But without gold or some other attraction, Mexico could not induce colonists to settle in what was increasingly seen as a backwater. By then the Russian threat had faded, prompting Mexico to secularize the missions by turning millions of acres and thousands of livestock over to Indian converts. But the Indians were woefully unprepared to manage their own affairs and the lands ended up being parceled out to wealthy and influential families in the form of large *rancheros*. Disenfranchised and demoralized, the Indians turned to working as laborers for their white overlords who often cruelly mistreated them. John Sutter was one of the early settlers to benefit from the breakup of these lands, having convinced the Mexican governor in 1840 that awarding him 48,000 acres on the American River would help stem the flow of Americans and British into California.

Still they came, although quietly and in small numbers. Like Sutter, easterners saw the Sacramento Valley as a promising place to ranch and farm, although most were drawn to the more accessible Willamette Valley in Oregon. Either way, these early pioneers followed the rough trails west laid by trappers and traders a decade earlier, a route they called "the California-Oregon Trail." Immigration west continued at a modest pace throughout the 1840s. By the eve of the Gold Rush there were about 3,000 Americans and an equal number of Mexicans in California quietly pursuing farming, ranching, and hunting.

But with Brannan's clarion call, a region the Spanish and Mexicans had long regarded as a worthless hinterland would never be the same. His news of gold in the Sacramento Valley spread like a prairie fire. Within weeks several thousand men from California's towns dropped what they were doing and raced for the Sacramento Valley to seek their fortune. Some traveled in ox-drawn wagons, others packed in on mules or on foot. By mid-June, San Francisco had emptied of three-quarters of its men. One newspaper suspended publication because all its workers had bolted for the gold fields. So many sailors deserted their posts that the Navy ceased posting them off the coast of California. As news of gold made its way to international ports, gold seekers began pouring in from every corner of the globe. And all that summer and fall, Brannan's store grossed $10,000 a month.

In the eastern states, separated as they were by time and distance, news of a gold strike was received with even greater cynicism than in California. Similar claims of El Dorados in North Carolina, Texas, New Jersey, and Maryland had all proved baseless. How was it, some asked, that the Spanish who had ruled the province for 200 years were unable to find what Americans had, just nine days before acquiring the province from Mexico? Some thought the rumors were circulated to generate business in the new American territory. Even those who knew gold was to be found in California thought it wasn't worth much. As a few acted on the news and headed west, the *Western Star* of Pulaski, Tennessee poked fun at the gullible foolhardiness of gold hunters in verse.

But by late summer, persistent reports of gold prompted the eastern newspapers to begin covering the story. On August 8, a St. Louis newspaper reported gold "collected at random and without any trouble." Papers in New York, Philadelphia, and Baltimore quickly followed suit with accounts of impressive gold finds throughout the Sacramento Valley.

As articles of fabulous gold strikes appeared again and again in the papers, skepticism gave way to curiosity and excitement built. In the shops and in the streets the talk was of "Gold, gold, gold!" People began to ask themselves and each other, "Is it true? Are such riches really to be had in California? And culled so easily from the earth?" What was really needed was proof, or at least confirmation from a source whose credibility was unassailable. They soon got both. After receiving a military report from the region, along with a Chinese tea caddy filled with more than 200 ounces of gold dust, President James Polk formally announced the discovery of gold to the Second Session of Congress on December 5:

The accounts of the abundance of gold in that territory are of such extraordinary character as would scarcely command belief were they not corroborated by authentic officers in the public service.

The hitherto skeptical *New York Herald* enthused that "The El Dorado of the old Spaniards is discovered at last. We now had the highest official authority for believing in the discovery of vast gold mines in California who have visited the mineral district, and derived the facts which they detail from personal observation."

The gold-filled tea caddy was put on display at the War Department, and thousands rushed to see the precious metal from the other side of the continent.

The presidential announcement had the effect of a shotgun start, as one historian put it. Suddenly, Americans who had dismissed gold reports as little more than wishful thinking now couldn't get to California fast enough. Americans sold or mortgaged their homes, emptied bank accounts, or borrowed the money from friends or family to finance the journey. From every state in the Union and every walk of life, men and women, old and young, doctors, lawyers, and merchants, the employed and unemployed—even Indians—dropped what they were doing and set out for California. On December 11, the *New York Tribune* giddily reported on the multitudes joining in the rush and the easy fortune to be made:

> *The gold mania rages with intense vigor, and is carrying off its victims hourly and daily . . . young men—including mechanics, doctors, lawyers, and we may add, clergymen—are taking leave of old associations, and embarking for the land of wealth, where the only capital required to make a fortune is a spade, a sieve, a tin colander, and a small stock of patience and industry.*

Masters brought their slaves to do the digging for them. There was hardly a town in the Union that did not lose some of its residents to the Gold Rush. More than a rush, it was a tidal wave of humanity that descended on California in 1849 and continued well into the 1850s. With the official news of gold, the frenzy had finally taken hold—fully ten months after Marshall's discovery.

Having finally accepted the veracity of the gold reports, people now believed it was in such abundance that nuggets could be picked from the rivers like daisies in a field. Newspapers reported the supply of gold to be virtually inexhaustible. A single handful of earth from the gold fields was rumored to contain at least an ounce of pure gold. Maps of the region depicted the plain west of the Sierras as completely gilded. A group of gold seekers from France brought rakes, intending to cull only large nuggets and leave behind anything so trifling that could not be caught between its teeth. Others bought "gold-finding" machines to facilitate their search.

And so the delirium went. Virtually everyone who set out had expectations of making a vast fortune, and in no time. Sensing they were part of a historic quest, emigrants referred to themselves as "argonauts," alluding to the mythical quest for the Golden

Fleece. They even had a name for the great adventure they were collectively embarking on: "seeing the elephant," which conveyed the sense of taking part in an epic adventure on a grand scale. In the cities, large stockholding companies were organized; those in small towns formed small groups or took their families. A few braved the journey alone, such as the man from Maine seen pushing a wheelbarrow across the frontier. Along the way, he refused offers to join large parties for fear they would hold him back. The lone figure averaged 25 miles a day.

For the young nation of America, the timing couldn't have been better, and President Polk knew it. An ardent supporter of Manifest Destiny, Polk had coveted the California province ever since reading a glowing book on the region, *Two Years Before the Mast*, by Richard Dana. At first, Polk offered to buy the province from Mexico, but the offer was rejected. Determined to extend America's borders all the way to the Pacific, he provoked Mexico into war to wrest the region away outright. After nearly two years of fighting, Mexico signed a treaty ceding the province of California—some one million acres—just nine days after Marshall's discovery of gold. To many Americans, the fortuitous timing was proof the country was being guided by the benevolent hand of Divine Providence.

* * * *

OF THE legions of people who caught the gold fever that year was one Joseph Goldsborough Bruff of Washington, DC. Like everyone else Bruff had been avidly following reports of California gold. But it wasn't until the reality intruded into his very work that he was moved to join in the mania. A draftsman in the U.S. Army's Bureau of Topographical Engineers, Bruff was tasked with making duplicates of Captain John C. Frémont's reports and maps of the gold regions for Congress. It was then that his interest in undertaking the journey was aroused.

If there was ever a man who embodied Bruff's ideal of the courageous soldier and the intrepid explorer, it was John Charles Frémont. A controversial figure who burned with ambition and daring, Frémont had been one of the first explorers of the West from the Great Plains to the Pacific. Known as "the Pathfinder of the West," he had twice crossed the frontier to California and published reports of his explorations. On his third trip to find a railroad passage to the Pacific in 1845, Frémont became convinced that war with Mexico was inevitable and, quietly encouraged by his expansionist father-in-law, Senator Thomas Hart Benton, suddenly bolted for California with sixty men. Fearing the explorer's intentions, the Mexican governor ordered him out of the territory two months after his arrival. Frémont retreated to Oregon but not before circulating rumors that American immigrants would soon be ordered out of California as well. When Frémont audaciously returned to the Sacramento Valley, a group of American settlers became emboldened and skirmished with a Mexican regiment on June 26. Raising a makeshift cotton flag depicting a prowling grizzly in Sonoma and at Sutter's Fort, the settlers declared themselves a republic. Never one to miss an opportunity for heroics, Frémont took control of the revolt and merged his forces with the Bear Flaggers into an American battalion.

When the U.S. declared war with Mexico, Frémont quickly threw himself into the fighting elsewhere. Forming a regiment that included James Marshall, Frémont fought from Monterey to Los Angeles, emerging as the outstanding hero of the war. It was actions like this on which Frémont's reputation thrived. Men envied his courage and audacity; women swooned over his swarthy good looks. The reports of his expeditions were read widely, making him one of the most celebrated men in America.

Bruff had once been a man as daring and adventurous as Frémont himself. Of medium height, erect bearing, hazel eyes, thick black mustache, and bushy black hair, he looked every bit the soldier he had failed to become. Indeed, soldiering and adventuring were in his very blood. The Bruffs (spelled Brough until 1792) were originally from the town of Bruff near Cork County, Ireland. Lt. Captain John Brough made the second voyage to Virginia with Captain John Smith, and a Captain Bruff commanded the first American troops that took Fort Niagara in 1796. Bruff's great-grandfather on his mother's side had commanded the Duke of York's yacht, and his maternal uncle, James Bruff, had been a Second Lieutenant stationed in nearby Maryland. With such a pedigree, it seemed Bruff was destined for a distinguished career as a military officer.

But when Bruff turned 12, a string of misfortunes conspired to derail him from his chosen path. His father Thomas, a dentist and inventor, was poisoned to death by someone who coveted his invention of a machine for making bullets. Coming at such an early age, his father's death impelled the young Bruff toward the self-reliance and resourcefulness he demonstrated later in life and on the trail. Four years later, Bruff enrolled in West Point, where he studied math, topography, and drafting. Although he distinguished himself as an outstanding student, he had a violent, uncontrollable temper. When a fellow student insulted him, Bruff challenged him to a duel in which he wounded the offending student. Since he had been a superb student, the school administration gave him a choice: He could resign or be dismissed. Reluctantly, Bruff resigned.

Shortly after, Bruff's mother passed away, perhaps overcome with grief over her son's dismissal. With no home to return to, Bruff tried to enlist in the Navy but was rejected. Like many young men at loose ends, Bruff, "having from childhood had a strong desire of traveling to distant parts," decided to indulge his desire for travel.

Unable to pay his passage, he signed on as a cabin boy on a ship bound for northern Europe. His first port of call was Cowes in the Isle of Wight. During the layover, Bruff toured the island and made sketches of its ancient castles, a skill he would make abundant use of on his journey across the American frontier. From Cowes the ship made for Texel, a Dutch island. On Christmas Day, the ship was caught in a violent snowstorm in which several of Bruff's shipmates were killed. With the ship listing, Bruff had to throw out its anchors to keep it from foundering on the rocks. He was then ordered to stand watch on deck the entire night in the howling snow.

When he returned to the U.S., Bruff found his sister bedridden from an unknown illness. She died shortly thereafter. Distraught and still at loose ends, he boarded a leaky schooner in Baltimore headed for the West Indies. In 1827, he returned to Washington, his wanderlust seemingly quenched. He took a job as a government clerk in the Gosport Navy Yard in Norfolk, Virginia, perhaps to be near his brothers who worked in the printing business there. When his superiors became aware of his drafting skills, he was promoted to draftsman but with no increase in his daily rate of $1.37.

It was during this time that Bruff joined the Portsmouth lodge of Freemasonry, a secular fraternal organization dedicated to moral and spiritual values. Bruff became an ardent member and practitioner who took seriously its tenets of brotherly love, charity, and high moral standards, all later evident in his compassionate behavior on the Gold Rush trail. It was most likely the following year that the adventurer decided to settle down for good and married Eliza Ann Thompson of Virginia, with whom he fathered a daughter, Mary Ann.

By 1837 Bruff was making $1.75 a day. But with two more mouths to feed, more than ever he felt underpaid for the two jobs he was performing. So he went across the James River to draw fortification plans for Fort Monroe, performing so well he was later awarded a cherished box of paints by President Andrew Jackson. Two years later, Bruff moved to Washington, DC, to join the Corps of Topographical Engineers when the Army Corps of Engineers was reorganized. If Bruff could not become an officer, then at least he could be part of the Army.

Established in 1838, the Topographical Corps was tasked with conducting the first scientific mapping of America's newly acquired territories. Called the "great reconnaissance," the scientific teams were composed of explorers, scientists, and artists who produced maps and lithographs of the flora and fauna of the region. The artists faithfully rendered everything from great California sequoias to breathtaking vistas of mountains and plains Americans were seeing for the very first time. The fascinating reports were published in the form of lavishly illustrated volumes that covered virtually every aspect of life in the West: biology, ethnography, geology, and so forth. The onetime adventurer Bruff was not on the front lines but served as a headquarters-based draftsman, applying his considerable skills in drawing and painting.

As Bruff sat at his draftsman's table reading Frémont's latest report of derring-do, his thirst for the swashbuckling days of his youth was suddenly rekindled:

> *It revived the spirit of adventure so long dormant and I was anxious to travel over and see what my friend had so graphically and scientifically realized: more particularly when a golden reward appear'd to be awaiting us at the nether end of the route.*

On the eve of the Gold Rush, Bruff was 44 years old and married with two young children, Zuleima and William. He had a stable—

if sedentary—government job. He drew the first map of the state of Florida and had drawn the route plans for the Mexican and Florida wars. When he wasn't drawing maps, he was engaged in the far less exciting work of designing buttons, insignias, and uniforms for the officers of the Corps. The maps in particular must have been a constant reminder of his adventures on the high seas and in foreign lands, long since abandoned. Approaching middle age and with a burgeoning family, Bruff knew that time was running out. The Gold Rush offered a last chance to recapture the adventure of his youth. It was also a chance for the former West Point cadet to vindicate his failed attempt at a military career and become the leader of men he felt destined to be. Along the way, the mapmaker planned to compile a guidebook for future travelers—not unlike the reports of his colleague Frémont—illustrated with notes and sketches of the American frontier. Quitting his job and resigning from the Freemasons, Bruff told his wife he would be gone eight months, during which time he would send ample remittances from his gold mining.

At first, Bruff mentioned his plans to a few friends he thought might be interested in joining him. But in the madness to get rich, thousands were looking to join a party heading west. Interest in Bruff's plan was so high that local citizens called for a meeting at the Apollo Hall in downtown Washington to form a party. At the meeting, Bruff was elected Chairman and twenty-five men were selected to participate in the expedition. As word of their plan spread, more men clamored to join the party, so many in fact that they eventually capped the membership at sixty-six, deemed the maximum manageable number for an overland crossing.

The sixty-six members were organized into a stockholding company, The Washington City and California Gold Mining Association, and they voted Bruff president and "Captain" of the expedition. What had started as a notion of Bruff and a few of his friends had morphed into a large, quasi-military expedition. Over the next few weeks, the men met regularly at Bruff's to formalize the exploratory organization and hammer out details of the trip to California. The planning, mapping, and other aspects of the journey were all eagerly handled by "Captain Bruff."

Membership in the Company required each man to purchase a share for $300—roughly a year's wages—to be used for general outfitting and provisions for the expedition. Those unable to afford the money were allowed to provide a substitute in kind entitling each man an equal share in the profits. Total stock in the company came to $11,000, not an inconsiderable sum in those days. A constitution was drawn up to which each man was required to swear allegiance, even though Bruff presciently observed, when push came to shove, it would have as much meaning as "singing psalms to a dead horse."

Membership normally entitled stockholders to share in the company's profits. Although no record exists of the Washington Company's constitution, it appears to have differed in being merely a vehicle for getting to California. Bruff felt that even if the Company survived the journey across the frontier intact (most didn't), it would be difficult maintaining unity once they reached the gold fields. Ergo, it was agreed upon that once in California, the organization would dissolve and free the men to prospect on their own—a provision Bruff would live to regret.

Similar companies were being organized in almost every city in the Union, usually bearing the name of their city of origin. There was the New York Company, the Boston Pack Company, the Charleston Company, the Michigan Wolverines, and the Pittsburgh Company. Although such large associations were at odds with the highly individual quest for gold, they provided greater security across the unfamiliar frontier and allowed gold seekers to benefit from their companions' much-needed skills, such as wagon repair or forging, that they might lack. Some companies had bylaws that prohibited liquor and swearing and enforced strict observance of the Sabbath. A few of the larger companies, like the Boston Pack Company, drove their own cattle across the plains as a kind of rolling pantry. The Spartan Band was perhaps the largest of the companies that year, fabulously provisioned with 57 wagons and 163 persons.

The Washington Company was organized into six "messes" of eleven men, each led by a director. Because most of the men who signed on with the Washington Company were government bureaucrats and totally lacking in skills needed on the frontier, some were chosen for their skills as carpenters, mechanics, blacksmiths, wheelwrights, and gunsmiths. Most of them hailed from the Washington-Baltimore area, but a few were from Boston and New Jersey. Several were married, although most were bachelors. There were no women.

In all likelihood, Bruff did not know all of the men in his company personally. Some were fellow Freemasons and several worked at the Treasury Department. A few were his friends, such as 43-year-old Swiss native Charles Fenderich, a celebrated lithographer. Members ranged in age from 19-year-old George Byington to the 59-year-old John M. Farrar. About half of the men were in their twenties. Some of the younger members were taken on because they were the children of Bruff's friends. If they were employed at all, they were probably making no more than a dollar a day. For this reason, they weren't screened, something Bruff would sorely regret once on the trail. Immature, eager for quick riches and a rollicking adventure on the frontier, they would prove a thorn in the Captain's side to the very end. At the last minute, several men who had fallen ill were replaced with eager new recruits. One of the older directors, William Dietz, insisted on going even though his son had just died tragically after gulping down a pint of brandy on a dare. Once on the trail, Dietz would irritate his companions with his behavior and gradually drift to the rear of the train, sullen and withdrawn over his loss.

One of the first decisions of the Company was how to get to California. One way—which became the preferred mode of travel for people of means who lived near the sea—was by ship. To meet the great demand for sea travel, all manner of ships were put into service that year: steamers, brigs, schooners, even old whalers were resuscitated. On one day in January 1849 alone, forty-nine ships departed from New York and another sixty-five from other Atlantic ports. Of the 124 Gold Rush companies that went to California in 1849, all but 22 went by sea.

Ships that embarked from ports on the eastern seaboard sailed around Cape Horn on the southern tip of South America to San Francisco. The 13,000-mile journey, however, took a year and was costly, ranging from $200-$500 depending on class of accommodation. Some shortened the time at sea by going by way of Chagres on the Atlantic side of the Isthmus of Panama, then two to three weeks traversing a dense jungle to the other side to Panama City, where a steamer took them to San Francisco. Crossing the Isthmus was risky, for the jungle was dense and dangerous, and ships waiting on the other side were often unreliable. Even though this route was longer in terms of distance, it was slightly shorter than the four to six months it would take to go overland. Once in San Francisco, the companies could outfit—assuming there were still provisions left—and only then would they have to begin hauling men and materials to the gold fields, a far less laborious journey than the heavily-laden trek of the overland travelers.

Despite his nautical background and proximity to the sea, Bruff, like tens of thousands of other gold seekers that year and in the years following, chose to go overland. Organized parties traveling in covered wagons had been the way an earlier generation had traveled to Oregon and California, usually via the California-Oregon Trail. The voyage overland came to define the California Gold Rush of 1849. It was deeply emblematic of the relentless westward movement of Americans who sought fortune in land they believed was decreed by Divine Providence as rightfully theirs.

There were a number of distinct advantages to going overland. It ensured the Company would be adequately provisioned for—by the time they got to San Francisco by ship, the demand for provisions would likely exceed supply. Going overland was also more cost effective, as the price of the sea voyage alone nearly equaled the cost for each man to join and provision the Company. Perhaps most important, overland travel offered the prospect of high adventure and the excitement of exploring the American frontier with its grand vistas and strange curiosities, like the primitive Indians and the shaggy-maned buffalo. To young and old alike, and especially to Bruff, crossing the American frontier promised to be the adventure of a lifetime and a chance to get rich at the same time.

But a host of dangers awaited overlanders: accident, disease, rain, extremes of heat and cold, storms, deserts, rugged mountains, deep snow, physical hardship, starvation, fetid water, hostile Indians—and just the plain uncertainty of it all.

If Bruff could not predict what he would encounter on the trail, he could at least be prepared for it. Thanks to his meticulous planning, the Washington Mining and Gold Company became one of the best organized and equipped expeditions ever mounted to cross the continent. A Supplies Committee was created and sent to Pittsburgh to order the manufacture of sixteen light Santa Fe wagons. Modified in the 1820s, the wagons were perfectly adapted for the rugged frontier. Wheels made of iron "tires" were four feet in diameter in the rear and smaller in the front for maneuverability. Although only 10 to 12 feet long and 3 or 4 feet wide, the wagons weighed 1,200 pounds and could carry three times their weight. A canvas cover waterproofed with linseed oil and beeswax provided protection from the elements.

In the Iron City, the committee also purchased most of the provisions they would need for the long journey: tents, rifles, blankets, muskets, ammunition, gunpowder, canteens, foodstuffs, cutlery, as well as tools for digging and smelting—even a portable forge for refining gold. Nothing was overlooked or left to chance in the great quest for fortune. Foodstuffs consisted of sacks of flour and beans, salt, huge sides of bacon, cornmeal, coffee, whiskey, and brandy. The men hoped to supplement the food with the abundant game along the trail. Because they would be headed into Indian country, each man was armed to the teeth with a rifle, a pair of pistols, a knife, and a hatchet. To instill harmony and discipline in the motley group of men, Bruff dressed his men (somewhat comically) in felt hats and uniforms of grey frock with rows of brass buttons and white shoulder straps—all designed by Bruff. It might as well have been called "Bruff's Army."

Exploration and migration had created three main routes to the Far West. The main route began at Independence and other towns along the Missouri, traced a northwest arc to the Platte River, and then followed the river's undulating course across the Great Plains to the North Platte. From there, the trail followed the Sweetwater River west. After stopping at Fort Laramie to rest and purchase goods, emigrants crossed the Rockies at South Pass, which marked the Continental Divide. Another trail, the Santa Fe, went south through Texas while the third, pioneered by the Mormons, followed the course of the north bank of the Platte.

Since the Washington Company planned to jump off at St. Joseph on the Missouri, Bruff sent another committee to St. Louis to buy 90 mules (a team of six mules for each wagon), 14 horses, and—somewhat superfluously—an ambulance.

When crossing the country in the nineteenth century, choosing your beast of burden was an exercise in juggling several vital considerations. Horses were strong and fleet of foot and made good riding animals. But their long legs and sensitive hooves made them unsuitable for pulling heavy loads along rough trails. They also required twice as much forage as a mule and could not endure the heat or long stretches of the trail where no water existed. More than half of overlanders chose oxen to pull their wagons, largely because they were considerably cheaper than mules and less likely to be stolen by Indians. But oxen were slower and less sure-footed than the mule. They also required more water—a critical factor in crossing the arid West. In their concern to cut costs, many spendthrifts later lived or not—to regret their decision.

Savvy emigrants chose mules to draw their wagons. A cross between a female horse and a donkey, the mule was the ideal draft animal for hauling wagons long distances over rough terrain. With their larger brains, mules were smarter than the horse and responded better to danger. They also had a keener sense of smell that allowed them to alert owners to the presence of predators like wolves or to game like antelope and buffalo. There were a few drawbacks to mules, however. They tended to be ornery and stubborn, especially in the hands of a greenhorn teamster. When set loose, they also tended to wander off—often right into the hands of waiting Indians.

The mules selected by Bruff and others like him weren't just any mule, but a new breed called the "Mammoth Jack." Stronger and larger than donkeys, the Mammoth Jack was first imported from Europe and bred by President George Washington. During the four-year course of the Gold Rush, this breed pulled thousands of wagons across 2,000 miles of frontier, making this hardy draft animal the unsung hero of the Gold Rush and of the Washington Company in particular.

At precisely 9 a.m. on April 2, the Washington Company paraded at Lafayette Park, across from the White House, amid great fanfare. In their natty uniforms and military deportment, the men looked more like soldiers going off to war than gold prospectors. At long last a commander (of a sort) of men, Captain Bruff drilled his men as a light infantry while a band provided by *Washington Star* founder Joseph Tate played a lively jig. Then, with Bruff proudly at the head, the Company marched in step in columns of six to the Executive Mansion to bid goodbye to his friend, President Zachary Taylor. To "Old Zac," Bruff explained:

> *The situation and circumstances, and informed him of the strength and character of my Company, its destination &c . . . That we were on the eve of an extraordinary journey, of great extent, and which must be fraught with ardious [sic] trials, seasoned perhaps with a due quantum of perils, &c and that most probably many of us would never again have the pleasure of greeting him . . .*

Wishing them all a safe journey, President Taylor then pressed Bruff's hand warmly in both of his.

Captain Bruff's last great adventure had begun.

Chapter Two

A DENSE MEDLEY OF HOOSIERS, WOLVERINES, AND BUCKEYES

As Bruff's train rumbled toward the Relay House Inn south of Baltimore, he reached into his knapsack and pulled out his notebook to map out the next day's schedule and activities. It was a ritual he would perform each day until the Company reached California. Careful planning of each day—mapping the route and distance to cover, identifying watering holes and grazing for the animals, where to stop for lunch, and so forth—would be essential to avoid delays and mishaps and arrive in California before the winter snows blanketed the High Sierras. It was a thankless and time-consuming task, Bruff felt, but someone had to do it. And who better than he?

After overnighting in Baltimore, Bruff and the men boarded the Baltimore and Ohio train to Cumberland, the gateway to the Appalachians and a major outfitting and staging point for westward migration. All were in high spirits as the party stopped in scenic Harper's Ferry for lunch. In Cumberland, a stagecoach took them to Brownsville, Pennsylvania where they boarded a riverboat—already crowded with gold seekers—down the Monongahela River to Pittsburgh, where the Company's wagons and provisions were waiting. At each town they stopped, Washington journalists were on hand to interview Captain Bruff and report on the Company's progress for a city participating vicariously in the adventure. Once on the trail, letters sent home to loved ones would be published in Washington papers so that readers could follow the exciting exploits of the city's preeminent gold mining company.

In Pittsburgh, Bruff hired a steamer, the *Robert Fulton*, to take the entire freight of wagons and provisions down the Ohio River to St. Louis. It took three days to load the ship with the provisions and wagons now boldly emblazoned with "WCC" on the wagons' canvas and sideboards. As he scanned the ship's deck, Bruff was stunned by the great number of people heading west. Little did he know he was merely glimpsing the tip of the iceberg. From cities and towns all over the Union, thousands of gold seekers were now converging on the Mississippi.

At 10 o'clock in the morning, Captain Bruff gathered his men on the ship's hurricane deck and drilled them in light infantry techniques. It was something he would do each morning until they began the journey in earnest. That evening, with some hours to kill, Bruff went to see a showing of *Richard III* starring the renowned British actor Janiun Booth, father of the presidential assassin John Wilkes Booth.

After eight days on the Ohio and Mississippi Rivers, the Company eased into St. Louis on April 15. The St. Louis *Republican* noted the arrival of the Washington Company favorably:

> *Yesterday morning the steamer* Robert Fulton *reached this port with one of the best organized and equipped Companies*

we have seen. It is from Washington, D.C. . . . with J.G. Bruff
as President and Commander . . .

Several hundred emigrants were now arriving in the city every day and the streets were thronged with men, mules, horses, and wagons. Hotels were sold out. One newspaper estimated 10,000 gold seekers a month were passing through St. Louis in route to the gold fields or looking to join up with one of the parties headed there. Dozens of steamers were moored along the shore as a motley crowd shouting in foreign tongues loaded and unloaded freight. Similar activity was occurring in ports all along the Mississippi: stevedores rolling barrels, lugging bales of hemp and cotton, and guiding wagons and pack animals onto waiting riverboats. Gunsmiths and saddlers could not turn out enough weapons fast enough. Overwhelmed by the mad crush of people, some emigrants decided to turn around and head home. It would not be the last time the Argonauts would lose their enthusiasm for the gold hunt. All the way to the Rockies, some gold seekers would, for one reason or another, quit the journey and return home. So many in fact they came to be called "go backs" or "turnarounds."

But the overwhelming majority of Gold Rushers could not get to the gold fields fast enough. To accommodate the large human traffic, steamers were departing hourly to and from the jumping-off towns on the Missouri River, Independence and St. Joseph. The great demand for riverboats had driven the price of tickets to St. Joseph sky-high, preventing Bruff from commissioning a single boat for his men and provisions. Using two steamers "crowded to excess," he sent two detachments and the wagons up while he and the rest of the men stayed behind to buy additional provisions and await a medical doctor who was to join the Company. When after two days the good doctor still had not arrived,

Bruff departed at midnight aboard the *Belle Creole*. The ferry was thronged with some 300 to 400 passengers from every state of the Union and many foreign countries, causing Bruff to marvel at the raucous scene:

> *We were on board amid such a dense medley of Hoosiers, Wolverines, Buckeyes, Yankees and Yorkers, including black legs and swindlers of every grade of proficiency and celebrity, as is seldom to be found, even on our western rivers. The decks, above and below, exhibited an equally stupendous assortment of wagons, horses, mules, tents, bales, boxes, sacks, barrels, and camp kettles; while every cabin and state room was an arsenal of rifles, fowling pieces, bowie-knives, hatchets, pouches, powder-horns and belts.*

Even though it was springtime, the rains were late and the Missouri was running low. With the ferry overloaded, it soon began to run aground on hidden sandbars. In the twilight, Bruff could see the ghostly outlines of steamers along the shore crippled with broken propeller shafts. As navigation became increasingly hazardous, the ferry master finally pulled ashore until daybreak.

On board, Bruff heard the first murmurings of a danger few could have anticipated: cholera. Normally making its appearance in summer, cholera had started early that year because of the great number of emigrants along the river. The disease had appeared in the fetid waters of Calcutta in the 1820s and made its way to European ports in the 1830s through infected rats stowing away on ships. By 1849 it had reached New Orleans and was now migrating upriver. The timing could not have been worse. With the mass of people converging on the river, the disease was now raging up and down the Missouri.

The very word sent a shudder through the passengers for the gruesomeness with which the little-understood disease attacked its victims. Once it entered the body through contaminated water, the bacteria multiplied by the millions until expelled by violent vomiting and diarrhea. While one may be infected—and infect others—and not know it for days, cholera could also strike with alarming swiftness. One could feel well at breakfast, complain of stomach pains by lunch, be struck by vomiting in the afternoon, and be dead by evening of dehydration. The crowded quarters and ignorance of sanitation on the *Belle* only fueled the spread of the disease. Just a week after Bruff left St. Louis, a steamer from New Orleans would arrive with 500 passengers, 47 of whom had died on board of cholera. Cholera had killed so many passengers on the *Monroe* in May that the ship was abandoned upstream in Jefferson City. By June, some 2,000 people would die from the disease in St. Louis alone. Steamers suspected of carrying infected people would be turned away or forced to dock on the opposite shore. Infected steamers would pile dead bodies on the deck and pull alongside river islands long enough to bury them in shallow graves hastily dug by nervous deckhands. That some steamer operators refused to tell passengers of the cholera outbreak for fear of losing business only worsened the epidemic. By July, the outbreak would reach epidemic proportions, prompting President Taylor to declare a day of prayer for the "fearful pestilence."

After four interminable days of dodging snags and running aground on sandbars, the *Belle* had only gotten as far as Camden (Tennessee), two hundred miles upriver. By now, most of Bruff's men who had taken the steamer *Alice* were already waiting in St. Joseph. In Camden the water had become too shallow to proceed, forcing the ferry master to turn around. After discharging its cargo and passengers in Lexington, the *Belle* returned to St. Louis. Feeling short-changed by the aborted trip, Bruff negotiated a reduced fare on behalf of the passengers.

As he wandered around Lexington, Bruff found it filled with "all sorts of inferior characters." Forced to overnight in the unpleasant city, he turned some hogs out of their shed, reversed the floorboards, and went to sleep on "the bleakest night of the season." It wouldn't be the last.

A few days later, the steamer *Meteor* came up to pick up the stranded passengers. As it continued upriver, the ferry struggled throughout the night, running aground or snagging on logs in the shallow water. The mood on board was once again somber as talk was all about cholera. Just shy of Ft. Leavenworth, the steamer stopped to repair the supply pump. Along the bank, Bruff spotted three Delaware Indians, an old woman and her children. The "wandering Jews of the West," the Delaware had been resettled several times, first from their home in eastern Pennsylvania to the Alleghenies, then to the Ohio River, Illinois, along the Mississippi, and finally among the Pawnee in Kansas, where Bruff encountered them. Their plight evoked pity in the Captain, who lamented, "No other tribe on the continent has been so much moved and jostled about by civilized invasions."

On April 27, Bruff's party finally pulled into St. Joseph, a week after the advance party had arrived. An outfitting town, St. Joseph was founded in 1843 by Joseph Rubidoux, a fur trader who named it in honor of his patron saint. Dubbed "St. Joe" by emigrants, it would soon eclipse Independence as the jumping-off point for the Oregon Trail. St. Joe was a rough-edged, frontier town filled with mountain men and trappers striding imperiously about the streets in buckskin boots and jackets and drunken Indians loitering in front of saloons and whorehouses.

But most Gold Rushers were too busy to take notice. Anxious

to get on the trail, they were frantically buying up horses, mules, provisions, clothing, muskets, and other articles of necessity for the journey. They invariably paid exorbitant prices for the goods, consoling themselves with the thought that they would more than make up for the added expenses when they reached the gold fields.

With its seventeen wagons, the Washington Company set up camp on Black Snake Hill outside of town, which afforded a fine view of the surrounding country and beyond. Looking west, the men got their first glimpse of the American frontier: a vast, flat expanse of dark green that stretched to the horizon. Gazing down on the town, Bruff could hardly see the city, for it was shrouded in a cloud of dust. Every road and path leading from it was seething with the movement of people and wagons. The hills around the city had become a vast sea of wagons and white tents displaying various mottoes such as "Rough and Ready," "Live Hoosier," and "Have You Seen the Elephant?" Mules had already consumed all the corn in the city. At that very moment, all along the Missouri, some 32,000 emigrants were outfitting their wagons and preparing to launch across the frontier. Seventeen thousand would start out from St. Joseph and another 15,000 from Independence.

Bruff's sketch of their camp revealed an idyllic scene of frontier life, of covered wagons and tents pitched among the oak and hickory trees with men lazing about smoking and chatting. It was on Black Snake Hill that Bruff began his practice of waking the men at 4 a.m.—much to the annoyance of several men who had begun to chafe at the Captain's overbearing martial style.

Camped near the Washington Company was a party of German and Swiss whose children had intermarried for the purpose of the expedition. Bruff was particularly intrigued by the patriarch of the group, a silver-haired old Swiss named Abbot. One morning Bruff found the old man lying under an oak tree reading *Kosmos* by the celebrated German explorer Alexander von Humboldt. The contemplative Swiss told Bruff he was "in easy circumstances" and had not come for enrichment but rather to enjoy the grandeur of the American West and hopefully find a pleasant place to end his days.

The next day Bruff went down to the Missouri River ferry to inspect the ferry operation. To his horror, he saw a dense line of wagons stretching from the river's edge up a 300-yard clay embankment and down the main street for half a mile. With only two ferries operating, getting the wagons across was moving at a snail's pace. Each time a wagon was put on the ferry, the long line of wagons slowly inched forward and closed ranks. In the desperation to get across, tensions among teamsters were running high. Near the head of the line, two men arguing over priority drew pistols and killed one another.

Day after day, in rainy, disagreeable weather, the agonizing crawl of wagons continued from dawn until midnight. Bruff and his men used the delay profitably, fitting harnesses to the horses and mules and taking inventory of their supplies. While Bruff was organizing the wagons, a man named Stinson approached and offered his services as a trail guide. He boasted he had traveled with the legendary explorer Kit Carson and knew the trail intimately. After sizing Stinson up, Bruff politely declined, saying the road west was wide and they would never be far from other wagons. But a Company vote overturned Bruff's decision, forcing him to hire a man he thought "knew as much about the Plains as the Plains knew about him."

It had been more than three weeks since the Company left Washington. With all the delays, the men were chomping at the bit to get on the trail. Indeed, they were now beginning to run behind schedule. Emigrants had a narrow window of departure for the long journey across the frontier. In normal weather they could not leave before April 25, as the spring grass was not sufficiently high for grazing. But to linger beyond May 25 ran the risk of being blocked by snow in the High Sierras, which often fell as early as October. That meant the Argonauts had about five or six months to complete the 2,000-mile journey—weather cooperating.

So the men marked time on Black Snake Hill. It was the Company's first encampment and already there were signs of discontent and discord among the men. The weather had been cool and rainy and many of the tents would not arrive for another week. Forced to sleep underneath the wagons, the men were grumbling "like young bears." Even more grousing arose when Bruff began assigning night guard duty. Some of the younger men protested, claiming they had never agreed to guard duty when they signed on, nor was it mentioned in the constitution. While it was an odious task, particularly after a long day on the trail, night guard was essential to protect men and animals from the predations of Indians. To set an example, Bruff himself stood guard duty, but it did little to placate the men. Indeed, guard duty became a sore that would fester to the very end—and with dire consequences for Bruff. Conflicts such as these caused some gold mining groups to break down entirely, with companies liquidating equipment and animals before heading home.

In the face of all the carping, Bruff remained stoic, focusing his energies on overseeing the branding and breaking in of the mules. Many of the mules were proving particularly ornery; the inflated cost of the animals had forced them to buy younger, unruly animals at $62 apiece. With the sudden surge in migration, huge herds had been imported from Texas and Mexico, but even that was insufficient to satisfy the demand. All along the frontier mule breeding had become a lucrative business. Taking mules only a few years old, breeders would run them a few miles in a harness and pronounce them ready for the journey. Obstinate by nature, green mules driven by an inexperienced teamster could easily lead to accidents or deaths caused by stampeding teams. As the Washington Company's mules brayed and bucked, the men, none of whom had experience breaking draft animals, struggled just to avoid being kicked to death. "Most of them knew as much about mules, when they arrived here, as the mules knew about them," Bruff quipped. With time running short, he finally hired an experienced mule breaker for $1.50 a day, which would prove to be a wise investment.

Freed from the burden of mule-breaking, the men turned to fitting harnesses, making reins, and weighing baggage and provisions. Like most emigrants, Bruff had purchased too many provisions, so he sent a few wagons into town to sell excess bacon, whiskey, salt, coffee, and lead. On May 2, Dr. Philip Austin, a physician from Johns Hopkins University Hospital, finally arrived along with the remaining tents.

On the morning of May 7, Bruff went down to the river to find two of his wagons near the head of the line. Approaching the wagon ahead, he asked the teamster when he expected to board. "Guess as how, if we have good luck, by 11 o'clock tonight," came the joyless reply. Bruff promptly ordered his wagons out of the line. Returning to camp, he called the men together to discuss their options. It had taken an exasperating 24 hours to get just two of the wagons within 100 yards of the ferry. At this rate, Bruff estimated it would take two weeks to get all 17 wagons across, assuming the ferries operating did not capsize or otherwise break down. (In fact, a local newspaper speculated it would take two months.) Thus far, the men had been lucky to avoid cholera. But each day they lingered in St. Joseph put them at greater risk of contracting the disease. Even if they were willing to take their chances, the

enormous number of pack animals had already exhausted the forage on the other side. To make matters worse, Bruff had learned of
the existence on the other side of several streams, tributaries of the
Kansas River, that had no bridge and were so difficult to ford that
wagons had to be emptied at each crossing. With all of these obstacles at St. Joseph, Bruff suggested they cross the Missouri at Old
Fort Kearny 90 miles to the north (in present-day Nebraska City).
Old Fort Kearny was closed the previous year after the military
deemed the site ill-chosen. At the old fort, corn would be available
for their animals and there would be fewer nettlesome creeks to
cross on the other side.

And so the next day the Company started north. Even though
Bruff had made a sound decision—or recommendation—they
had lost valuable time lingering in St. Joseph. With 2,000 miles
between them and the Sacramento Valley, they needed to be east
of the Rockies by August 1 to avoid the snow over the High Sierras. To slow them further, May was proving to be an extremely
wet month. The prairie sod had become a quagmire and was
deeply rutted from the passing of other wagons, slowing their
pace to a crawl and wreaking havoc on wheels. Wagons, which
normally averaged two miles an hour on the trail, now crept
along at an agonizing five miles a day. Thirteen miles up near the
town of Savannah, two of the wagon axles broke from the strain.
That evening, the Company pulled into an oak and walnut grove
to camp and repair the wagons. At a farmhouse nearby, Bruff
learned of a ferry operating across the Missouri called Duncan's
Ferry and decided he would try to cross there. The distraught
farmer told Bruff his wife had divorced him and joined a gold
prospecting company formed in Savannah. Although the wagons
had been repaired in a day—thanks to Bruff's foresight in bringing a spare—the rains had returned, making the trail as sticky and

sodden as molasses. The caravan of wagons lurched and crawled, and more axles broke. It seemed as if the expedition would never get to the frontier.

One evening the skies cleared and Bruff laid his bedroll out in the open air. As he lay down on the mossy ground, he took in a chorus of hooting owls, crying whippoorwills, and barking foxes. One of the men began playing "Home Sweet Home" on a bugle, causing him to think wistfully about "the friends and comforts we had bade a long farewell to and to which some us might never return."

On May 22, the Company came to the Nodaway River, a broad swift-moving stream about 100 miles southeast of the Platte River. Lewis and Clark had camped at the mouth of the Nodaway in 1804. After they crossed the river, Bruff went off to buy some flour and encountered an agitated man from a gold mining company from Pittsburgh. The man, now on his own, told Bruff that weeks earlier he had abandoned his group because there had been so much fighting and discord that he had come to fear for his life. The luckless company had foundered before breaching the frontier. Thinking of his own already frustrated group, Bruff prudently ordered guards to stand watch with loaded weapons that night.

The next day the Company reached a narrow stream fringed by deep, soft banks. As the bridge over it was precariously narrow, Bruff cautioned the teamsters to proceed with care. The first two wagons passed over safely. As the driver of the third started over the bridge, the wagon—with two sick men inside—tipped over. As it careened over the edge, the driver leaped off the mule saddle and the two sick men jumped out the back seconds before the wagon tumbled into the water. Despite the spectacular fall, the only damage had been a broken axle.

On May 26, about 57 miles out of St. Joseph, the Company reached Duncan's Ferry. With one company ahead of them and the spring waters roiling and turgid, Bruff offered to assist their crossing in return for same. The first crossing of oxen went smoothly. On the second trip, Bruff put several of his men on board to assist with the other company's wagons. As the ferry was crossing, it struck a partially submerged log and capsized in deep water. One of the wagons disappeared in the raging current with all its contents. Several of the men frantically swam to the bank—as did the oxen, which were surprisingly good swimmers in a pinch—while others clung to a log until rescued by a canoe. Old man Duncan, who was steering the boat, drowned, but he proved to be the only casualty. None the worse for the wear—apart from the tragic loss of Duncan—Bruff and the Company headed north in search of another crossing point.

The morning broke cold and clear. To make up for lost time, Bruff roused the men at 3 a.m. with a bugle call. After breakfast, they set out in the early morning darkness. By evening they had reached the Nishnabotna River and ferried all the wagons across. Although the men were flagged, Bruff resolved to take advantage of the dry weather and ordered an all-night march along the Nishnabotna. The marshy trail made going slow and from time to time the wagons had to be emptied or pushed to get through the sticky mud. The next morning Bruff realized Stinson, who claimed to know the area intimately, had overlooked a much drier trail some distance from the river. It would be the first in a series of bungles by the feckless guide. In the evening they spotted an old farmhouse that turned out to be occupied by several Mormons awaiting the arrival of a large Mormon train to take them to Salt Lake. Described by Bruff as "clever fellows," they prepared a hearty dinner for Bruff and his officers.

Near the headwaters of the Tarkio Creek they noticed a tidy farmhouse that looked as though it had been recently vacated. In front of the house was a haunting reminder of the tragedy at the ferry the previous day. A tall pole bore a hand-painted sign swinging eerily in the wind, "TO DUNCAN'S FERRY, 9 MILES, THE BEST ROUTE TO THE GOLD REGIONS." Alas, the ferry was Duncan's no longer.

After stopping for a late breakfast, Bruff sent two of his men 10 miles north to Old Fort Kearny to engage a ferry. That evening, the men returned with bad news: Heavy spring rains had raised the river to a level not seen in years. With so much dangerous debris hurtling downriver, ferry operators had suspended service. The Company would now have to cross the turgid, muddy river at Council Bluffs 120 miles farther north. There it was lower although still quite dangerous. Upon hearing this, some of the "weakest minds" clamored to return to St. Joseph. Bruff insisted on sticking to his plan and crossing at old Fort Kearny. That very day he had spoken with a man who had successfully crossed the Missouri a month earlier at that locale. But that, the men countered, would have been before the river's rise. Convinced his was the right approach, Bruff summoned the man and persuaded him to lead them to the crossing, called Indian Point, just south of the old Fort.

When they arrived under a light drizzle, Bruff gazed down from the bluff and saw a churning mass of muddy water. "Banks oerflow'd, running like a mill-race and thick with drift, much of which was large trees." It was a half-mile wide with treacherous, shifting sandbars lurking just below the surface. Even more hazardous were the submerged logs hurtling downstream that could rip the hull of a ferry wide open. Undeterred, Bruff examined the ferry and deemed it too low to handle the raging current. He ordered his mechanics to raise the sides of the scow and cut new, larger oars for steering. To compensate for the powerful drift, he ordered the ferry be launched a half-mile upriver, necessitating the cutting of a towpath through thick brush. Wielding hatchets and bowie knives, the men slashed bushes and bramble, felled trees, and dragged logs and stumps to the side. All day they worked and by nightfall a path had been cleared.

The next day brought clear skies. Using the nautical skills acquired in his youth, Bruff rigged the ferry with a sail that consisted of a tent pole for a mast and yardarm and a tent canvas for the square sail. To test the unusual sailing ferry, he sent one wagon and four mules across. As they eased the craft gingerly into the water, the ferry captain watched for any floating debris or boils that signaled a submerged log or sandbar. Several men stood astern with poles to fend off mammoth logs of oak, walnut, ash, and elm shooting downriver like torpedoes. The scow was so low and the river so turbulent that when the ferry was mid-stream, they could see only the white canvas of the wagons and the heads of the men bobbing up and down. From the bank, it looked as if the entire group was drifting downriver on the many logs churning in the river. A tense half-hour later, the ferry safely reached the other side. Satisfied with the success of his experimental nautical craft, Bruff ordered the remaining wagons to be taken across the river, a painstaking process that took three days. Once his men and wagons were all safely on the other side, Bruff took the last boat across. So grateful was the ferry driver for the uncanny nautical knowledge that he gave Bruff a discount on the fare.

It was June 4, almost two months since the men had left Washington. By this time, the first great wave of Gold Rushers was already at South Pass in the Rockies. All the delays notwithstanding, Bruff's decision to cross at old Fort Kearny had been vindicated. Faced with tough decisions and seeming insurmountable obstacles, he had shown unerring judgment and gotten his Company to the Great Plains without mishap.

The heavy rains had ceased and summer was just beginning. Before them lay the great frontier.

Chapter Three

THE END OF EVERYTHING

IN CROSSING THE MISSOURI RIVER, BRUFF AND HIS men had passed from the known to the unknown, from the settled, civilized Union into the wild and untamed American frontier. It was a vast area more than twice the size of the Union that only recently had begun to be mapped and explored.

Exploration of the West began in the sixteenth century when the French and English undertook the search for a Northwest Passage, a presumed river route across the continent to the Pacific. While exploring for the elusive passage in 1789, Scotsman Alexander Mackenzie became the first white man to cross the continent. More than a decade later, President Thomas Jefferson dispatched Lewis and Clark to find the passage and improve commerce with the Indians. Their Corps of Discovery followed the Missouri to its headwaters then struck overland to the Columbia River. Although the intrepid explorers also failed to find a Northwest Passage, they had returned with a wealth of information on the region's geography, peoples, and resources, and more than 100 maps of their travels. Robert Stuart, a fur trader for John Jacob Astor, later pioneered a more southerly route to the northwest than the Lewis and Clark trajectory. Accessible to wagons, the trail traced an undulating line that ran from the town of St. Joseph up the Missouri River and into the Platte River Valley toward Fort Hall in present-day Idaho. Using this route, trapper and trailblazer Jedidiah Smith became the first American to cross the Great Plains in the 1820s. Continuing west, Smith forged a trail through the Rockies at South Pass, which marked the Continental Divide. An entire generation of traders, trappers, farmers, and Mormons would adopt Smith's route—dubbed the Oregon Trail—as the most practical to northern California and Oregon. By the early 1840s, the first wagons began rumbling along the trail, mostly farming families headed to the fertile Willamette Valley of Oregon with a smattering settling in the Sacramento Valley.

If early explorers and traders had forged the way west, it was the Mormons who paved it. Having fled persecution in the east, Mormons originally thought their Promised Land lay in Illinois. But it wasn't long before they became reviled by the locals, as much for their uncanny success in business as their strange practice of polygamy. After their charismatic leader, Joseph Smith, was murdered in 1844, the Latter-day Saints began to search for a new religious haven. Two years later, Mormon families started drifting west, but with no idea where they would settle. Because most were leaving from Nauvoo, Illinois, the Saints followed much the same route as the Oregon Trail. When they reached the Great Salt Lake Valley, their new leader, Brigham Young, decided to settle there on the thinking that such a harsh place would be unlikely to attract large numbers of Gentiles. Once in Salt Lake, Young established winter camps in Iowa and Nebraska to facilitate early spring departures by Mormons. To ease the difficult passage, the enterprising leader established river ferries, free for Mormons and $3 for all others. He published mileage guides and established inns along the way with baths and barbershops. Cattle and vegetable gardens along the route allowed the Saints to replenish food stores. By the time of the Gold Rush, the Oregon Trail had become more of a road than a trail.

But the region west of South Pass was still terra incognita. Mormons had only gone as far as Salt Lake City and most other travelers had been farmers bound for Oregon, not California. There were parched deserts to cross—or circumvent—and labyrinthine mountains that could lead the unsuspecting emigrant astray.

By far the most formidable obstacle was the Sierra Nevada ("snowy range"). Running like a wall north to south for 400 miles along California's eastern flank, the Sierras were some of the highest mountains on the continent and snowed in for long periods of time. So deep was the snow in winter that it buried entire trees. Explorers and travelers had invariably perished—or nearly so—trying to cross the 14,000-foot range. In 1848, in the fourth of five expeditions west, Frémont had recklessly attempted to find a route over the Sierras that would be passable for railroads in winter. Trappers, traders, and even the Washoe Indians in the area scoffed at the notion and warned him he would die trying. Indeed, the Sierra peaks were still littered with the remains of previous failed attempts: pack saddles, packs, bits of clothing, and carcasses of mules and their owners. Frémont, however, was convinced he could cross and make an even bigger name for himself in the process. Using a seasoned guide, he set out in January but quickly encountered trouble in the impossibly deep snow. Ten men in his party of thirty-three froze or starved to death. Frémont narrowly escaped death himself, managing to cross the mountains at present-day Carson's Pass and stumble, starving and emaciated, into Sutter's Fort in March.

Unclear as to the best way over the Sierras, or even the best route beyond South Pass, like many Gold Rushers, Bruff had charted a course only as far as the Rockies, intending to learn more about the way forward from soldiers and emigrants as he advanced.

If any Argonauts knew where they were going—at least to a point—they knew considerably less about what they would encounter along the way. The entire Great Plains north of the Kansas River was designated Indian Territory by the government. Except for a few licensed trappers and traders, the region was strictly off limits to whites. With the exception of a few thousand white squatters who had ignored the ban, no one but Indians lived on the Plains. If there had been any major settlement of the Plains, it was as a result of the removal of Indians east of the Mississippi.

To meet the sudden demand by Gold Rushers for information about the trail, publishers began churning out "emigrant guides." More pamphlet than book, the guides provided advice on what provisions to bring, the type of animal suitable for drawing wagons, how to ford rivers, as well as information on sources of water, pasture, trees for firewood, flora and fauna to avoid, and obstacles. Distances were provided between watering holes and pastures as well as natural landmarks along the trail. Bruff bought several of these guides, the best being William Clayton's twenty-four-page *The Latter-Day Saints Emigrants' Guide: Being a Table of Distances, Showing All the Springs, Creeks, Rivers, Hills, Mountains, Camping Places, and All Other Notable Places, from Council Bluffs, to the Valley of the Great Salt Lake*, published in 1848. Clayton had traveled with Brigham Young from Illinois along the north bank of the Platte in their historic bid to find a Mormon home.

Yet, much to the frustration of emigrants, guidebooks were often unreliable. Maps and distances were often inaccurate and vital grass, watering holes, and creeks were not where the guide-books said they would be. Since two-thirds of the 2,000-mile jour-ney was over arid land, failure to find water in particular could lead to disaster.

Every emigrant who could read had doubtless read Frémont's published reports of his first three expeditions in 1842, 1843–44, and 1845. In the first, Frémont had made a five-month journey along the Platte to South Pass under the guidance of Kit Carson. Although the second journey aimed to map the route to Oregon beyond South Pass, Frémont managed to forge a new pass over the Sierras that he named Carson's in honor of his guide. Each of his reports contained detailed descriptions of the trail, Indian inhabi-tants, important landmarks, and geological features, as well as use-ful maps.

Like other emigrants, Bruff had also read the twenty-one installments in *Knickerbocker's Magazine* of the historian Francis Parkman's account of travel on the Oregon Trail. Presented as an adventure story, Parkman's articles provided a detailed, if at times distorted, account of life on the Plains. In particular, his descrip-tion of an unfortunate emigrant party he met near the South Fork of the Platte River played on the usual white fear of Indians:

> *They were ill-looking fellows, thin and swarthy, with careworn anxious faces, and lips rigidly compressed. They had good cause for anxiety; it was three days since they first encamped here, and on the night of their arrival they had lost a hundred and twenty-three of their best cattle, driven off by the wolves . . . Since leaving the settlements they had met with nothing but misfortune. Some of their party had died; one man had been killed by the Pawnees; and about a week before they had been plundered by the Dahcotahs [Sioux] all of their best horses . . .*

Parkman's portrayal of Indians was as much a reflection of common attitudes toward Indians as it was a shaper of them:

> *They [Indians] were thorough savages. Neither their manners*
> *nor their ideas were in the slightest degree modified by contact*
> *with civilization . . . their religion, superstitions, and preju-*
> *dices were the same handed down to them from immemorial*
> *time. They fought with weapons that their fathers fought with,*
> *and wore the same garments of skin. They were living represen-*
> *tatives of the stone age . . .*

Parkman's account perpetuated the greatest misconception most easterners had about the frontier: that it was seething with murderous, thieving Indians. The stereotype of the savage native had long been nurtured by dime-store novels and newspapers seeking to appeal to easterners' appetite for tales of adventure and danger on the frontier. Travel narratives of explorers and traders, while acknowledging Indian bravery and nobility, also exaggerated the Indian penchant for violence and treachery. Lurid accounts of intertribal warfare, scalp-taking, and other atrocities eventually shaped the popular perception of Indians as essentially danger-ous, uncivilized creatures who stood in the way of progress and of whose treachery whites should forever be on guard.

In fact, a statistical analysis has shown that between 1840 and 1860, only 362 emigrants were killed by Indians along the trail, about 18 a year. During the same period, whites killed 426 Indi-ans. Bruff's own experience would confirm the essentially positive behavior of the Plains Indians toward the whites in 1849. The hos-tile California Pitt Indians were another breed altogether, how-ever. Of course, none of this was known at the time, and emigrants ventured across the Plains expecting the worst and were appropriately armed to the teeth. Not surprisingly, the general fear and suspicion of the Indian sparked wild rumors along the trail about Indian savagery as stories passed along the trail about Native atrocities grew inflated with each telling. One mother was so convinced of Indian barbarity that she wove burial shrouds for each member of the family prior to embarking. Sadly, the mistrust engendered by popular perceptions created more problems between Indians and whites than any innate hostility on the part of the Indians.

There were also a host of other unknowns and unpredictables along the trail. Weather on the Plains could be extreme. Too much rain would turn the trail into a quagmire, too little would make it dusty and not produce the grass needed to feed the animals. Accident, disease, wild animals, poisonous plants and insects, and conflict with other emigrants and each other would prove to be their constant companions on the journey.

The morning of June 5 broke clear with a light breeze blowing out of the southeast. As the men looked west across the Plains, they beheld a vast undulating carpet of tallgrass prairie stretching disconcertingly to the horizon. It was a strange and unfamiliar landscape unlike anything they had seen back east. Flat and featureless, the landscape was nearly treeless except for the cottonwoods and elms along the creek banks. Flowers like leadplant, stiff goldenrod, primrose, and spiderwort lent a measure of color to the monotonous, dark green sea. When Willa Cather moved to Nebraska as a child, upon seeing the prairie she was so overcome by its strangeness she cried, "It was the end of everything."

At 8 a.m. the Company prepared to embark. Teamsters organized the Company's wagons into a sinuous train about a football field in length. With Bruff at the head, the men gathered alongside the wagons, making last-minute adjustments of their backpacks and checking that their pistols were loaded. Raising his arm high,

Bruff thrust it forward giving the signal to start. Whips cracked, teamsters cried out, and wheels creaked forward as the Washington Company began the long march to California.

The trail up the valley of the Platte River could not have been easier for tender-footed emigrants and their overloaded wagons. Following the south bank of the Platte River, the trail was nearly as flat as a pool table. All the way through Nebraska it ascended to the Rockies so gradually as to be imperceptible. Even the heaviest wagons could make the trip. The Platte trail was also wide, allowing wagons to fan out for three to five miles to avoid the choking dust and deep ruts of other wagons.

The Platte River was as strange and unfamiliar as the prairie itself. It derived its name from the French *la rivière plat* or "flat river." The Pawnee called it *ni bthaska* meaning "flat water." Fed by the melting snows of the Rockies, the river was broad, flat, and silvery. With no trees bordering it, the river looked like an enormous culvert carved through the prairie. Even though it was a mile to two wide, the Platte was dangerously shallow, and its braided channels and sandbars made fording perilous. Its water was brackish and perpetually muddy, prompting the emigrant refrain, "too thick to drink, too thin to plow."

The Company covered 23 miles the first day. After all the frustrating delays and false starts, the men had finally begun the journey in earnest. The trail was teeming with canvas-covered wagons, so many that it looked like a great caterpillar winding and twisting its way west. While one could take comfort in the safety of numbers, in dry weather the large number of wagons raised huge clouds of dust, irritating to those in the rear. To protect their eyes, many teamsters fashioned goggles with glass and leather frames. Others fanned out to the side—in some places for miles—to avoid the dust. Wet weather was little better, for the wagons simply marred the trail with deep ruts, making travel rough for those in the rear.

Not that emigrant parties were concerned about those in the rear. A coldly competitive attitude prevailed among Gold Rushers as if those first to arrive would somehow be rewarded for their efforts. On the trail a few days ahead of Bruff, emigrant William Swain observed:

> *The whole emigration is wild and frantic with a desire to be pressing forward . . . Whenever a wagon unluckily gets stuck in the mud in crossing some little rut, the other trains behind make a universal rush to try to pass that wagon and to get ahead of each other. Amid the yelling, popping of whips and cursing, perhaps a wagon wheel is broken, two or three men knocked down in a fight, and twenty guns drawn out of the wagons. All this is occasioned by a delay of perhaps two minutes and a half.*

If Bruff was in a hurry, he didn't show it. As he marched up the valley, he delighted in the beauty of the tallgrass prairie with its rolling green hills and unusual flora and fauna of Indian apples, wild roses, plovers, killdeer, curlews, and grouse. They feasted on nature's garden of wild gooseberries, strawberries, onions, and prairie peas.

The next morning, the Company traveled 14 miles before halting near Weeping Water, a tributary of the Missouri where Lewis and Clark had stopped on July 20, 1804. In the afternoon Bruff came across three starving army deserters from Grand Island and gave them some food. Desertion from military posts was common in 1849, as many men had enlisted merely as a cheap means of getting to the gold fields at the government's expense. To their chagrin, these men had not been assigned anywhere near the gold fields.

Near the headwaters of the Nemaha River, Bruff spotted a small party of Pawnee Indians, a tribe deemed friendly by the government, in the distance. Their ragged appearance revealed nothing of the proud race of warriors they had once been. Armed with only quiver and bow and without any mounts, these Pawnee were a sad lot—ragged, starving, and gaunt. Opening their dingy robes to expose their prominent ribs and breastbones, they begged for food. Fearing if he refused, they would attempt to rob his rear wagons or a small unarmed family, Bruff gave them some bread, bacon, and a hatful of tobacco. Out of pity, some of the men offered bells and whistles and a silver "peace medal" that the government and emigrant parties routinely presented to peaceable Indians. In gratitude, the weary Pawnee chief laid a skin on the ground and motioned for Bruff to sit to his left, cross-legged like the others. The chief then lit a long pipe and, after taking three long puffs, passed it to Bruff. Bruff later made a sketch of a smoking Pawnee that was used as a decoration in the U.S. Treasury headquarters.

The beleaguered Pawnees that surrounded Bruff were the remnants of a great nation of 20,000 warriors once feared by all the Plains Indians. For generations they lived and prospered along the Platte, Loup, and Republican Rivers. In spring, they planted corn, squash, and beans in their villages before traveling to their favorite buffalo hunting grounds south of the forks of the Platte. In late summer they returned to their villages to harvest their crops before returning to the rivers for the fall and winter hunts.

Then began their tragic demise. In 1832, a smallpox epidemic killed thousands of Pawnee. The outbreak was followed by an even greater and more enduring scourge, the Sioux. Driven out of their ancestral home in northern Minnesota by the Cree, Assiniboine, and Chippewa, the Sioux moved south and west over the Plains where they thrived. When the Oglala Sioux moved into the area of the Laramie Fork, they began sending their own hunting parties to the forks of the Platte in 1835. Finding it rich in buffalo, they decided to claim the territory as exclusively theirs. During the next decade the Sioux waged relentless attacks on Pawnee villages, stealing horses and driving them from their hunting grounds. By 1848, the thirteenth year of the war, the harried Pawnee were virtually homeless, a broken and dispirited tribe with no friends. The previous winter, hunted by the Sioux like animals, the Pawnee had returned from their hunting grounds south of the Platte with so little game their trail could be followed by the bodies of those who had starved to death. Those who made it to their fields on the Platte bottoms found all their corn burned up by a drought.

Now only 5,000 Pawnees remained, relying mostly on begging and stealing horses to survive. Bruff's Pawnees were probably moving from their old villages south of the Platte to safer ground along the Missouri. Although they were still capable of mounting an attack, the chiefs usually held warriors back, afraid to engender the animosity of the white man. Bruff aptly summarized the state of the haggard Pawnee before him in light verse:

The dark and savage Pawnees came,-
And asked for something to eat;-
But oh, how chang'd & tame!-
They wanted bread and meat.-

And the murd'rous thieving Sioux,-
Pursuing the fallen Pawnee foes:-
Who have little but lives to loose [lose],-
Their race is near its close.

As the men resumed their journey, several desperate Pawnee attempted to follow but gave up after several miles. At nightfall the Company arrived at Loup Fork, a tributary of the Platte, and made camp for the night among a few cottonwoods near the Platte bottoms. The next day the Company passed through a deserted Pawnee village with hundreds of empty earthen lodges. Littering the ground were moccasins, wooden mortars and pestles, dried herbs, reed mats, and other artifacts.

With good reason, Bruff assumed the Pawnee had been driven out by the Sioux. But they may well have been fleeing another, all-too-familiar, enemy—cholera. The disease had followed the emigrants up the trail, where it was now killing Indians and whites alike. The Pawnee knew painfully well that, like smallpox, this disease followed in the white man's wake. In 1837, a deckhand working for the American Fur Company brought cholera upriver that had swept them off "like chaff before the wind," according to a government Indian agent. That year, the Pawnee lost a quarter of their people to the dreaded disease. Entire villages had teepees full of dead bodies. Other tribes that lived along the Platte—the Cheyenne and Sioux—were also affected. The Blackfeet and Mandan were nearly wiped out entirely.

Little did the Indians or emigrants know that the Platte Valley was the perfect incubation ground for the disease. As the salty river flowed over its low banks, it created standing pools of brackish water where the *Vibrio cholerae* organism thrived. Add to it the human and animal waste of thousands of emigrants along the river, and the river became a moving vector that affected thousands of travelers downstream. Even though most understood the disease was related to contaminated water, the large number of people and lack of good drinking water along the Platte made it difficult to ward off. That year, cholera would kill 1,500 emigrants on the trail east of Fort Laramie and would pursue them all the way to the Rockies and even beyond. Little did some know when they had set out on the journey with such excitement what gruesome fate awaited. For survivors, the grief of having to bury a loved one along the trail drove many to quit and go home. Dug in haste, many of the graves were so shallow that wolves had no trouble exhuming and devouring the bodies of the fallen.

A few miles from the ghostly village, a hunting party of Indians approached from the hills displaying a white flag. The head of the party said he was a nephew of the Pawnee chief, Shaitarish, or "wicked chief." Consulting his pocket notebook, Bruff found his name, which he had obtained in St. Louis, and uttered "Shay-taar-eesh." Upon hearing this, the chief was struck with delight. He embraced Bruff "with the warmth of an affectionate bear and just as odiferous," telling him buffalo could be found in two more days.

The Company's good fortune in meeting friendly Indians contrasted with the bad luck of others. The previous day, the Company had crossed paths with a government party headed for Missouri that had been robbed of all its provisions by a war party of 500 Cheyenne. Like the Pawnee, the Cheyenne had been driven from their home in the Upper Plains by the Lakota Sioux. At first the whites, bent on resistance, closed their wagons and "stood to their arms." Waving a white flag tied to a rifle, the chief and three of his emissaries rode over to the party. Speaking Spanish, the chief calmly reasoned it was folly for the whites to resist and risk losing their men—they might just as well give up their provisions and save their lives. Conceding the wisdom in the good chief's advice, the men complied. After the Indians had finished pillaging all the wagons, they threw down some moccasins and beadwork, saying it was payment for the provisions they had taken. Having lost everything, the unlucky party bought from the Washington Company enough food to reach the Missouri.

A few days later, three Mormons, one sick, stopped in their camp to rest saying they had been robbed by a party of Crow Indians who took everything including their horses. Once again, Bruff sold them provisions to get them to their destination. Ever concerned about the welfare of others on the trail, the devout Freemason also allowed a small party of Argonauts fearing Indian predation to join his Company.

On June 17, the Company arrived at the new Fort Kearny, named after Brigadier General Stephen Watts Kearny, a hero of the Mexican War. Fort Kearny was one of three forts Frémont had astutely recommended be established on the trail (the others were Forts Laramie and Hall) to protect wagon trains headed to Oregon. Congress approved funding for the construction of the military posts in 1846 but building had been delayed by the war with Mexico. Construction on Kearny having only recently begun, it consisted of little more than adobe battlements, tents, and sheds for the 170 men stationed there.

Overlanders were deeply appreciative of the forts along the trail and organized their perilous journey around them. Part way station, sentinel post, supply depot, and message center, the forts offered emigrants a taste of home. Kearny had a store, a blacksmith shop, a sawmill, and a boarding house run by a Mormon. Not surprisingly, all around Kearny were encampments of companies from virtually every state of the Union. A correspondent for the *St. Louis Republican* described the scene:

> *Every state and I presume almost every town and Country in the United States is now represented in this part of the world. Wagons of all patterns, sizes, and descriptions, drawn by bulls,*

cows, oxen, jackasses, mules, and horses, are daily seen rolling
along toward the Pacific, guarded by walking arsenals.

Bruff called on the officers there, one of whom, Col. Andrew
Porter, was an acquaintance. Porter was surprised to see Bruff, having received word that the captain had succumbed to cholera. The
Commander of the Fort, Lt. Col. Benjamin Bonneville, invited
the captain to dine with him. Also a veteran of the Mexican War,
Bonneville was something of a legend in the military. In the 1830s,
he had taken a leave of absence to explore the West. He was gone so
long incognito that the War Department eventually dropped his
name from the military registry. During his absence, Bonneville
explored the Great Salt Lake area and correctly concluded, con-
trary to earlier belief that the briny body of water drained into the
Pacific, that it had no outlet to the sea.

Over breakfast, Bonneville regaled Bruff with amusing stories
of the "pious gold pilgrims" along the trail. As thousands were
camped opposite the fort, Bonneville had observed the petty
squabbling and breakup of the numerous joint stock companies
with sworn constitutions. The Argonauts would then divide the
property, some proceeding on foot or mules while others turned
back in disgust. Bonneville could well appreciate the demands of
Bruff's position:

> *He says I have a most trying, thankless, and unenviable task*
> *in this matter myself, and he thinks, that if extraordinary*
> *patience, forbearance, and determination, I succeed in keeping*
> *the Company together, to California, I shall do wonders.*

Walking back to camp, Bruff came across several gravestones of
cholera victims. Having kept a detailed record of each gravestone

he passed, his journal later served as a valuable registry for the many casualties of the trail that year.

Before leaving Kearny, Bruff shed more unnecessary equipment, including the ambulance that he deemed "a perfectly useless article, except to encourage lazy men to ride." Henceforth, each man would be limited to 50 pounds of provisions, much to the grumbling of the men. The Washington Company was not the only one jettisoning excess articles. So many parties were lightening their load that the area around the fort had become a huge dumping ground. There were discarded sawmills, pickaxes, shovels, anvils, featherbeds, rocking chairs, furniture. Dozens of other useless articles that had once seemed so essential for the journey were now being left by the wayside. So much abandoned property littered the trail that some of the merchants who first sold the items in Missouri towns were rushing out to collect and resell it to next year's travelers.

The Company also left behind one of the older members of the party, 48-year-old Richard Culverwell, who had become too ill to continue. Refunding $75 of his money, Bruff advised him to return home and recuperate. So determined was he to get to the gold fields that Culverwell went to Salt Lake City, where he hooked up with a party traveling via the southern route. Culverwell would later break with the party and meet his death, appropriately, in Death Valley.

For the Washington Company, it was smooth sailing. Summer had arrived clear and calm. Days were warm and nights deliciously cool. The men dined on savory buffalo meat and marveled at the prairie's curious inhabitants: the black wolf with its icy, enervating stare, chirpy prairie dogs, and wary coyotes. From time to time, as commander of the party, Bruff would be invited to dine with other emigrant parties, or saunter off on his own either to hunt game or simply to seek respite from the burden of his duties.

Notwithstanding the trail's more pleasant moments, uneasiness about Indians hung over the Company like a cloud. Of late, Teton, Sioux, or Cheyenne—no one was quite sure which—had been spotted in the distance mounted and wearing war paint. Until 1840, white-Indian relations were generally good as contact had been based primarily on trading from which Indians benefited. But in the decade preceding the Gold Rush, Indians of the Plains and Rockies had watched anxiously as roughly 5,000 white emigrants passed through their territory, scaring off and plundering all the game. Their conclusion: Nothing good ever accompanied the white man. As throngs of Gold Rushers now poured across the plains, they were as destructive as a plague of locusts. These strange and inscrutable creatures were killing and scaring all the game, polluting the streams, destroying grass and timber—and giving nothing in return. For this reason, the Sioux dubbed the white people *wasichu*, "one that eats the fat."

Of all the offenses of the whites, the worst in Indian eyes was the wanton killing of buffalo, the mainstay of the Plains Indians. Indians depended heavily on the shaggy beast for food, shelter, and clothing. Between 1824 and 1836, Frémont noted, one would always be among large bands of buffalo between the Missouri River and the Rocky Mountains. But large-scale harvesting of buffalo by hunters interested only in their hides and tongues (considered a delicacy) had drastically reduced their numbers. Hunters left the meat—nearly 2,000 pounds per animal—for the wolves or to rot in the sun. The total number of buffalo killed during the decade, Frémont concluded, had been "immense." Indeed, during the eight years from 1834 to 1842, the American Fur Company, Hudson's Bay Company, and a few smaller enterprises shipped an astonishing 90,000 buffalo robes annually.

Traveling on the Plains in 1843, the naturalist and painter John

J. Audubon lamented, "Even now, there is a perceptible difference in the size of the herds, and before many years the Buffalo, like the Great Auk, will have disappeared . . ." Two years later the Cheyenne chief, Old Soldier, complained to Stephen Watts Kearny that the slaughter of bison was so great that it threatened to destroy the Cheyenne way of life. Indeed, the very next year some of the Cheyenne and other tribes had begun to starve from the lack of bison along the Platte and Santa Fe trails. The government was well aware of the problem but powerless to control emigrant behavior on the open Plains.

Decades of carnage had left the Platte Valley littered with buffalo bones, as emigrant John Bidwell observed in 1841:

> *The scenery of the country of the Platte is rather dull and monotonous, but there are some objects which must ever attract the attention of the observant traveler; I mean the immense quantity of buffalo bones, which are everywhere strewed with great profusion, so that the valley, throughout its whole length and breadth, is nothing but one complete slaughter yard.*

Some inventive pioneers and Gold Rushers found they could communicate with wagons behind them by scribbling messages across the broad foreheads of those bleached-white skulls and setting them on stakes driven into the ground beside the trail.

Notwithstanding the senseless slaughter, as many as 60 million buffalo may still have been on the Plains at the time of the Gold Rush. Huge herds in the distance appeared to awestruck travelers as swirling dark clouds. When buffalo were on the move, they meandered along in massive columns or stampeded with a thunderous shaking of the ground beneath.

Unlike hunters, Gold Rushers had different motives for the

killing: for meat, to allay boredom, or simply to demonstrate male prowess. Emigrant parties killed as many as fifty in a single day, usually leaving all but a few to rot on the Plains. Seized with the excitement of the hunt, most whites were generally unaware of the dangers of hunting buffalo. When pursued, buffalo usually took flight to difficult ground, which resulted in accidents to horse and rider alike. The resulting confusion could leave the hunter stranded and exposed in the prairie for days. While crossing the Plains, Bruff several times bore witness to the perils of buffalo hunting:

> Men charg'd by wounded bulls, unhorsed, and many badly hurt - the horses generally running off with the band of buffa-loes, for the indians to pick up hereafter. Lots of rifles and pis-tols lost, as well as horses: and many a poor fellow, after a hard day's hunt, on an empty stomach . . . has a long and tiresome walk, after night, to his own, or the nearest camp he can make.

Another time he saw a hapless hunter almost gored to death after wounding a bull:

> A young man by the name of Wright being in advance, dis-charged his piece into the bull's flan, wounding him, - when he charged, causing his horse to throw him and run off: the bull tossed him on his blunt horns, - made a circuit, came up, and put his head down to gore him, when with great presence of mind, he drew a heavy bowie-knife, and chopped the enraged animal across the snout, - causing him to throw up his head, snort, and run off, pursued by another hunter . . .

As the Indians watched with consternation the thousands of *wasichu* drifting up the Platte Valley, little did they know it was the beginning of the end, as much for the buffalo as for themselves who depended on them. Although buffalo could still be found in great numbers on the Upper Plains, by 1848 the vast herds in the lower Platte River Valley had disappeared. By 1890, the buffalo would vanish from the Plains entirely.

Chapter Four

DELAYS AND DISSENSION

AND SO THEY ROLLED, RUMBLED, AND MARCHED UP the Platte River Valley. For the most part, the late spring weather was cooperative, although one never knew what the mercurial Plains would serve up. One day a cold front swept across the Plains, plunging the temperature from 80 to 20 degrees Fahrenheit in a matter of minutes. There were days when the wind swept across the flat landscape so ferociously the men had to brace themselves against it as they walked.

By July, the excitement with which the men had embarked on their grand adventure had given way to listlessness born of the tedious routines of the trail. Each day the men rose at 4 a.m. After breakfast they struck camp and, come sun or rain, set out around 6 or 7. Around midday they "nooned" for lunch for an hour, sometimes longer depending on their progress. Rather than alleviate the monotony, the break for meals only reinforced it, consisting as it did of the same dull fare day after day: biscuits, dried meat, greasy bacon, and coffee, supplemented occasionally by buffalo or antelope when they were lucky in the hunt or could purchase it. Fruit and vegetables were nearly nonexistent on the trail. After lunch, they resumed their march until dusk with perhaps a stop or two to rest or make repairs. At dusk they halted for the day. Even though the men were exhausted from 12 hours of walking, before they could rest there was camp to set up and the animals to tend to. Then there was guard duty for part of the night. Day after day, they repeated the same pokey routine.

The pace of movement only added to the ennui. The wagons rumbled along at an agonizing two miles an hour, maybe three if the weather and trail were good. If you were a teamster, you bounced and jostled for hours on the hard wooden boards; if not, you walked so as not to burden the animals. Either way, heat, dust, mosquitos, and flies were their constant companions. Had they felt some progress being made on the trail, it might have alleviated the tedium somewhat. But at an average pace of 13 miles a day, the trail seemed endless. Indeed, they had not yet completed a quarter of the journey and the hardest parts were yet to come.

Whether it was the harsh conditions of the trail, accident, death, or simply squabbling within the party, other emigrants were returning to the States almost daily. Usually returning on foot or horseback, many were so ashamed they could not look the oncoming Gold Rushers in the eye. Some even avoided the trail entirely rather than have to explain the reasons for their loss of heart. These "go backs" had thought they had seen the elephant when in fact they had glimpsed only its tail. Later, as travelers struggled through punishing deserts and deep Sierra snow, some would regard the "go backs" as the wisest of the bunch.

Despite the hardships, the men of the Washington Company had ample reason to be grateful and they knew it. Unlike other companies that had already foundered over petty squabbling, what dissension that had arisen—usually over guard duty or Bruff's irritating military style—had thus far been manageable. Nor had they met with hostile Indians, theft, or serious accident. The numerous graves they passed each day, grim though they were, were a blessed reminder they had fended off the specter of cholera and were getting farther from it with each passing mile.

One day Bruff decided to take a break from his onerous duties. Ordering his second in command, Gideon Brooke, to take charge, he struck out on his horse over the hills to hunt and enjoy the scenery. He had ridden some distance when he spotted an antelope grazing near some buffalo that he took down. By this time, he had drifted far from the trail and out of sight of any of the wagons. Suddenly, he noticed several mounted Cheyenne armed and dressed in war paint. Alarmed, he slipped off unnoticed back to the security of the trail. By the time he had regained the trail, his Company was so far ahead that he did not rejoin it until noon the next day.

By the end of June, the Company had reached the South Fork of the Platte in western Nebraska. Here the land was a vast plain of white sand glaring in the sunlight. With no direct pass through the eastern face of the Rockies, they looked for a place to ford the South Fork in order to follow the northwest course of the North Platte. As they approached the river, Bruff asked Stinson to look for a shallow place to cross. The worthless guide promptly went off buffalo hunting instead.

As the Company meandered along the river looking for a shallow place to ford, two Mormons approached Bruff to offer their ferry service. After assessing the condition of their ferry and the sandy condition of the ground on the opposite bank, Bruff politely declined. As he moved on, he heard a commotion in the rear of the train. Ordering the wagons to a halt, Bruff went back to investigate and found two of the Mormons making their pitch directly to his men. One of the Mormons defended his action saying, "the sense of the Company should be taken about it," and Bruff flew into a rage. Tensions were already simmering in the Company and he certainly didn't need strangers stirring up more. Fingering his pistol tucked in his belt, he thundered, "Be off or I'll blow you to blazes!" Given his violent history at West Point, the temperamental Bruff may well have been dead serious.

Unbeknownst to Bruff, the enterprising ferry operators were supporting the growth of Salt Lake City. When Brigham Young passed through here in 1847, he, too, could find no easy passage across the river for his wagons. Resourcefully, Young sent his men upriver to cut two large cottonwoods 30 feet long from which two canoes were hewn and lashed together. With two more trees they made planks of wood and fastened them to the canoes far enough apart to be under the wheels of the wagon. The ferry had proved so successful that Young ordered his men to remain and assist other Mormons coming along in a few months. In the meantime, Gentile wagons had begun to arrive and were being charged $1.50 per wagon to cross. The arrangement proved lucrative, and Young dispatched men each summer to keep the ferry going. Revenue it generated would be used to fund construction of their new community in Salt Lake City.

After a hard tramp along the South Fork, the Company arrived at the mouth of Deer Creek and made camp. Congregated all along the banks of the creek were hundreds of people, wagons, and tents. What excess baggage they had been unwilling to part with at Fort Kearny they were now dumping along the bank with a vengeance. Virtually everything to be found on the trail and at home was strewn along the banks, including many improbable items. There was a diving bell, large anvils, forges, bellows, India-rubber boats, heaps and heaps of bacon, bags of beans, salt, tents, harnesses and poles, trunks of clothing, armoires, and rocking chairs. Beans were often the first foodstuff to be jettisoned because they were heavy to transport and tended to cause indigestion. Emigrants who viewed the Gold Rush as a competition of sorts preferred to destroy what they could no longer carry rather than leave it for others. Tools and utensils lay on the prairie deliberately bent and broken. Kegs and trunks had been chopped to bits with a hatchet. Clothing was shredded. Bruff observed one man angrily pouring turpentine over an unwanted heap of sugar. Rummaging around the refuse, Bruff found some fresh slabs of bacon. After trimming the fat and "rusty exterior," he replaced his own stocks with some choice cuts from the abandoned piles.

The discarded junk along the trail had actually been accumulating for years. Three years earlier, in precisely the same spot, Francis Parkman had observed:

> It is worth noting that on the Platte one may sometimes see the shattered wrecks of ancient claw-footed tables, well waxed and rubbed, or massive bureaus of carved oak . . . Brought, perhaps, originally from England; then, with the declining fortunes of their owner, borne across the Alleghenies to the wilderness of Ohio or Kentucky; then to Illinois or Missouri; and now at last fondly stowed away in the family wagon for the interminable journey to Oregon. But the stern privations of the way are little anticipated. The cherished relic is soon flung out to scorch and crack upon the hot prairie.

Passing through here the year after Bruff, Franklin Langworthy, a minister from Illinois, also was appalled by the waste that had accumulated:

> The destruction of property upon this part of the road is beyond all comprehension. Abandoned wagons literally crowded the

way for twenty miles, and dead animals are so numerous, that
I have counted fifty carcasses within a distance of forty rods
[200 yards] . . . The Desert from side to side, is strewn with
goods of every name . . . log chains, wagons, and wagon irons,
iron bound water casks, cooking implements, all kinds of dishes
and hollow ware, cooking stoves and utensils, boots and shoes,
and clothing of all kinds, even life preservers, trunks and boxes,
tin bakers, books, guns, pistols, gunlocks and barrels. Edged
tools, planes, augurs and chisels, mill and cross-cut saws, good
geese feathers in heaps or blowing over the Desert, feather beds,
canvas tents, and wagon covers.

So abundant were the books on the trail that the good minister was able to read discarded books all along the way. When he finished one, he would simply jettison it and pick up another.

Beyond the creek Bruff found a suitable place to ford where the river was about a quarter-mile wide and three feet deep. Crossing at an acute angle, the wagons slowly followed a sandbar to the opposite shore. Safely on the other side, they were now 175 miles from South Pass in the Rockies. To the west the men could see the 10,000-foot Laramie Range looming in the distance, the highest land they had seen thus far. They now had to cross more than 100 miles of dry sagebrush plains—the worst stretch of trail thus far—to Fort Laramie.

On July 1, the Company arrived at Ash Hollow, a picturesque setting with a small, spring-fed stream lined with ash trees. The hollow and the many small ravines feeding into it were filled with vegetation of all sorts: wild grape, cherries, plums, currants, and gooseberries. Wild roses and other flowers were in full bloom, suffusing the air with a sweet perfume. Above the hollow were rolling green hills where grass for the animals was plentiful.

Yet the thin carpet of green belied the fact that the land was becoming drier. Lush prairie grasses were slowly giving way to hardy tufts of bluestem, western wheatgrass, needle-and-thread, and blue grama. Here and there were also prickly pear cacti and poisonous wormwood. Soon the soil would turn from beige to pink, grasslands would give way to sagebrush, and forage would only be found along creek bottoms and springs.

After a day's rest, the Company descended the high table-lands into the North Platte Valley. Here was a magnificent land-scape of stunning rock formations that provided a measure of relief to the monotony of the trail. Eons of wind, ice, and rain had washed away a landscape that had been uplifting for mil-lions of years, leaving 300-foot-high formations that towered above the plain like guardians of the high passes that lay ahead. Buttes of rock, sand, and clay bore such an uncanny resemblance to fortresses and redoubts that emigrants had named them accordingly. First was Courthouse Rock, which so much resem-bled a Missouri courthouse that it actually deceived many trav-elers. Frémont had measured it at 300 feet in height. Beyond this monolith stood Chimney Rock, a towering, yellowish 300-foot spire of eroded sandstone that Bruff was moved to sketch. Every part of the rock within arm's reach had names inscribed upon it. Called "Elk Penis" by the Sioux, it was the most famous of the stunning geological formations appearing along this section of the trail.

Beyond Chimney Rock, the trail became soft and sandy and the mules were pushed to the limit. Grass was now getting harder to find, appearing only around springs and in creek bottoms. The dry air was suffused with the pleasant aroma of sage. Scattered among the rocks above were stunted cedars that fueled their campfires with their fragrant wood. The men were moving from the Plains into the great West, from a landscape of green to one of beige, and from flatness to one with dramatic vertical heights.

The Company celebrated Independence Day with a feast. The New York Company, whose commander also affected the title "Captain," joined in the celebrations and was received, Bruff-style, with military honors. A thirteen-gun salute honored the original thirteen colonies. By request, Bruff gave a speech and the men sat down to a sumptuous dinner of pork and beans, buffalo meat, rolls, soup, and stewed dried apples, with apple pie for dessert. The feast was followed by brandy and port wine, with abundant toasting to the success of the Company thus far.

Several miles on, they entered a broad valley at the far end of which stood the last of the Plains monuments: Scott's Bluff, a massive, uplifted butte of sandstone and chalky marl. The imposing rock formation encroached on the river, forcing the trail to make a wide, sweeping turn along the southern fringe of the bluff. All around its base were fresh graves of emigrants. A few had no date of death, indicating they were actually food caches that would eventually be plundered by passing travelers. Here was a trading and blacksmith shop run by Antoine Rubidoux, the son of the founder of St. Joseph.

Adjacent to the depot, Bruff found an enterprising Sioux trader selling whiskey for $5 a gallon. Liquor had had as profoundly a disruptive effect on Indians as disease, war, and resettlement. Traders were originally allowed to bring it into Indian Territory for their own use. But they soon found liquor could be used to good effect in the bargaining process, which often left Indians bereft of everything when trading was done. The government tried to ban importation of spirits into Indian Territory altogether, but to no avail.

As he skirted the sand bluffs, Bruff encountered an old teamster leading two wagons back to Missouri. The driver told Bruff that the head of the party had died west of the Laramie. His dying request was that he escort the family—a widow and children—back to Missouri. But when the driver reached the rear of the train, he told the men he was returning because the emigrants had used up all the grass west of the Laramie. To yet a third he told a different story. Bruff never learned the truth.

Early the next morning as he was mounting his horse, Bruff was informed that one of the men, 25-year-old Charles Bishop, was seriously ill. He immediately ordered the wagons wheeled down to the river and circled. Walking back to the tent of the sick man, he found Dr. Austin inside tending to Bishop. Austin said he was showing all the signs of Asiatic cholera. Bishop's messmates confirmed that several days earlier he had carelessly drunk slew water, which Bruff had expressly cautioned the men not to drink. At 11 a.m. Bishop became deranged and began shouting he wasn't afraid to die. For a few hours he writhed in pain, begging his mates to shoot him. By 1 p.m. Bishop was dead.

The men of the Company were in shock. They'd witnessed death all along the route, but this was the first Company casualty of the journey. Moreover, cholera had struck far from its source along the Missouri, raising fears they were still being haunted by the terrible disease. Bishop's messmates solemnly laid out his body, wrapped him in his blue blanket, and placed him in a bier formed with his tent and poles. For three hours Bruff labored in the hot sun, making head and footstones for the grave. Because Bishop had served in the military, his body was draped with the stars and stripes and laid to rest with his bridle reins on a ridge 400 yards from the trail. As the sun cast its dying rays, the men, ordered to don clean clothes for the occasion, marched in an elaborate funeral procession to the mournful sound of bugles. That evening Bruff penned a long verse to Bishop, the first stanza of which read:

The adventurer's train,
On the Platte river plain,
Was halted at early hour;
For a comrade was ill,
Whom no medical skill,
Could save from a Higher power!

Solemnly, the men resumed their march to Fort Laramie. As they approached the fort, Bruff sent three of his men ahead. It was hot and the men were chafing at the dust being raised by trains in front. Looking across the river to the Mormon Trail, Bruff noticed huge clouds of dust being raised by still more wagons. Everywhere he looked he saw wagons, mules, oxen, horses, and men. Indeed, since leaving St. Joseph, one never felt far from American civilization—or far enough. On the trail by day, were wagons after wagons, front and rear, a great caravan of billowing white canvas winding along like a serpent. By night, instead of the silence of great open spaces, one was forever bombarded by the noise of other emigrant encampments: campfire chatter, clanging of dinner bells, bugle calls, children shouting, music playing. One of the journey's great disappointments for Bruff—and no doubt others—was the multitude of emigrants on the trail that had robbed the frontier trail of its natural wonder. For the first time during the arduous journey—and in a manner quite out of character—he began to bristle at petty annoyances such as the emigrant penchant for inscribing their name on everything:

> *The peculiar vanity has been displayed all along the route, from our frontier down into the valley of the Sacramento. Nothing escapes that can be marked upon, - Buffalo-sculls [sic], stumps, logs, trees, rocks, etc, even the slab at the heads of graves, are all*

marked by this propensity of "penciling by the way." The singular feature is that of marking initials; for instance A.S.S. as if everyone should know who he was.

It wasn't just Bruff who was feeling the stress. One of his men, a sergeant, had violently struck another in the face in an altercation. Although Bruff had high regard for the aggressor, he needed to make an example of the man to keep the Company in line. He immediately halted the wagons and gathered the men. In his customary formal, military style, Bruff convened a "court martial" and the offender was demoted and assigned to four guards.

Shortly after the incident, the Company arrived at the Laramie River, named after Jacques La Ramie, a Frenchman who had drowned in it. Depending on the rainfall in the mountains, the river could be alternately a raging torrent or a placid stream. Now mid-summer, the river wasn't high and the wagons crossed without mishap. They had finally reached Fort Laramie.

Fort Laramie couldn't have come at a better time to ease tensions and boost the men's sagging morale. Situated on a bluff overlooking the confluence of Laramie Fork with the Platte River, the fort had recently been purchased by the government to protect western-bound Gold Rushers along the trail. Even though the large adobe structure was in bad repair, the government deemed the fort important, for it lay in the midst of several powerful and hostile Plains tribes such as the Sioux and Crow. Since the 1830s, the post had served as a major crossroads where Indians and trappers came in large numbers to trade buffalo robes and furs for blankets, guns, powder, lead, tobacco, and other dry goods, or simply to congregate or relax. The fort offered everything a traveler could want: grass, wood, clean water, and even luxury items like whiskey and cigars.

In a meadow near the trading post the Company set up camp along with hundreds of other Gold Rushers pausing to rest a few days. At the blacksmith shop, Bruff had the wheels shortened in preparation for the rougher trail ahead. The proprietor of the Trading Company told Bruff a letter for him had been received, but that someone from a company from Tennessee or Kentucky had inexplicably claimed it.

The next day, while enjoying a cigar purchased at the post, Bruff sketched the dilapidated fort. Scattered all around it were discarded goods, including an enormous 20,000-pound heap of bacon. Having learned at the fort of the punishing nature of the Black Hills just ahead, emigrants were lightening their wagons to spare the animals. That evening Bruff dined with the fort's commander, Major Simons, and a colleague from the Topographical Corps. On his walk back to camp, he passed an old graveyard for mountaineers and traders being used to bury Gold Rushers still dying of cholera.

After two days of rest, recuperation, and repairs at Laramie, the Company was back on the trail. The fort had marked the end of the main stem of the Platte River section of the journey. The muddy Platte had been their constant companion for the past 41 days and 600 miles, and they were now entering the rain shadow of the Rockies. They had climbed to 3,000 feet in altitude and would ascend 4,500 more feet on their way to South Pass through the Sweetwater Valley. Compared to what lay ahead, the Platte had been a cakewalk. From Fort Laramie to California, they would have to traverse five distinct mountainous regions: the Foreland Ranges of the Rockies, the Overthrust Belt, the Snake River Plain, the Great Basin, and the highest of them all, the Sierra Nevada.

Following the North Platte, they moved northwest along a 100-mile arc into the Black Hills, the foothills of the Laramie range.

The plains were bright with goldenrod and white and purple this-tle, along with yucca plants and sagebrush. The constant jarring of the wagons over the Black Hills' rough, stony ground led to fre-quent breakdowns. But with little rain to soften the trail, the Com-pany was making good time, some days traveling as much as 23 miles. Bruff delighted in the unique beauty of the sand hills, which he thought "grand." When they stopped to repair yet another bro-ken axle, he strolled over to a stream and netted some mullets and trout with a seine he had bought at Fort Laramie.

By mid-July they were at 5,000 feet where the sun was now beating down like a hammer on the anvil of the High Plains. Here the trail was a constant grind up mountain spurs and down steep ravines. With summer in full force and many wagons ahead of them, forage had become scarcer. But there were benefits to the Black Hills. In the harsher environment, Indians had become absent. Cholera, too, had nearly disappeared from the trail, thanks to the higher altitude—although emigrant graves continued to pop up disconcertingly here and there.

A few days out from the fort, the usual problems resurfaced. On the evening of July 13, Bruff found two of his men sleeping on guard duty. The next night a man brazenly refused to stand duty. When two others were assigned duty in the recalcitrant man's place, they also refused. Over the next week, several more men spurned duty or were caught sleeping at their posts. For their infractions, Bruff had no choice but to mete out punishments, which only widened the rift between him and the delinquents.

The next day the Company was greeted by one of the Great Plains notorious calling cards: a vicious hailstorm. As the Com-pany was ascending a hill, two menacing cloud formations—cold, Artic air and a warm, southern mass—collided directly above the party. Amid the crashing of thunder, rain fell in sheets and lightning struck the hills all around them. At first the animals appeared on the verge of stampeding, but Bruff astutely ordered the mules turned with the rear of the wagons to the gale, thereby averting a disaster. All the animals stood fast except Bruff's mule, which had bolted, causing Bruff to fall from the wagon and be struck by a falling keg of water. The party ahead had unyoked their mules, which promptly stampeded down the hill. Enormous hailstones then began to pummel them, bruising and cutting men and beast alike. Bruff's back was so lacerated it looked as if it had been lashed with a switch. "I thought that in my younger days, in the tropics, and at sea, I had seen some tall storms, but this one beat all my experience," he wrote. The storm passed as quickly as it came on, leaving an eerie silence in its wake. As they inspected the damage, they found the wagons in the other party had been cut to pieces, but the Washington Company's, being of softer wood, were unscathed. When it was all over, the temperature had plummeted 40 degrees.

While the men were nursing their wounds in camp that evening, a soldier rushed into camp on horseback with a man and a boy. Identifying himself as Captain Duncan, he had departed Fort Laramie three days earlier and had ridden his horse to exhaustion 140 miles in search of four army deserters. One of the deserters, Duncan said, had "ravished" an emigrant's wife and stolen money and a box of Colt revolvers from their tent. The previous day, Bruff had seen four suspicious looking men in dark clothes riding along the Mormon Trail on the opposite side of the river. At the time, he thought they were Indians, but now realized his mistake. Bruff lent Duncan some fresh horses and the posse dashed off in search of the deserters.

As the Company advanced west in late July, the trail veered away from the Platte as the river turned sharply south. The trail was good, although the landscape was mostly barren with desiccated sage and greasewood bushes scattered here and there. The only water was a mineral spring that Bruff knew from his reading of *Clayton's Guide* was poisoned. As they descended a steep hill, an axle broke, forcing them to lay over with no grass or water for the animals. All the next day they searched for water. When they finally arrived at the bottom of a ravine, they found only a fetid, coffee-colored alkali swamp. All around the swamp was a ghastly sight: hundreds of bodies of oxen, bloated and stiff, which had imbibed the tasteless water.

Even though it was dark and men and animals were exhausted, they pushed on in search of potable water. At length they came upon several dozen dead oxen Bruff surmised had been struck by lightning from the same violent hailstorm that had lashed them a few days earlier. At last, around midnight they came to a creek with good water. As if to signal their good fortune, enchanting emerald veils of light shimmered in the skies above—the aurora borealis. Although flagged, Bruff and Dr. Austin loaded a mule with canteens filled with water and took them to needy travelers a mile in the rear. It was early morning when Bruff finally lay down to sleep but was kept awake by the sound of wagon trains rattling along in the darkness.

With water becoming increasingly scarce along the trail, the next day Bruff ordered the men to discard excess weight, sparking yet another conflict within the Company. After a particularly heated argument with some of the men, Bruff angrily discarded several sacks of beans and stormed off to dine alone. In his journal the tempestuous Captain fumed at their behavior:

All the bad traits of the men are now well-developed,- their true character is shown, untrammeled, unvarnished . . . some of whom at home were thought gentlemen, are now totally unprincipled.

The next day Bruff learned that the disaffected men had formed a faction against him. Two factions, in truth: one group sought complete autonomy within the Company and freedom to elect its own officers; another wished to travel without any obedience to Bruff and pack its own mules and food. But the majority of men stood, whom Bruff gratefully praised as "the right stripe in every particular," steadfastly behind their commander. Internal discord had already led many of the larger companies to divide and subdivide until there were now only families or small groups of friends traveling together—and with an attendant risk to their safety in the smaller numbers.

As they resumed the journey, they ascended Prospect Hill in present-day Wyoming and were rewarded with a commanding view of the surrounding country. To the west was a breathtaking view of the shimmering Sweetwater River. To the north lay the jagged, purple peaks of the Rattlesnake Mountains behind which loomed the majestic Wind River Range. To the south, the silver thread of the Platte River wound away into the distant Black Hills dappled in sunlight.

With most of his men now squarely behind him, Bruff jettisoned more iron implements, a large keg of gunpowder (one man intended to use it to blast gold from quartz), and an India-rubber boat. Once again he ordered the men to limit personal effects to 50 pounds, an indication they had ignored his earlier instructions. With light fading, they made camp at Greasewood Creek and savored its cool mineral waters. Bruff sent Stinson ahead to reconnoiter. The guide returned with disturbing news of snow already at South Pass. It wasn't yet August. Other emigrant wagons, far in advance, were already approaching the Sierras.

They were now three weeks behind schedule, and the worst was yet to come.

Chapter Five

OVER THE GREAT DIVIDE

AT FIRST GLANCE, THE SWEETWATER RIVER VALLEY in present-day Wyoming appeared to be the kind of pristine idyll the men had imagined the trail experience to be when they set out. The valley was wide and offered breathtaking vistas of the open range and the purple Rattlesnake Mountains to the west. Between the gaps in the Rattlesnake, the majestic, snow-crested Wind River Range loomed in the background. The bottomlands were filled with lush grass and beautiful wildflowers. As for its water, it was as good as its name: sweet, cool, and delicious.

But the trail itself was not so benevolent. Even though it was a smooth climb to South Pass, the river swirled wildly with many infuriating oxbows, requiring the wagons to ford it several times. There were also long stretches when the trail diverged from the river—sometimes by as much as 15 miles—where it was hot, dusty, and devoid of water.

As they made their way through the picturesque valley, they came to a prominent trail landmark noted by virtually every explorer of the west: Independence Rock. A high granite mound a half-mile long, the rock protruded from the flat desert floor like a humpback whale. It was given its name by a party of trappers led by William Sublette who camped here on July 4, 1830. It was believed that if a party made it to this point by July 4, they would be able to cross the Sierras before the onset of snow. The Washington Company arrived on July 26, but Bruff registered no concern for their lateness. For more than a decade, passing travelers had carved or painted their names or the names of their companies on the rock to commemorate their historic achievement thus far. The numerous inscriptions on the monolith eventually gave rise to another of its names, "The Registry of the Desert." The demand to mark one's name was so great that it eventually spawned a group of stone carvers who would carve a name for a fee. Over time 20,000 names were inscribed on the rock, including that of the ill-fated Donner party that passed in 1846. Even Bruff could not resist inscribing the Washington Company's name, although only after looking long and hard for an empty spot on the rock. When he finished, he sat down and sketched the gargantuan formation.

From Independence Rock, the trail veered away from the river through a barren landscape of sagebrush, dwarf pine and cedar, shelves upon shelves of black granite, and more emigrant graves, broken wagons, and dead oxen. As the trail swung back to the river, they circled around a 400-foot-deep granite defile, Devil's Gate, through which the Sweetwater rushed. Here the company halted and the men clamored atop the gorge, firing their pistols, amused by the sound reverberating between the canyon walls. Despite their merriment—or perhaps because of it—that very night two men were "reported" for refusing guard duty.

One morning Bruff came across an ox wagon on the road with a woman sitting alone, distraught and weeping. She told Bruff how her husband had gone in search of a lost pony and was afraid he would not return by nightfall. For a moment, Bruff thought to assign one of his more reliable men to look after her cattle grazing at the river bottom, but he assumed the husband would be back by evening. That evening, however, a German man with his sick son in tow entered Bruff's camp and asked to spend the night. Saying nothing of his encounter with the man's wife, Bruff invited them to supper and offered them "the privilege of a bed on the first floor." Two days later, as he was passing Devil's Gorge, he once again encountered the unfortunate German woman, this time weeping over her now gravely ill son. Once again the husband was off chasing wandering cattle. Solitary families such as these were often no match for the rigors of the frontier and were easily overwhelmed. Bruff foresaw a grim future for them:

> *This poor woman sees hard times indeed; the son will probably die, the indians or emigrants, some of whom are little better than savages . . . will carry off their oxen, and finally the husband will take care of himself!*

While passing Bitter Cottonwood Creek, bone-dry in late July, Bruff noticed a pile of sandstone resembling a ruined tower a half-mile from the trail. Walking over to inspect the curious formation, he found it to be very different from what it had looked from a distance. It was more of a cave than a tower, and filled with bats, owls, and swallows. The exterior was marked with the names of passing travelers, most of which had been worn off. Upon close inspection he was able to make out two of the names, [Caleb] Greenwood and [William] Sublette, men whose names were associated with a shortcut through the mountains they would soon take.

For a week they meandered along the Sweetwater River, sometimes fording it twice in a single day, other times straying miles from its winding course. Twice when Bruff needed water, *Clayton's Guide* had failed him. Where the guide had indicated Sage Creek, he did not even see so much as a creek bed, and the second creek was but a dusty trough at the base of a hill. A day later, however, the *Guide* correctly indicated precisely where they would find the unusual "ice springs," deliciously cold ice water a foot beneath thick turf, which acted as insulation during summer. Emigrants invariably found the natural ice house a great curiosity, although it was quite similar in principle to the domestic ice houses back east. Still more of the Sweetwater's bounty was found in the many grouse, hares, and prairie dogs they shot and cooked over fires made with the wood of broken wagons. Here and there some stray buffalo were also to be found, but were too fleet of foot for the men to bring down. Bears and wolves were also plentiful but rarely made an appearance by day.

On August 1, with the Sweetwater now a mere trickle at its headwaters, the Company reached the Continental Divide at South Pass. Although a major geological feature of the continent, the Pass was an utter disappointment, being barely distinguishable from the barren slope leading to it. Frémont, who had crossed the 7,500-foot Pass in 1843 with Kit Carson, had also been struck by its lack of drama:

> *I should compare the elevation with which we surmounted immediately at the pass, to the ascent of Capitol Hill from the avenue, at Washington . . . It will be seen that in no matter resembles the places to which the term commonly applies— nothing of the gorge-like character and winding ascents of the Allegheny passes in America, nothing of the great St. Bernard and Simplon passes in Europe . . .*

The anticlimax notwithstanding, the Divide was still an important milestone of the journey, for it marked the division of east and west and the Atlantic and Pacific waters. "Uncle Sam's backbone," as it was popularly called, also marked the halfway point of their journey—thus far, they had crossed 1,000 miles of frontier. Looking north, Bruff could see the towering peaks of the remote Wind River Range whose 100-mile-long ridge line formed the Continental Divide and whose waters fed all three of the West's great rivers: the Colorado, Missouri, and Columbia.

That night, as Bruff was taking notes by the campfire, he heard the rare merriment of his men, inspired by the crossing of the Great Divide to the east:

> *Camp all still except the occasional snore of the weary sleeper, or the hearty laugh of the sentinels below, watching the mules grazing, at some joke to wile away the hour . . . The men were lively on striking these waters, and sat up some time after supper, spinning yarns, singing, and performing on various instruments of music.*

Their exuberance would soon be tempered by the rigors of their next hurdle, the forbidding Green River Basin, a bleak sagebrush plain stretching as far as the eye could see. It was a deflating reminder of how much distance—over 1,000 miles—they had yet to travel and over some of the roughest terrain thus far. Emigrant William Wilson put it best in a letter home to his family that year: "You may think you have seen mountains and gone over them, but you never saw anything but a small hill compared to what I have crossed over, and it is said the worst is yet to come."

Worst was an understatement. Until now, except for the 100-mile slog through the Black Hills, the trail had been mostly level through broad valleys. Water and forage were rarely far from reach. Even when wood was absent, buffalo chips made handy fuel for their fires. All that was about to change as they were now entering the rugged North America Cordillera. The Cordillera was a rumpled mass of faults and folds, of basins, plateaus, and mountains that ran all the way to the Sacramento Valley. The entire landmass ran north-south, which meant each hill, canyon, and river became an obstacle to surmount. Because the rivers generally ran transverse to the trail, water would be far harder to find. Sage and greasewood would now replace buffalo chips and wood for fuel—unless of course they came across an abandoned wagon.

At the first hollow they came to, they were relieved to find a small spring—Pacific Springs—bubbling up from a slight depression in the ground. The spring fed into a narrow brook not more than a few feet wide and lined with thick grass for almost a mile. Here they halted for two days to rest and water the animals in preparation for the long, waterless trek ahead. While Bruff was making camp, Captain Duncan rode up. Duncan had captured the four deserters farther up the trail and was taking them back to Fort Laramie. Seizing the opportunity, the men hastily penciled some letters home for Duncan to post at the fort.

At times, the trail became a meeting ground of the West's mid-century pioneers. A few days on, while Bruff was lunching in the shade of the wagons, a party heading east halted nearby. Curious to learn why the men were heading in the opposite direction, Bruff went over and found a Mr. Babbitt and his two sons from Salt Lake City. One of the sons had walked the previous year alone from Salt Lake to Missouri—in winter, no less. Babbitt was bound for Washington with a copy of the Mormon Constitution he planned to submit to Congress. The Mormons, he said, intended to seek admission to the Union as the "State of Desertia." Babbitt then produced the constitution, which Bruff, despite his dislike of the unconventional Saints, found "beautifully written and very neatly put up."

Employing his skills as a draftsman, Bruff made drawings of his surroundings throughout his voyage west. Above is Bruff's sketch of a fellow forty-niner and his horse.

Here, Bruff depicts an accident that befell the group while trying to cross a log-filled river.

Above: The terrain of the trails was unforgiving to the wagons. Many capsized along the wa

Below: Ferries across the Missouri River were perilous. Cholera was rampant among the travelers, and Bruff's company was no exception.

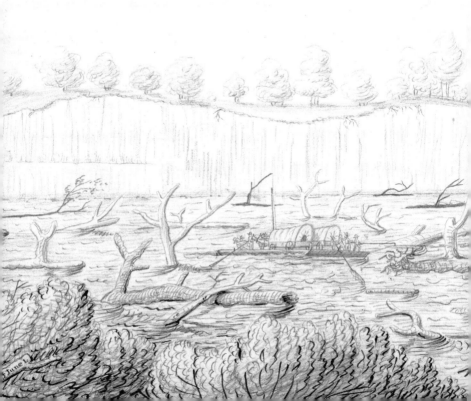

Above: Presence of mind often meant the difference between life and death.

Below: A deserted Pawnee Village the group encountered

Top: Mealtime provided the only respite from the tedium of the march westward.

Right: Chimney Rock

Bottom: A depiction of the company ferrying the Platte River above Deer Creek on July 20, 1849

4 ms: from road

2 ms: S.W. by S. from road.

Above: Courthouse and Jail Rock on the Platte River

Below: A burial for one of the emigrants

CHS. BISHOP
of
Washington City,
Died July 8. 1849
of Cholera,
Aged 25 years.

C. B

THE EMIGRANT'S GRAVE

The Emigrant's Burial

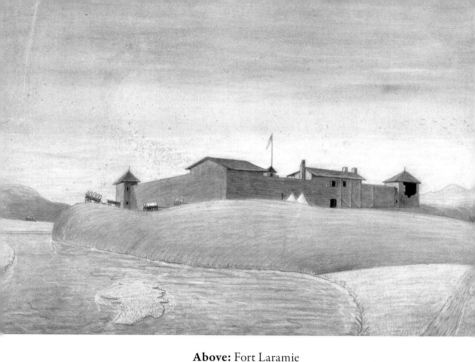

Above: Fort Laramie

Below: A tremendous hailstorm in the mountains almost broke the group's resolve.

The Devil's Gate,
Sweet-water river.

Above: The Devil's Gate on the Sweetwater River

Below: The view from the Summit of Independence Rock looking to the southeast

Henry Austin, M.D
John Bates
Chs. G. Moxley
J. Goldsborough Bruff, Capt.
Washington City Company
July 26, 1849.

S.E. View from the top of Independence
Rock, Sweet-water river, &c &c &c. and mountains
View from the Summit of Independence Rock,
looking to the S.E. exhibiting the Imp of water river, & mountains
The Washington City Comp.y corralled below, noon July 26. 1849.

the Wind River Chain of Mountains.   Two Lupps Started.   A little on the plains.

Great dividing-Ridge of the Rocky-Mountains, between the waters of the Atlantic and Pacific Oceans,
looking back towards the SOUTH-PASS: the Pass about 8 miles distant.

Above: South Pass: the great dividing ridge of the Rocky Mountains between the waters of the Atlantic and Pacific

Below: Steamboat Springs, August 17, 1849

Steam Boat Springs   aug

Babbitt, who had been one of the first gold miners in California, then produced two heavy finger rings and a $10 coin made of California gold. The Mormons in Salt Lake, he boasted, had a "barrel of gold dust" given as church tithings from Mormon diggers in California.

Babbitt's claim was likely true, for Mormons had been in on the ground floor of the Gold Rush. In 1846, at the request of President James K. Polk, Brigham Young had sent a group of young Mormons from Salt Lake City to California to fight in the Mexican War. At war's end, the men mustered out of the army, some of them choosing to seek work in California rather than return directly to Salt Lake City. Some of the Mormon veterans were at work digging John Sutter's millrace when Marshall discovered gold there in January 1848. After harvesting the surface gold during the spring of 1848, many returned to Salt Lake City in summer leading wagons over Carson's Pass, the route blazed by Frémont.

On the third day out from South Pass, the Company reached a fork in the trail. The left branch led to Salt Lake City and the right toward "Sublette's Cutoff." At the fork, a stick had been driven in the ground, bearing a board on which were posted notes to travelers in the rear as to which branch they had taken and urging those in the rear to hurry along. Wishing to avoid further dissension from his "ill-disposed men," Bruff called a meeting at 10 a.m. to reach consensus on which route to take.

Because the original California Trail beyond South Pass was so indirect, explorers during the 1840s had blazed several shortcuts, called "cutoffs," at various points between the Green Valley and Nevada's Humboldt River. The cutoffs ran like fingers reaching across the Cordillera, offering Gold Rushers several options for reaching California. Each cutoff had its own advantages and disadvantages and there was no single best way through the rugged wilderness. Most were opting to take one cutoff or another—even though some weren't cutoffs at all.

The original Oregon Trail went southwest along the Big Sandy River to Fort Bridger and then veered sharply northwest toward Fort Hall on the Snake River. This was the route taken by those bound for Oregon but was not ideal for travel to California. After the Mormons settled in Salt Lake in 1847, many emigrants chose to go to California by way of Salt Lake City. To do that, they followed the trail to Fort Bridger and then, instead of turning northwest toward Fort Hall, they proceeded southwest through the Wasatch Range to the Mormon settlement. From there, either the Salt Lake Cutoff or the Hastings Cutoff connected them with the Humboldt River—the final leg of the road to California. Although a more directly western route, the Mormon trail forced travelers to traverse one of the most punishing deserts in North America, the Great Salt Lake Desert, a vast sea of glaring, white sand 100 miles across with no access to water. Although a less familiar route, about a third of emigrants chose this route, which alleviated emigrant pressure on the other cutoffs.

Another option was to bypass Fort Bridger entirely by taking a more direct westerly route from Pacific Springs: Sublette's Cutoff, which connected up with the Fort Hall Road in the Bear River Valley. If Bruff didn't need to resupply at Fort Bridger, the 100-mile-long Sublette's was his shortest and best route west.

One of the first to forge the Sublette Cutoff was Caleb Greenwood, commander of the Townsend-Murphy party in 1844. One of the members of the party had claimed to know a shorter way to the Green River from having taken it with the Bonneville expedition in 1832. The Greenwood shortcut was later called Sublette's Cutoff after William Sublette, who also used it—even though, like Greenwood, Sublette had no hand in discovering it.

Of all the cutoffs, Sublette's was the only one that saved significant time and distance. From Pacific Springs, it was an almost straight shot across the Green River Basin, reconnecting with the original trail at Bear River in present westernmost Wyoming. It also had the advantage of passing north over the desert and delivering the travelers at the headwaters of the Humboldt River. By cutting out the dogleg down to Fort Bridger, the Sublette Cutoff shaved off about 50 miles and three or four days of travel. But the distance saved came at a high price: The trail was diabolically rough and had a punishing stretch of 50 miles without water or forage until the Green River. Many cattle perished on this stretch, inspiring the joke about how easy Sublette's Cutoff was to follow—just look for the path of bleached bones. As one historian put it, "if Fort Bridger was the long way, then Sublette's was the hard way." Bruff wrongly estimated Sublette's would save them ten days—it saved four or five at most. But it was still the best route and all the men agreed to take it, as did most 49ers.

That evening Major Horn, who was traveling with his wife, set up camp nearby and invited Bruff to supper. In a delightful change from Bruff's usual fare, the Horns served up light rolls, baked prairie hen, stewed dried peaches, and coffee "with sugar in it!"

In the late morning they struck the Big Sandy, a stream fed by the snows of the Wind River Range 25 miles to the northwest. It was a narrow stream, only 10 feet wide, but it had water. In preparation for the long, rough, waterless trek ahead, the men filled their canteens and some casks for the animals.

As they resumed their march, a fresh breeze blew fine white dust into their faces, giving the men a ghostly appearance and requiring the animals to be cleaned at every halt. All along this arid section of the trail were bodies of dead oxen and mules that had begun to fail in large numbers from sickness, dehydration, and fatigue. So many animals had died along this stretch that it was difficult to find a camping spot that was not littered with carcasses. One of their own mules had become sick and was abandoned "to the wolves." When they finally found a place with tolerably fewer carcasses, they made camp. Nearby were the graves of a couple who had succumbed to cholera two weeks earlier.

Late in the afternoon of the third day out they arrived at some high sand and clay bluffs overlooking the Green River Valley. It was a "grand sight": sandstone buttes worn into truncated cones standing like sentinels on the hills and the silvery Green River winding through the willow trees deep below. But the valley's breathtaking beauty belied its danger, for the Green River Basin was a desolate, 6,000-square-mile wilderness of sand and rock. Even worse, the Basin was riven by north-south trending canyons that made for a grueling up-and-down grind. Although there was abundant water, the high rock walls flanking it made river access difficult; nor was there any timber, grass, or game.

Walking to the rim, Bruff looked aghast at the steep descent before them. About a third of a mile in length, the hill was angled at 45 degrees and covered with an unstable mix of clay and scree. The wreckage of dozens of wagons and dead oxen strewn at the base of the hill testified to the difficulty of the descent. "From the crest, down to the base, right and left, were fragments of disasters, in shape of upset wagons, wheels, axles, running-geer, [sic] sides, bottoms, &c. &c. Nothing daunted."

Easing the first wagon to the precipice, the teamster double-locked the brakes, holding firmly onto the bridles of the lead mules as the wagon skidded down. One wagon after another repeated the delicate maneuver. Astonishingly, all the wagons descended without a single accident. Only after all the wagons had successfully negotiated the hill did Bruff learn, to his exasperation, that Stinson had failed to notice a trail branching off that would have spared them the steep descent *and* save three miles in the process.

Exhausted, the Company limped down the valley a quarter-mile and made camp. All around the camp was stark evidence of the toll the descent had taken on other emigrant trains as dozens of dead oxen and shattered wagons lay strewn about. To the emigrant graveyard Bruff added another of his mules that had collapsed in the harness, "a tribute to the lean, lank wolves."

In the morning, he sent the feckless Stinson ahead to find pasture while he bought more mules from traders operating along the trail. As he was negotiating with the mule owner, he noticed that the clique that had been lobbying for his removal was buying liquor from a trader operating a "Missouri whiskey cart." When the Company constitution was drafted, Bruff had anticipated that, if they made it as far as the Sacramento Valley, selfishness and animosities arising from the hardship of the journey would cause the men to scatter as soon as they reached the Sacramento Valley. For this reason, he had insisted that the leadership be dissolved upon arrival at their destination and that each member go off on his own to mine. Some of the men who objected to his proposal were the very same young Turks who were now clamoring for his removal.

> But they all knew better than me, and I was compelled to preside over all these proceedings, and see men swear, on the Holy Evangelist, &c. to abide by and uphold the same....and but few cared one cent for, ere they had gone half across the continent.

Fuming over their perfidy and lack of gratitude, Bruff stormed off by himself in a light rain to fish. Casting his seine in the river, he caught some salmon and trout near the grave of an Alabaman who had died the previous week.

After abandoning a broken wagon, the Company resumed its march across the valley floor following the river as it swirled through hills of grey and brown sandstone. Bruff paused to sketch an Indian engraving on the sandstone cliffs depicting forty-three rifles set upright around a chief and a horse while four Indians looked on. Symbolizing the tribe's power, the sketch was later published in the Smithsonian's *Annual Report*.

At length, they came to La Fontanelle, a tributary of the Green River named after Lucien Fontanelle, an American Fur Trading Company employee who camped there in the 1830s. Near the river a Frenchman named Thomas was operating a trading post "trying to cut-off the 'cut-off folks,'" Bruff quipped. The son of a French Canadian father and an Iroquois Indian mother, Thomas had three Shoshone wives. Keen to meet the intriguing half-breed, Bruff found him in a buffalo tent lying on his back and being tended to by a doctor from another emigrant party. Thomas was pale and ill with a broken arm, with his wives looking on mournfully and wiping the sweat from his brow. Inside another conical skin lodge, Bruff found several men seated on animal skins playing three-card Monte for silver while "nearly white" children cavorted in the background.

In contrast to the harshness of the Basin, the Fontanelle was a lush, beautiful enclave, the only such one along this leg of the trail. Scaling a clay embankment near the camp, Bruff took in the enchanting view of the valley and stream below:

> *The beautiful silvery creek, meandering in every variety of curve, and islands mostly of an oveal* [sic] *shape, filling up nearly, the concavities of the bank, with bright green grass and*

*willows, and little grooves of bright willows interspersed along
the grassy edge of the stream Cattle grazing; the camps;- and
people; and blue smoke curling up in delicate and graceful spi-
rals form the campfires, the warm tints of the bluff, darker hills
above, and the distant blue mountain; made a picture I gazed
on with admiration, for some time.*

Moments like these along the trail were few and hard-won,
especially for the busy Captain. Partaking of the creek's riches,
he netted some fat trout and mullet. He also caught some fat
black mice living in holes along the stream bank that he roasted
and found "very tender and sweet." So taken was he with the
valley that he sent the wagons ahead so he and Dr. Austin could
linger in the enchanting environment a bit longer. Momentarily
free of his duties, he and Austin hunted grouse skittering among
the sage bushes. After quenching his thirst in a cool brook, Bruff
lay down on a mossy bank under some tall pines and smoked his
pipe, savoring the beauty and peace of the American wilderness
with geraniums, boxwoods, blue bells, and holly carpeting the
hills. Marring the otherwise idyllic setting were the graves of two
recently deceased emigrants. So long did the two linger that they
did not catch up to the wagon train until nightfall, when they
spotted their campfire glowing like a beacon in a distant meadow.
When they arrived, waiting for them was hot coffee, corn cakes,
fried bacon, and "sweet repose."

On they marched through the rugged foothills of the Bear
River Mountains, over ridges, down steep ravines, and back up
again to ever higher ridges, an exhausting rollercoaster ride of
ups and downs, ups and downs. On the evening of August 10,
they arrived bone-weary and coated with a thick layer of dust at
Smith's Spring. In the valley was a trading post run by a Virgin-

ian named Joseph Greenwood, whose father Caleb had been the first to take wagons across Sublette's Cutoff. Tall, rugged, and handsome, Greenwood was bedecked in a suit of smoked deerskin consisting of a frock, pantaloons, and moccasins. His three wives were Shoshone, two of whom Bruff thought "ugly as mud." Young Greenwood told Bruff that in June alone 3,200 wagons had passed through the valley. That evening Bruff accompanied a dozen of his men with their musical instruments over to Greenwood's. Inside a cramped "skin lodge" they played "Dan Tucker," "Carry Me Back to Old Virginia," and "Zip Coon" to the delight of everyone, especially the "squaws."

One of the traders told Bruff of an emigrant out hunting who was accosted by a party of Snake Indians, a name loosely applied to any number of tribes in the region. According to the trader, the Indians tied him to a tree and shot him in the back. When the man failed to return to camp, his comrades went looking for him and found his lifeless body still tied to the tree. They followed the Indians' trail to their camp, where they demanded the chief punish the murderers. After holding counsel, the chief offered to tie the murderer to a tree and allow the white men to take their revenge. But the emigrants demanded the chief himself punish the culprit. The chief then summoned the murderer's brother and ordered him to cut the culprit's throat. He obliged. Bruff also heard that Pawnees had killed two express riders who had passed Bruff in Bear Valley on their way from Fort Hall to Fort Laramie. One of the men was seen with several arrows protruding from his body.

Whether the stories were true, wildly exaggerated, or completely false, Bruff had become inured to alarmist tales of marauding Indians and quietly slipped off to hunt and fish. When he returned, the men asked to stay two more days at the spring so the animals might graze on the fine grass and the men harvest the abundant game of ducks, grouse, and mud-hens in the valley. Bruff himself preferred the sweet, black mice with which he made a delicious pie that evening. The presence of so many wagons in La Fontanelle gave it the appearance of a bustling village with men and women tending cattle, others reading in the shade of a tree or washing clothes in the river. Bruff used the downtime to refine his notes and wash clothes. The evening was again filled with music and singing.

The next day, three Bannock Indians with yellow wolf dogs in tow wandered into camp to barter horses and an old woman. One of the Indians, clad in a teamster's linen frock emblazoned with U.S. buttons, offered Bruff the woman for a copper powder flask. Little did he know that the Bannock, second only to the Comanche in their hostility toward whites, had been attacking travelers along the trail.

Chapter Six

THE CUTOFFS

August 14 broke clear and calm with light frost. The day marked six months since the Company's constitution had been formed. In accordance with its provisions, a new election of officers was to take place. If ever there was a time for the young Turks of the Company to usurp Bruff, it was now. But when the votes were tallied, to their dismay, three-quarters of the men had reelected their Captain as Commander and President. His supporters heartily congratulated him, which was deeply gratifying to him, especially as "the office conferred me no advantage, but rather imposed onerous duties." Notwithstanding the vote of confidence, that sixteen men—a quarter of the membership—had voted against him assured continued strains within the Company. As his first act in his "second term," Bruff abolished the position of the adjutant, further consolidating his authority and increasing his duties.

While the men were relaxing in camp the next day, they were visited by one of the West's most colorful and celebrated characters, Pegleg Smith. Forty-eight years old, the portly Pegleg ran a trading cabin nearby where he lived with his 16-year-old Indian wife and his son. Born in Kentucky, he ran away from home at 16 and found work on a flatboat on the Mississippi. When he reached St. Louis, he signed on with John Jacob Astor as a trapper and trader. His first trading excursions took him along the Sante Fe and Oregon Trails. Life on the frontier suited him and he spent the next 40 years in the wilderness, trapping and trading between the Colorado and Missouri Rivers. Pegleg befriended the Indians and eventually learned to speak several Native American languages. Indians admired the mountaineer for having fought alongside the Utah in a war against the Snakes. While trapping on the headwaters of the Platte in 1827, Pegleg was shot in the leg by an Indian's arrow. The arrow had entered just above the ankle, shattering both bones. Pegleg was in such pain he begged his friends to cut off his leg, but no one had the stomach for the job. He then summoned the cook to bring him the butcher knife and gruesomely severed the leg below the knee. He wintered on the Green River, ministered by forty Utah Indians. In spring, a crude wooden leg was carved from a tree and thus was born the nickname. To the Indians he was *Wahetoco.* In the last years of his life, Pegleg retired from the wilderness to a ranch outside San Francisco—although he continued to wear his trademark beaver skin hat.

The Company was advancing through the short but rugged Bear River Valley in present-day Colorado. Even though it was summer and the temperature soared into the 90s by day, nights were often freezing at the higher altitudes. Patches of snow were already visible in the Bear Mountains to the west. The valley was home to a large number of friendly Shoshone, many of whom wandered into emigrant camps to trade or beg for gunpowder and food. At mealtime, the hungry Indians invariably gathered near the messes, waiting to pounce on the slightest morsel offered or discarded. Their craving for food was equaled only by their desire for Western clothing. At every opportunity they pestered the men

to trade their shirts and coats for dried fish and fowl. One particularly natty Indian wearing the perforated tin of a lantern as a visor
to a scotch bonnet unsuccessfully begged Bruff to give up a shirt
for some trout. Despite the petty annoyances, Bruff found them
good-humored. In one instance, when Bruff patted a child on the
head remarking, "Good Papoose," an old Indian stunned him with
the rejoinder, "Yes, very good papoose, God damned!"

The Shoshone were on the move with all their possessions in
tow. Horses and mules were dragging log pole sleds filled with
sacks of corn, mats, and skins. As they drifted by his camp, Bruff
was taken by the sight of them, "well-mounted, and accoutered
with savage finery, having long rifles, quivers, and bows..." Finding
one young brave particularly striking, he took out his pencil and
drawing pad. He had just completed the face when an elder spotted
him, raced over, and cried out, "*No schwap!*" The elder made additional signs signifying that if Bruff were to draw him, the brave
would die that very night. The elder then spoke some words to the
youth who promptly mounted his horse and raced off.

Back on the trail, the Company came to the valley's main attraction: a fascinating cluster of effervescent "soda and beer springs."
Some were deep churning wells like pots of boiling water while
others shot up like miniature geysers. Several produced cones of
deposited mineral sediment ranging in color from white to beige
20 feet in height. Others oozed water that ran red as blood. The
largest and most impressive of them, Steamboat Springs, shot
a plume of steam and mineral water every fifteen seconds like
clockwork. The spring was so named because it produced a hiss-
ing sound that resembled a steamboat's boiler. Despite the bizarre
colors of the waters, emigrants uniformly praised the taste of these
springs. Sampling the water bubbling up from one beige-colored
fountain, Bruff thought it "only needed lemon syrup, to render it

perfect soda water." Behind the spring was a cedar tree on which was etched, as high as could be reached, the names of passing travelers that Bruff paused to sketch. "These springs are really worth a travel so far to see," he concluded.

At the north end of Bear Valley, the Company arrived at yet another fork in the trail. Being unaware of any other route, Bruff had originally planned to continue to Fort Hall on the Snake River and then to the Raft River where the trail to California branched off to the south. But 10 days earlier, he had learned of a man who had discovered a shortcut that could accommodate wagons. On July 19, Benoni Hudspeth and J. J. Myers, two gold seekers seeking to shortcut the swing up to Fort Hall, blasted a 134-mile pass directly to the Humboldt River. Called Hudspeth's or Emigrant's Cutoff, it was the only cutoff on the entire trail created by 49ers.

But Hudspeth wasn't like the previous cutoffs in a number of respects. To begin with, it was a complete unknown. No trappers or traders had ever been through the area, and emigrants had no idea as to the trail's difficulty, the height of mountains, whether the Indians were hostile or where—or even if—water could be found. Nor did they know that Hudspeth wasn't any shorter than Fort Hall. The Hudspeth route swung to the south and west while the Fort Hall route swung to the north and west; the two routes together actually formed equal sides of an oval. Notes posted at the entrance to Hudspeth falsely advertised it would take them to the headwaters of the Humboldt River in 100 miles; it was closer to 250. The Hudspeth route also led over high mountainous country, far higher than the route to Fort Hall. Despite all the unknowns, most wagons were heading blindly down it in the hopes of shortening the journey.

The cartographer Bruff wasn't taken in by the sign or the promise of a shortcut. But he still had to convince his men of the risks of taking it. Taking a piece of charcoal, he proceeded to draw a map of the two trails on the side of a wagon, showing that Hudspeth was likely to be no shorter than Fort Hall. In any case, any distance saved, he argued, would be offset by the trail's shortcomings. Having just been forged in mid-July, the Hudspeth was certain to be more rugged. And because so many emigrants were now taking it, there was likely to be less forage for the animals. Since it was an unexplored region, there were no landmarks to indicate their location. As one emigrant on the Hudspeth later lamented, "We feel puzzled to know our locality. We are here but do not know where here is."

After listening to Bruff's arguments, the men voted unanimously to ignore his advice and take the Hudspeth on the grounds that all the other Gold Rushers were taking it. It was a case of the blind following the blind and it wouldn't be the last—or the worst—of the Company's cutoff gambits. Although overruled, Bruff decided to go via Fort Hall to obtain information about the best route over the Sierra Nevada.

On August 18, the two parties parted ways. The Company gave Bruff what he described as "an old broke-down horse." Still, it would be the first time he had ridden the trail, having walked the entire 1,200 miles from St. Joseph thus far. Three men accompanied him: William Barker, Augustus Capron, and Stinson, whom Bruff vowed to cut loose at the fort.

The Fort Hall trail took them through twisted volcanic rock formations and high basaltic cliffs. Here and there were more soda and sulfur springs whose mineral deposits colored the rock basins bright orange and blue. As they passed a Shoshone village, several Indians rushed out to the trail to "schwap." One Indian, nattily—if incongruously—attired in a black frock coat, blue striped shirt, blue suspenders, and a black hat offered a deerskin for some tobacco and ammunition. Unwilling to part with the ammo, Bruff appeased the Indian with a few ounces of tobacco. Stinson traded a six-cent looking glass and his worn-out boots for a pair of new boot moccasins.

As darkness fell, Stinson's horse refused to go on, so they stopped for an early supper before proceeding to camp on a high ridge. Near midnight, they were ascending the ridge when the men were startled by the caterwaul of a cougar in the willow trees. For nearly an hour the cat had been stalking them, but the men had been unable to see or shoot it among the willow trees. At dawn Bruff woke to relieve the guard. In the half-light, he went down to inspect the trail ahead. Not 20 yards from camp, he came across the cougar's footprints in the dust. Farther down, he found bear tracks and scattered markings in the dust and concluded the cougar had pounced upon the cub, only then abandoning its interest in the men.

In the morning Bruff and Barker went off to climb a ridge that afforded a magnificent view of the Snake River plain. As he and Barker were enjoying the panoramic view, an Indian from the previous day, apparently having followed them, suddenly appeared on the ridge. Whatever the brave's intent, having lost all confidence in Stinson, Bruff enlisted the Indian to guide him to the military cantonment near the fort. Pointing to a dark blue line in the distance, Barker asked what it might be. Bruff said he thought it was the Bannock River. Upon hearing this, the Indian burst out "Panak!" and bounded off like a deer out of sight, never to be seen again. Such was poor Bruff's luck with guides—native or otherwise.

Now his own horse, feeble to begin with, had given out. As he descended the ridge on foot, he had to drag the tired animal down, determined to reach the military cantonment by nightfall. Around sunset they came upon a small party of Bannock in a meadow by

a stream. Like the Shoshone, the Bannock coveted western clothing and many of them were parading gaily about in scotch plaid
bonnets given to them by the Hudson's Bay Company. Noticing a
beautiful, cream-colored pony, Bruff offered to barter for it with an
old brave, but his two wives protested. The old man then brought
over a fine white horse for which Bruff traded his own, a gun with
a broken stock, and an old coat. When the old man demanded
more, Bruff threw in a pair of brass bracelets, a plug of tobacco,
some gun powder, and 50 percussion caps. Presuming Bruff was
the advance of a large emigrant party they could trade with, the
Indians inquired by signs as to the number of wagons in the rear.
Fearing if he told the truth they might follow him and steal one
of the horses, Bruff enthusiastically signaled ten wagons would be
coming along momentarily and slipped off. By now it was almost
dark. As the trail was dangerously riven with marshes and deep
sand, the old Indian kindly offered to guide the men to the Loring
Cantonment. When they were within sight of several wagons and
a tent, the old man said he was not allowed to proceed farther and
bid Bruff and his men goodbye.

At the cantonment, Commander Colonel Andrew Porter, who
had himself just arrived at the site, warmly received the men and provided them a hearty supper, some brandy, and real beds. In the morning Bruff persuaded Stinson to enlist as a mule driver for the post.
At long last he was rid of him and rather handily, too, as none of the
Company men was around to protest his sly legerdemain. But Bruff's
chief reason for going to Fort Hall had been wasted for the officers,
all new at post, could offer no information about the trail west.

After four days' rest at the cantonment, the men moved on, even
though Barker and Capron were ill. Colonel Porter gave the men
ten days' rations of bacon, bread, coffee, sugar, and a new military
saddle and holster, refusing to accept any money for it from Bruff.

Five miles along, the men pulled into Fort Hall. Built by Nathaniel Wyeth in 1832, Fort Hall was the westernmost of the fur trading centers. Located on the south bank of the Snake River, Wyeth had selected the site for its close proximity to a number of tribes with whom furs could be profitably traded. It wasn't long before the site's value was noticed by the Hudson's Bay Company, which promptly set about driving Wyeth out of business by over-bidding him in fur prices paid to the Indians and underbidding him in the prices of goods sold to them. By 1837, Wyeth was forced to sell to the only buyer around: Hudson's Bay. The company's timing was perfect. With the opening of the Oregon and California Trails in the early 1840s, profits from emigrants redoubled those earned from the fur trade. The fort remained an important trading post and emigrant waystation until 1863, when a flood had so demolished the walls of the fort that only the Indians and a few pioneers knew where the once-bustling trading depot had been.

After setting up camp, Bruff strolled over to the fort to meet the manager, Captain Grant. A Scotsman from Canada, Grant told Bruff he had recently replaced a Mr. Thing, who was demoted for having committed a grievous error. One day, a party of Blackfeet arrived at the fort and asked to enter. Thing not only gave them entry but feted them, even allowing them to sleep within its confines. At dawn the next morning, Thing had discovered the guests had carried away every animal from post!

Concerned about the welfare of his men, Bruff asked Grant for information about Hudspeth's Cutoff. Grant knew nothing except to say he had sent his son in search of it but he failed to find it. He believed the cutoff to be the work of a man who, owing him money, sought to evade him by creating a path around the fort. Bruff was put off by Grant, whom he found "very English" and "anti-Yankee," given to complaining at every opportunity of the taxes the government imposed on his trading. While listening to Grant kvetch, Bruff's attention was suddenly directed to a young Indian woman who had entered the room.

I was struck with her beautiful and graceful figure, and very neat dress.-She was about 18 years of age, rather tall, and slender, of a very light yellow complexion, glossy black hair, done up in long braids, with ribbons.- like our school-girls, black eyes and long silken lashes; Her dress was pure white deer-skin-A frock, reachinging [sic] a little below the knees; pantaloons-to the ancle-moccasins [sic], and a purple figured Merino shawl, thrown gracefully around her waist, and over one arm.... Pretty black eyes, and handsome Grecian nose; but alas! her mouth interfered with perfection! - very thin lips,- merely a long straight line!

Smitten by the native damsel, Bruff commented to Grant that she was the most beautiful and cleanly-attired Indian woman he had ever seen. Alas, Grant's reply quickly demolished Bruff's romantic infatuation with the fair princess. She was married to Grant's herdsman, a Frenchman, and lived in one of the "black, dirty, and sooty skin lodges nearby the Fort."

At dawn the next day, Bruff and his men set out south over grassy plains along the Bannock River. While "nooning," a friendly Wallah Wallah youth rode up armed with a quiver full of arrows, bow, and rifle. Dismounting, he greeted Bruff with a hearty "How do?" Bruff offered the boy some coffee and tobacco and they chatted. The boy, who spoke some English, said proudly he could take down a buffalo with his bow and arrow—no mean feat. In fact, he was on his way to the fort to trade several buffalo robes taken with his bow and some clothes for a horse he intended to acquire.

Barker bought one of the buffalo robes from the boy for a silver dollar. When the exchange was completed, the boy politely said, "Good Bye, Sir," mounted his horse, and rode off. Buffalo had once ranged in large numbers west of South Pass. Since the 1830s, white hunters and Indians seeking hides had slaughtered huge numbers so that by the time of the Gold Rush only a few were left in the region for the young brave to hunt.

All this time Barker and Provost, it turned out, had cholera, a shocking turn of events considering how far from the Platte they were. To control the diarrhea, Bruff gave them some laudanum, a bitter tasting opiate. At length they came upon several abandoned wagons, an indication the Gold Rushers had decided to pack in the rest of the way to California. Rather than leave the wagons for a needy company, the owners had selfishly smashed them to pieces.

On August 26, Bruff and his companions arrived at American Falls on the Snake River in present-day Idaho. Being late summer, the falls were "more froth than water" but moved Bruff enough to sketch the scene. While he was drawing, several stark-naked Wallah Wallah Indians came over a hill, calling out "schwap feesh?" Bruff purchased five large, fresh salmon in return for four rifle balls. The next day they reached the Raft River, a tributary of the Snake and a major junction in the trail. To the west the trail led to Oregon and to the south along the west bank of the Raft River was the route to California. All emigrant traffic now turned southwest up the valley of Cassia Creek, a tributary of the Raft. In a few miles they would rejoin the main trail and the rest of the Company.

From his camp on the head of the Raft, Bruff could see smoke curling up in the distance and concluded it was from the campfires of the detested Digger Indians. The term "Digger" was a pejorative used by whites for certain bands of the Shoshone and Paiute Indians who hunted with only bow and arrow and lived off seeds, grubs, snakes, rodents, and insects. Frémont was perhaps the first American to record their unusual hunting-gathering practices during his first expedition in 1843:

> *Shriveled and hapless specimens of humanity at best, danger-ous thieves and murderers at worst. Roots, seeds, and grass, every vegetable that affords any nourishment, and every liv-ing animal thing, insect or worm, they eat. Nearly approach-ing to the lower animal creation, their sole employment is to obtain food; and they are constantly occupied in struggling to support existence.*

Bruff shared Frémont's contempt, but with a Darwinian slant: "They are the original and most numerous class commonly called the Mountain Diggers, perfectly untamable and the lowest species of the genus Homo, next to them is the baboon."

But the Diggers were anything but harmless scavengers. Daily they threatened emigrants along the trail from the Raft to the Humboldt River. Rarely confronting emigrants directly, they pre-ferred to circle about the wagons and shoot arrows into the mules or oxen, knowing that the travelers would have to leave the animals behind. Another Digger trick was to sneak into the camps at night and quietly lead the cattle away for slaughter. Only when they reached the Humboldt, a region too harsh even for the lowly Dig-gers to live in, would emigrants be beyond reach of their predations.

In the morning, the men were awakened by howling wolves to find themselves coated with a thick mantle of frost. Bruff's long hair was frozen to his saddle and he had to wrench it loose in order to get up, leaving some of his long curls "as a memento for the wolves to examine."

Moving south they entered the "City of Castles," a breathtaking valley of fantastic rock formations in present-day Idaho. There were green and white rocks heaped in huge blocks, rocks rounded in shapes like mushrooms, and deep caves with arched entrances. Many travelers had marked several large blocks for their uncanny resemblance to houses and castles. One emigrant thought the rock formation reminiscent of a city:

> *Here was a mass of common buildings, the streets, the town pump, the taverns with their chimneys, the churches with their spires, the monuments of the graveyard, the domes, the cornices, and the columns. They all had their representation in this wild scene of nature.*

One rock inscribed with tar read "Napoleon's Castle," another "Castle City Hotel." Against his better inclination, Bruff marked one rock "Sarcophagus Rock."

While Bruff was sketching some fungi-shaped rock formations, two Mormons from Salt Lake rode up. Bruff asked if they had ever taken the trail to California. Replying in the affirmative, one of the Mormons offered to sell Bruff a copy of *The Best Guide to the Gold Mines*, which he bought for 50 cents—more out of curiosity than belief in its usefulness. Examining it, Bruff noticed it was merely a single sheet of paper folded into four sections but "tolerably correct." Indeed, along with *Clayton's Guide* the industrious Mormons became the first to produce a continuous travel guide from the Missouri River to the Sacramento Valley. The map in *The Best Guide* showed the preferred trail to California going through Carson, an alternate route taken in 1848 by the Mormon Battalion returning from the gold fields to Salt Lake City who wished to avoid the difficulties encountered by the Donner party on the Truckee.

At Steeple Rock, Bruff arrived at the main trail, once again crowded with wagons, where they overtook a single wagon party of seven from Illinois. By now, the rest of the Company was far ahead. Farther along they overtook several more emigrant parties, some of whom Bruff had dined with back on the Platte. Descending 2,000 feet through a steep mountain pass to Goose Creek, they entered a narrow gorge where Bruff found a note from his company posted on a stick. The note indicated the Company's date of passing, destination, and that all had gone well on the Hudspeth. On the left was a sign:

Public Sale:
Will be sold, on Sunday, 2 Sept, on the head of Mary's [Humboldt] River, Stores, and a lot of merchandize. Emigrants in the rear will do well to be there, as great bargains will be sold. Aug. 29th 1849. (signed) Wm. Mullin & Co.

Many at this stage of the journey had to pack in to the gold fields on foot, often because they had lost all their animals to Indians or fatigue.

On the first of September, the men woke to subfreezing temperatures. Along this stretch of the trail there was no good water, only marshes, sinks, and noxious alkali ponds that deposited a white powdery residue on the trail. As the sun rose and the wind picked up, the men were blasted with a vile coating of alkaline powder. With no good water, unsuspecting emigrants had allowed their animals to drink from the poisonous alkali ponds and their carcasses were now strewn all along the trail. Some of the bloated bodies of oxen had burst and were seething with maggots.

At midday they passed the grave of a "W. Maxwell, Teamster in the Pioneer Line," who had died the previous week from cholera and scurvy. One of the more spectacular failures along the trail that year had been that of the Pioneer Line. Created by Messrs. Turner and Allen of St. Louis, the Line purported to offer first-class commercial passenger service from St. Louis to the gold fields in the unrealistic time of 60 days. The price of passage including rations was $200 a person and included 100 pounds of luggage. A rather good bargain, except for the fact that the second line (the first seems to have gone through) consisting of a massive 38 wagons, started woefully late and ended in disaster. Before the wagons had even started out, the guide had died of cholera in Independence. Along the Platte, many teamsters deserted, and passengers with no mule-driving experience were forced to drive the wagons. Almost two dozen passengers died from cholera. With fewer passengers, they began dumping enormous quantities of food, including a ton of cured meats. Fifty gallons of liquor was poured into a stream. When they reached the Rockies, their green mules became spooked by thunderclaps and the wagons failed. With no one to fix them, the train broke down entirely. The remaining passengers walked, worked, or begged their way 700 miles to California. Some, like poor Maxwell, never made it.

In the morning with the temperature a biting 18 degrees and the wind howling, Bruff hurriedly ate a quick breakfast of bread and coffee and hit the trail. Around noon he was informed that his Company had halted not far ahead and was waiting for him in a narrow ravine. Racing to a rise overlooking the ravine, Bruff signaled the men below. "There's the Captain!" one of the men shouted when he caught sight of Bruff. After a separation of 14 days, he was relieved to find his men all well and in good spirits. Indeed, compared to what they were about to enter, the past month of meeting colorful mountain men, drinking from delicious soda springs, and trading with friendly Indians had been a leisurely stroll through the park.

Chapter Seven

THE HUMBUG AND BEYOND

BEFORE THE COMPANY COULD MOUNT THEIR ASSAULT on the High Sierras, the most formidable obstacle on the trail, they had to cross the Great Basin, a vast, inhospitable, desert depression 500 miles in diameter and 5,000 feet above sea level. Named by Frémont during his second expedition, the Basin was the geological equivalent of a black hole: none of the rivers flowing into it went to the sea. Instead, they fizzled out in the desert or drained into small, briny lakes.

The trail through the Basin followed the wildly meandering course of the Humboldt River for 350 miles across the desert floor. Once variously called "Swampy" and "St. Mary's," the river was renamed by Frémont for Baron Alexander von Humboldt, the renowned German scientific explorer. It was a rather poor way to honor the man, for the Humboldt had no aquatic life, was coated with algae, and tasted vile. Although it was potable, the river only grew fouler downstream as evaporation concentrated the salts. Emigrants arriving at the river were invariably dismayed by its small size, for in most places it was no more than 20 feet wide and two feet deep. Writing home, William Swain described the river as "nothing more than a mud ditch winding through the alluvial deposit of the valley in the most crooked course that could be marked out for it."

Indeed, the Humboldt's crookedness only added to the travelers' misery. For many miles, the river twisted and turned in sweeping oxbows, often bending back on itself or cutting it itself off entirely. The meandering created a bottomland of countless stagnant, swampy pools bordering the main channel. Each time they needed to water the animals, travelers had to cross the sloughs to reach the water in the main channel, an unpleasant and exhausting task that required emigrants to slog through acres of muck. Livestock, desperately thirsty from hauling heavy wagons through the desert heat, had to be restrained from charging headlong for the river, where they might easily mire down in the muck and drown. Many did. To water the animals safely, men often had to fetch bucket after bucket of water and armloads of cut grass. Besides being a killing field for livestock, the fetid sloughs were fertile breeding grounds for mosquitoes, often covering the helpless animals entirely. Emigrants caustically dubbed the river "the Humbug."

With no tributaries, the Humboldt grew weaker as it flowed until it disappeared altogether in a miasmic swamp called the Humboldt Sink. Forty-Niner Reuben Shaw offered this dour impression of the Sink:

> *There we found a mud lake, ten miles long and four or five miles wide, a veritable sea of slime, a 'slough of despond,' and ocean of ooze, a bottomless bed of alkaline poison, which emitted a nauseous odor and presented the appearance of utter desolation.*

But their hatred of the Humboldt was equaled only by their need for it. Despite its small size, the river spanned the entire desert east to west, offering water and grass for the animals most of the way. Without it, the desert simply could not be crossed and emigrants would have had to go by way of Oregon to get to California. Gaining the headwaters of the Humboldt was one of the great milestones of the westward journey, for it brought them within striking distance of the Sierras. While the arrival at the Humboldt meant that the wearisome journey was three-quarters over, it marked the beginning of the most hellish hardships of the trail.

Upon reaching the Humboldt, the Company found a note pinned to the side of an abandoned wagon that read:

Aug: 3, 1849. This wagon and plunder is left for the use of the emigrants: Please dont [sic] destroy this wagon, for it might be of great service to some poor Emigrant like ourselves. (Signed) Barnet R. Light.

Poor Light had frozen to death in the arctic night. He must have known he was near the end—how else to explain his dying missive? Considering himself one of the aforementioned "poor emigrants," Bruff proceeded to cannibalize the wagon's fore wheels, axle, and tongue to refurbish one of his damaged wagons.

At breakfast the next morning, several Diggers entered Bruff's camp wearing a quiver of arrows he knew were being used to bring down emigrant animals by the score. Wishing to inspect the poison he believed was on the arrow tips, Bruff attempted pull one of the arrows from its quiver. But when the Indian objected strenuously, he backed off fuming:

These brutal wild wretches had committed so many rascalities upon the emigrants, that the least pretext would have been sufficient to ensure their destruction. I said to one of them, "Dig-

ger?" - he replied with a shake of the head, and downcast look,
"Shoshonee."-but I knew he lied.

The reviled Diggers circulated the camp looking for handouts, but got nothing and eventually wandered off. From his camp, Bruff could see pale blue smoke of their campfires curling up over the ridges. As a precaution, he added extra sentinels to watch over the animals that night.

Having taken ill, Bruff was too weak to walk or ride in the saddle and took refuge in a wagon. As the wagon rumbled over stony hills and slogged through deep sand, he gazed listlessly at the desolate landscape of barren plains and fetid alkali ponds. To avoid the punishing sun, the Company was now traveling in early morning and evening and resting in the shade of the wagons during the day. Water and grass were now far apart, and men and animals had to pace themselves lest they dehydrate. Thanks to Bruff's foresight, they had brought large water caskets that they could fill at each hole—assuming it had good water. Other emigrants had not been so prudent, for the trail was littered with dead oxen and mules. Among the rotting carcasses, Bruff noticed the gravestone of a man who had the unique misfortune of having been killed not by disease, Indians, or the elements, but in a dispute with another emigrant.

The Humboldt wound endlessly, sending the party northwest and then back to the southwest over and over, forcing the Company to ford the diabolically crooked river several times. Halting for lunch at several springs with good water, Bruff noticed a solitary ox in a copse of willows by the stream. The creature was so weak it had fallen in trying to drink at a spring and was now struggling in vain to extricate itself. By nightfall, the wolves would have set upon the helpless animal.

On September 12, some of the men called for an urgent meeting to discuss sending six men ahead to the Sacramento Valley to make "advance mining arrangements" for the Company. Bruff found the idea "pure folly" because they were still a great distance from their destination. The proposal clearly deviated from the original plan to dissolve the Company only when it reached California. Now that they were within striking distance of their destination, some of the men were simply in a hurry to break free and get to the gold fields. Although Bruff protested vigorously, he was overruled once again.

In the forenoon they came to a broad alkali plain, its parched surface cracked and glazed white. Dwarf sage bushes coated with the fine powder only added to the bleakness. Beyond the plain, they entered Pauta Pass in the Blue Mountains, a deep winding gorge 60 miles long. Bruff thought the Pass to have been the site of a fight a man named Jefferson had in 1846 with the Pauta Indians, who stole most of his cattle (although Jefferson survived.)

A few miles on, Bruff noticed a makeshift board on which was pinned a note stating that 10 miles ahead all the grass had been cut by emigrants and to turn abruptly where abundant grass could be found in a half-mile. Immediately Bruff turned right and found the grass, reassured for once that not all the travelers on the trail were thinking only of themselves. The Company made camp in a grassy meadow and cut and bundled enough forage for three days. Several other parties were camped in the glade, including the Wolverine Company of Michigan and a family with two small girls.

The next morning the six-man advance party, which Bruff derisively referred to as "the useless project of the Company," departed for the gold fields. As for the rest, they would soon be faced with the most significant decision of the journey: how to cross the mighty Sierras.

One of the main reasons most early emigrants ended up in Oregon was because it was simply far easier to get to than California. The Columbia leading there was the only river to cut through the Sierra-Cascade chain of mountains. From its confluence with the Snake, emigrants followed the river to a saddle in the range that took them all the way to the Pacific. Getting through the High Sierras to California, however, was a different matter altogether. With no river to provide easy passage into California, emigrants had to ascend the mountains—not just any mountains either but some of the highest and steepest on the continent. At more than 14,000 feet, the Sierras were the highest range in the West, with winter snow so high it often covered the treetops.

Emigrants were generally aware of two passes over the Sierras, the Truckee and Carson's, both of which had a grim history of disasters and near disasters. Both required travelers to follow the Humboldt its entire length to the Sink, beyond which lay a pitiless sand desert 40 miles across. A desert as small as "Forty Mile," as some called it, could normally be crossed in a few days, but for 15 miles the trail consisted of heavy sand that reached nearly up to the wheel hubs. If they made it through Forty Mile, travelers then chose one of the two routes leading over the Sierras, their final assault on the gold fields.

The Truckee Trail followed the Truckee River into the mountains where it then ascended over a relatively low but steep 7,000-foot notch in the mountains. The first to cross it in wagons was Eliza Stephens in 1844, guided by the 81-year-old mountain man Caleb Greenwood. Stephens had followed the Oregon Trail to Fort Hall and then to the Humboldt. Near the Sink, an old Paiute chief named Truckee showed them the way over the mountains by drawing a map in the sand. As they approached the summit, heavy snow forced Stephens to leave some of the men, women, and children in the party in the mountains where, miraculously, they survived until they were rescued in the spring.

Stephens honored the good chief by naming the pass after him, although it was later changed to Donner Pass after one of the worst emigrant tragedies of the nineteenth century. In 1846, George Donner and James F. Reed had led their own and several other families overland to California from Independence. As they attempted to breach the Truckee Pass in November, an early snowstorm struck and they were marooned for the winter on the eastern approach to the pass. Reed and several others had gone to the settlements for help but were unable to mount a rescue until February. Over the long winter, only 45 of 81 emigrants managed to survive, several, including Donner himself, resorting to cannibalism to avert starvation. When Stephen Watts Kearny's party passed through in 1847, they found the grisly remains of skulls whose brains had been gouged out and eaten and bones broken for their marrow. That the gruesome incident had occurred just three years earlier meant Gold Rushers were all too aware of the dangers of Truckee.

★   ★   ★   ★

JUST SOUTH of Truckee was the equally steep Carson's Trail, which followed the Truckee route to the Carson River south of Lake Tahoe to Carson's Pass. The Pass was blazed at great cost by Frémont during his second expedition in 1844, and his account offers a cautionary tale for anyone contemplating crossing the Sierras in winter. After mapping the Oregon Trail from South Pass into Oregon, he and his guide, Kit Carson, headed south along the eastern flank of the Sierras. In late January they halted near the headwaters of the Truckee River to seek guidance from the Washoe Indians on crossing the mountains. Using hand signs,

Frémont explained he had come from far away and had been traveling for a year and now wished to cross over the Sierras "into the country of the other whites." An old Indian indicated that before winter it was "six sleeps" to the place where the whites lived but crossing now was out of the question due to the deep snow. He urged Frémont to follow the river to a lake (probably Lake Tahoe) where there was plenty of fish and no snow and they could wait out the winter. So many times had the old Indian repeated the word *tah-ve* that Frémont realized it was their word for snow. Not that it mattered, for the reckless Frémont was determined to tackle the Sierras regardless of the dangers. He insisted his men and horses were strong and that they could "break a road through the snow."

Spreading out bales of scarlet cloth and trinkets, Frémont showed the Indian what he would give in return for a guide. After a short discussion between the Indians, the old man said that if Frémont could break through the snow, at the end of three days he would come upon grass, which would be about six inches high, and where the ground was entirely clear. That far the old man had been hunting for elk, but beyond that—he closed his eyes—he had not seen.

But there was one among them who had been to the whites. Going out of the lodge, the Indian returned with a young man who said he had seen the whites with his own eyes and swore, first by the sky and then by the ground, that what he said was true. After Frémont lavished the Indians with gifts, the young man agreed to guide them. They gave him the name Melo, signifying "friend" in the Washoe language. Melo was thinly clad and his moccasins were nearly worn out, so Frémont gave him some fresh skins for the journey.

Inauspiciously, the next day it snowed heavily as Frémont and his men prepared to ascend the Sierras. Leggings and moccasins were re-stitched and blankets repaired. Frémont gave a pep talk to his men, reminding them that they were only 70 miles from Sutter's Fort as the crow flew but that the journey ahead would be the harshest they had undertaken thus far. Provisions were already so low they had to kill a dog who had been their companion ever since the Bear River Valley.

In the morning, the sky cleared to reveal the icy pinnacles of the Sierras towering like angry sentinels above them. Everyone was grimly silent as they began their journey. On their ascent, they passed two huts that were buried so deep in snow they almost escaped notice. Soon the snow became even deeper and it became necessary to "break a road." This consisted of taking the strongest horse and driving a clearing through the snow until it became fatigued. As the lead horse moved to the end of the line, it was replaced by another horse. Sometimes the process was done on foot. Astonishingly, they covered 16 miles the first day, reaching an altitude of 6,700 feet.

Two days later they encountered what Melo described as the first "deep snow." In some places, the snow was over 15 feet deep. Attempting to force a road through a pass indicated by Melo, the horses gave out after 300 yards and refused to go on. With horses floundering in the snow and the trail now strewn with equipment temporarily abandoned, Frémont made camp and sent the horses back to pasture where they had grazed the previous night. It was 10 degrees, and a stiff wind blowing made it the coldest night of Frémont's entire year-long journey. Out of nowhere, two Indians appeared and one of them, an old man, immediately began to harangue them, saying that they and the animals would perish in the snow if they continued. If they would go back, the Indian would show them a better way across the mountain. According to Frémont, the Indian painted a dire picture of the way ahead:

We had now begun to understand some words, and, with the aid of signs, easily comprehended the old man's simple ideas. 'Rock upon rock—rock upon rock—snow upon snow,' said he; 'even if you get over the snow, you will not be able to get down from the mountains.' He made us the sign of precipices, and showed us how the feet of the horses would slip, and throw them off from the narrow trails that led along their sides. Our Chinook, who comprehended even more readily than ourselves, and believed our situation hopeless, covered his head with his blanket, and began to weep and lament. 'I wanted to see the whites,' said he; "I came away from my own people to see the whites, and I wouldn't care to die among them, but here'—and he looked around into the cold night and gloomy forest, and, drawing his blanket over his head, began again to lament.

Frémont held fast to his plan, however. As he waited for the baggage to be brought up, the men made snowshoes and sledges to transport the luggage. The next night it was so cold that Melo deserted. Instead of seeing the native's flight as a sign of just how dire the situation had become, Frémont took it as a disconcerting example of Indian treachery and faithlessness.

On February 6, Frémont set out with a party to reconnoiter in their snowshoes. They marched in single file, tramping down the snow as they went. After 10 miles, they reached one of the peaks near a pass indicated by Melo. Far below, Frémont could see a large snowless valley, bounded on the western side by a low range of mountains 100 miles in the distance. Immediately Carson recognized them as the mountains bordering the coast. "There," he said, "is the little mountain—it is fifteen years since I saw it; but I am just as sure as if I had seen it yesterday." Between them and this low coastal range lay the Sacramento Valley.

But at that height, distances were deceiving. Frémont and Carson realized that between them and the plains they had miles of snowy fields and broken ridges of pine-covered mountains to cross. That night they stumbled into camp exhausted, having walked 20 miles in their snowshoes that day. They were now at 7,900 feet and the thermometer registered 3 below zero. The next day all their energies were directed to bringing the animals and sledges up. Fortunately, the sun and wind had cleared snow from some areas, providing grassy spots where the animals could graze.

The next day they were at 8,050 feet and still climbing. The glare of the snow had rendered many of the men nearly blind, but they were fortunate in having some black silk handkerchiefs which, worn as veils, gave them some relief.

On the evening of February 11, Frémont received a message from one of his men in the rear indicating that the mules and horses had plunged through the snow road and were now nearly buried. Frémont ordered the men to shovel the animals out and return them to their pastures of the previous day. Running low on provisions, they killed one of their dogs and a mule for dinner. Three days later, they reached the highest part of their trajectory over the Sierras—nearly 10,000 feet. To the west, Frémont took in a beautiful view of a mountain lake entirely surrounded by mountains. After spending two days bringing up all the animals, he reconnoitered ahead with Carson. Although they would now be descending, they still had deep snow, ice, and rugged terrain to deal with. Some of the men had the misfortune to wear moccasins with *parflèche* buffalo soles that were so slippery they were forced to crawl across the snow beds. Along the way they ate their pack animals to survive. Out of sixty-seven horses and mules with which they began the Sierra crossing, only thirty-three made it to the Sacramento Valley and then only in a condition to be led along.

It had taken Frémont more than a month to reach Sutter's Fort. He named the pass after Carson in recognition of his skill as guide in leading them over the mountains.

*   *   *   *

BY 1848, Mormons leaving California for Utah were leading wagons across the 8,700-foot pass, paving the way for more of their brethren. But they had the advantage of departing in springtime and summer when weather was benign. Emigrants approaching from the east, however, invariably arrived in late fall or, if delayed, at the onset of winter when the chance of encountering snow was high. Carson's offered a bit more grass and water but like the Truckee was just as steep an ascent. The appeal of both the Truckee and Carson's was that from the Humboldt Sink, they traced a fairly direct line southwest to Sutter's Mill. The downside was that even if they were to make it to one of these passes, going this way meant making a frontal assault on the Sierra Nevada's high eastern escarpment.

By the time the Washington Company hit the Humboldt, word had begun filtering back along the trail of the suffering of travelers who had gone via Carson's or Truckee by way of the Humboldt Sink. There were terrifying stories of wagon wheels mired in Forty Mile's scorching sands, hundreds of animals too weak to move left to rot in the desert, and men dying of dehydration. Those who had tried to breach the steep Carson were in difficulty, and those at the Truckee were faring little better.

As he rumbled along the Humboldt, mulling which route to take, Bruff came upon a party of Mormon families on their way back to Salt Lake from the gold fields. The patriarch of the group, Thomas Rhodes, had just crossed at Carson's Pass. Rhodes had gone overland to California in 1846 with his wife and 12 children.

But when his wife died the previous year, he decided to move his family to Salt Lake. Despite his dislike of Mormons, Bruff found Rhodes kind and trustworthy and knowledgeable about the various routes.

Rhodes said that the Truckee Pass had very little grass on the approach to it and no potable water. Because of its steepness, very few wagons had gotten over it and most animals were giving out before reaching the top. Rhodes also strongly warned against going via the Humboldt Sink. For 10 miles on the approach to the Sink there was no grass and nothing but sulfur water. As if the desert beyond the Sink weren't harsh enough, there were also many Digger cattle thieves to contend with.

With all the frightening news coming from Carson's and Truckee, Bruff and his cohorts began to consider a lesser known route—Lassen's Trail. A wildly circuitous trail, it required travelers to exit the Great Basin 60 miles above the Sink and veer sharply northwest on the Applegate Trail to Goose Lake on the northwest corner of present-day California. The Applegate Trail was forged in 1846 by Jesse Applegate and Levi Scott, who were looking for a safer passage to Oregon after Applegate's son and nephew perished in the rapids of the Columbia River on a journey in 1843. Once established, the Applegate Trail was used regularly by Hudson Bay trappers to travel from Oregon to California. Ergo, the Applegate was never conceived as a route into California from the east but, as its trajectory indicated, as an alternative route between California and Oregon.

From the Applegate's terminus at Goose Lake, Lassen's Trail struck southwest for 150 miles before depositing them at Lassen's ranch. It was a long, roundabout route, but its appeal lay precisely in the fact that no one knew much about it. Some even believed it was a shortcut. Despite its length, Lassen's did offer an alternative to the frontal assault required of the southern passes by making a long end run around the northern end of the range. But there were known disadvantages to Lassen's as well. At 6,100 feet, the pass was relatively low, but because it was so little used, it was a rocky, rugged passage. In addition, even though the trail allowed the group to avoid the worst section of the Basin, one still had to cross the equally forbidding Black Rock Desert to get to the Applegate Trail. If there was one thing all three passes had in common, it was danger. Emigrants invariably died or nearly died trying to cross them.

★   ★   ★   ★

LASSEN'S TRAIL was named by a Danish-born rancher, Peter Lassen, who had emigrated from Missouri to California in 1839. Shortly after his arrival, Lassen began working at Sutter's Mill. After watching with envy as Sutter profited year after year from the arrival of emigrants at his fort, the enterprising Lassen decided to find some land on which to build his own ranch. When Sutter sent him 100 miles up the Sacramento Valley as part of a posse to recover horses that had been stolen, Lassen found his new home. The valley's lush, green hills offered ideal pasture, and there were majestic views of the snow-covered peaks of the Cascades to the north. As soon as he returned to Sutter's Fort, he applied for Mexican citizenship—a condition for land ownership—and a land grant. In 1844, he obtained a grant of 22,000 acres and, with Indian labor, began building his ranch.

In 1847, Lassen returned overland to Missouri, presumably to collect friends to populate a new city he was planning to create. Led by Commodore Robert Stockton, who had just assumed command of military operations in California, the party consisted of forty-five men, including head guide Joseph B. Chiles and trailblazers J. J. Myers and Milton McGee.

In July, the party reached Truckee Pass, where melting snows had exposed the grisly remains of the Donner party, which Kearny (passing through a week before them) had buried. Lassen resolved then and there to avoid the Truckee and equally steep Carson's trails and discussed with Myers, McGee, and Chiles the best way to return. Whatever he had decided, the party was already advising westbound parties they encountered to take the Applegate Trail to the headwaters of the Pitt River and follow it south, even though the route was little traveled. To what extent Lassen had anything to do with the advice is uncertain, although it served his purposes. How else to attract newcomers to his ranch and populate the new city he intended to build?

After wintering in Missouri, Lassen set out for California in early May 1848 in a train of forty-seven wagons guided by Joseph Chiles. With Lassen was Master Mason Sashel Woods who was carrying the Masonic Charter with which they planned to establish the first Masonic Lodge in California. In August, as they neared the Humboldt, Lassen's party met a group of eastbound Mormons carrying astonishing news. According to a member of Lassen's party, Richard May:

We met a train of packs from California 23 in Number Several of them had specimens of the Gold Lately discovered in that Country about 70 miles above Sutter's establishment They represented the Mines as being very Rich yielding on an average of two oz of gold to the days Labor and that one particular Man had made 700 dollars in one day.

It was the first news of the gold discovery, and it must have come as music to Lassen's ears. Farther along they met more Mormons who had come by way of Carson's and asserted it was a better route over the mountains than the Truckee. But when Lassen reached the Humboldt River, he turned sharply west, leading his small band on the Applegate Trail toward Goose Lake. (Chiles, however, split and went over the Sierras using the more traveled Carson's Pass.) When Lassen reached Goose Lake, he turned southeast into California following the Pitt River. He then made a long, 150-mile trek south along the ridgeline through mostly uncharted regions of the northern Sierras. South of Big Valley, they had trouble getting their wagons through the thick forest and had to cut them down to carts to negotiate the narrow passages. As they wandered through the Sierras, they ran low on food and nearly starved to death before finding a pass that delivered them to Lassen's ranch.

Historians disagree on whether Lassen got lost or simply had difficulty getting his wagons through the thick forests. It is unlikely Lassen was lost, for he knew Frémont, Kit Carson, Chiles, and other seasoned guides from whom he had gleaned vital information about the passes over the Sierras. He himself had explored the area, sometimes on his own and sometimes with Frémont when the latter passed through in the spring of 1844. By opting not to descend into the valley as soon as they crested the Sierras but riding the high ridgeline instead, Lassen knew very well what he was doing: forging a route that would lead emigrants to his doorstep, much as the Truckee led to Sutter's. Once at his rancho, Lassen organized a meeting with emigrants who praised him as an able guide and endorsed the new "Lassen Cutoff." Their glowing testimony to Lassen and his trail appeared in the *New York Herald* in February 12, 1849:

> *We found the ascent and descent to and from the mountains, very gradual and easy; and upon the whole, your committee consider the pass discovered by Captain Lawson, one of the fin-*

est in the world . . . in the opinion of your committee, a most practicable road can be made, with very little labor through this pass . . .

Your committee think Captain Lawson entitled to the thanks of this meeting, for the energy and decision displayed by him in surveying the route . . .

★   ★   ★   ★

SUCH WAS the situation when, on August 11, Milton McGee, who was guiding an emigrant party, veered off the Humboldt and followed some faint tracks west toward the Applegate, a trail that no gold seekers, mostly out of ignorance, had yet taken. When three days later, the highly respected Benoni Hudspeth followed suit, other emigrants blindly took his cue—even though they had no idea as to its length or the conditions on the trail. Most emigrants were opting for Lassen's on the hope that it was no worse and quite possibly even better than the alternatives. Others, who had no knowledge of any of the trails, found the prospect of a "cut-off" appealing, believing they would arrive in the gold fields in 10 days.

On balance, Bruff, too, favored Lassen's. The potential threat posed by the Diggers was a constant concern he wished to avoid. By contrast, Indians on the west side of the Humboldt were friendly—or so he thought. Nor did he wish to traverse the grueling Forty-Mile Desert beyond the Sink. But it was mostly because of J. J. Myers that Bruff liked the trail. Indeed, Bruff believed it was Myers, not Lassen, who had led the first train of emigrants from Missouri over the Pass, after which Lassen followed. In his research of the trail earlier that year, he had found a letter dated February 13, 1849 from Myers, the blazer of the useless Hudspeth Cutoff, to Brigadier General R. Jones. In the letter Myers claimed to know intimately the mountains and rivers of California and to be able to guide any party from the Humboldt River to the Sacramento Valley "not over 150 miles distant." Only Myers was wrong: From the Humboldt, Lassen's wasn't 150 miles but more than 300 miles. Even though Bruff claimed to know this, he planned to strike directly west as soon as he crested the Sierras by following a little-known route once used by Frémont. If he failed to find it, his error would add weeks to the journey, extending it into the inclement winter months for stragglers such as themselves.

If there were any doubts as to his decision, they were soon dispelled by Lieutenant Hawkins. Hawkins was leading a government supply train from Oregon to Fort Hall to resupply the Mounted Rifles. Having just come by way of Lassen's Pass, Hawkins confirmed the water and grass from there all the way to the Sacramento Valley were good. There was one drawback: Near the Pitt River, the supply train had been attacked by Paiute Indians, who killed a soldier and wounded two others, prompting many soldiers to desert. Bruff learned of more Indian attacks the next day from a note tacked to a board for the rear division of the Nemahaw Company stating that Indians had stolen all their cattle and wounded one man but that the cattle had been recovered. Farther along the trail, Bruff heard more stories from travelers who had lost their cattle to the hostile Paiutes.

When Bruff called the men together the next day to make a decision on which trail to take, it was more than to avoid dissension in the ranks as the other consultations had been; it had the potential of being a life or death decision. Taking the wrong trail earlier—such as the Hudspeth—had only resulted in a slightly tougher trek. Crossing over the High Sierras in early winter was a different matter entirely. After weighing all the pros and cons, the men unanimously agreed with Bruff: Lassen's it would be.

On the eve of their arrival at the fork, James Wardell read an address to the Company he had written on his own. Wardell praised the men for their "suppression of evil passions" over the course of the journey and congratulated them for their extraordinary good luck thus far in avoiding accident, illness, and hostile Indians. At the end of his speech, the men gave Wardell a rousing three cheers and sat down to supper. Whether the men knew it or not, in advocating for Lassen's, their Captain was gambling heavily on finding Frémont's shortcut.

Chapter Eight

LASSEN'S GAMBLE

On September 19, the Washington Company arrived at the turnoff to Lassen's. If Bruff was superstitious of omens, he might have read meaning into the nearby grave of Mary Jane McClelland, who, at 3 years and 4 months of age, had died the previous month—the youngest death he had recorded on the trail so far. Not far from the grave stood a shiny, red barrel the size of a whiskey keg. Riding over to examine it, Bruff saw it had iron hoops and a square hole cut in its head. Printed neatly on its side in bold black letters was "POST OFFICE." Peering into it, Bruff found it half full of letters and notes. Adjacent to the rudimentary post office was a billboard plastered with notes urging those in the rear to hurry along or indicating which fork had been taken. Here, emigrant parties had paused to read the notes and discuss with passing emigrants what they knew of the new route. Anxiously, they weighed what was known about Carson's and the Truckee with what wasn't about Lassen's. With most wagons now turning off toward Lassen's, it was enough to convince the undecided to follow suit. All told, some 9,000 wagons—two-thirds of the remaining wagons on the trail—would opt for Lassen's by the end of October.

One might normally have taken solace in the greater number

of wagons. But the trail was littered with putrescent, rotting oxen that were now failing in staggering numbers from dehydration, heat, and sheer exhaustion. On the first day alone on the Applegate, Bruff counted two dozen dead oxen, a couple of dead horses, and countless wheels, hubs, chains, harnesses, and other wagon fragments. The next day they passed fourteen more dead cattle, one on its last breath, and one stuck horridly in a spring with its hind quarters protruding in the air. The killing field looked apocalyptic. The stench was nauseating.

At Antelope Springs the Company found some water oozing from clay cliffs. At the base of the cliffs, emigrants had fashioned large basins to catch the trickle so the animals could drink. Bruff was annoyed to see other Gold Rushers had selfishly allowed their oxen to stand in the basins, muddying the water for others. Nearby was a block of wood on which was written, "THIS IS THE PLACE OF THE DESTRUCTION OF THE TEAM." Strewn around the sign were several dead oxen and broken wagons, indicating the demise of the party's draft animals had forced the party to pack in. To the rear, families who had fallen back were also abandoning wagons, leaving women and small children to walk the rest of the way.

Farther on, the Company found water at Rabbit Hole Springs, named for the innumerable rabbit tracks leading to it. All around the springs lay dead oxen, including several stuck upside down in the pools. To avoid the stench, Gold Rushers had widened the trail, only to leave more dead animals and broken wagons in their wake. Traveling a few days behind the Washington Company, a member of the Wolverine Rangers described the scene:

> *I had associated with the name 'wells' a vision of an oasis—*
> *verdure, trees, and cooling water. The whole environment*

as far as the eye could reach was simply an abomination of desolation . . . ash heaps of hills into which slowly percolated filthy-looking, brackish water. More than half the wells were unavailable as they were filled with the carcasses of cattle which had perished in trying to get to the water. To add to the natural horrors of the scene, about the wells were scattered the bodies of cattle, horses, and mules which had died here from overwork, hunger, broken and thirst; broken and abandoned wagons, boxes, bundles of clothing, guns, harnesses or yokes, anything and everything that the emigrant had outfitted with . . .

Beyond Rabbit Hole was a barren tableland studded with greasewood and sage. On the far side were several wells dug 3 to 6 feet deep with cool, clear water—if only the men could get to them! "There is scarcely a space for the wagons to reach the holes, for the ox-carcasses," Bruff complained. It didn't matter, for by now many of the holes were plugged with dead oxen whose bodies had swelled up so as to fill the holes entirely. In one gulch 100 yards long were wells choked with dead oxen and ox carcasses. Covering his face against the putrid air, Bruff called the gruesome scene "the very heart of Golgotha." One of his own mules now gave out; he promptly consigned it to the "depot of carcasses." But with water nearby, they had no choice but to camp in the wretched place.

While the men fed the animals with grass they had cut a few days earlier, Bruff walked to the edge of the plateau to survey the next day's challenge: the forbidding, waterless Black Rock Desert. Gazing down from the rim, Bruff spotted old acquaintances from the Platte in the ravine below: Major Horn and his wife. Having forgotten to cut grass for this barren section of the trail, Mrs. Horn was baking bread for the animals. She invited Bruff to dine on the "horse-rations," which he found, along with the fried pork fat and coffee, far from the sumptuous meal they had prepared for him back on the Platte, but delicious under the circumstances. At nightfall the Horns moved on. Throwing down his blanket among the carcasses, Bruff slept "as well as the effluvia would permit."

Early the next morning he was awakened by a commotion. A few of the younger members were attempting to steal his horse, some of the same rascals who had been so long a thorn in his side. Drawing his pistol, the hot-tempered Bruff was on the verge of making "a bloody example of them" but checked himself out of consideration for the boys' parents.

A short way into the Black Rock Desert, they halted to ration some grass and a quart of water for each animal. Black Rock was a vast, barren plain where the sun baked the ground so white it looked like a sheet of ice. Surveying the landscape around him, Bruff observed a desecration of property and life beyond all imagination: nearly a hundred dead oxen and a vast sea of broken, burnt, and abandoned wagons. Animals still standing were being prodded beyond their limit. One emigrant described the surreal scene:

> *People are driving their poor, exhausted cattle [across the desert]...and when they lie down from exhaustion, they will sometimes wait awhile for them to rest. At other times they will beat them or split the skin on their tails or set a dog on them if they have one., or go through all these operations in succession, and if the poor creatures can bear all these operations without moving, then they are abandoned.*

At length the Company came upon a party of Cherokee Indians from Washington County, Arkansas on their way to the gold fields. Ironically, the Cherokee had been forcibly driven from their homeland in the southeastern U.S. when gold was discovered there in 1838. Led by Captain Louis Evans, the one-time county sheriff, the Fayetteville Mining Company had originally consisted of an impressive 40 wagons and 130 men. In striking out from Arkansas, they had blazed a 300-mile trail never before traveled later dubbed the Cherokee Trail. After a member of the party drowned in the Green River near Pueblo, Colorado, the company began to fracture into several parties, each taking different routes over the Sierras. Although the Cherokee were renowned as pathfinders, that winter they would be no match for Lassen's Trail, where they lost all their animals in snow 3 feet deep.

Ahead, the mountains appeared as baked clay in shades of yellow, orange, and red. At the base of one range, the men were astonished by the sight of a light-blue lagoon bordered by tall, cedar-like trees. Bruff was the only one who knew it to be a mirage, with the pretty trees merely a reflection of dusty sage bushes. "The whole landscape was aerial except the outline of the mountains," he explained to his baffled men. So real did the image appear that oxen had stampeded for the illusory lake in a desperate attempt to quench their thirst. Now dozens of cattle lay bloated and dead on the crusty alkali plain. Three oxen were still alive, one looking back anxiously toward the trail "for succor from suffering and a slow death." To end its misery, Bruff shot it, knowing the wolves would soon finish the others.

By evening of their third day on the desert, they arrived at Black Rock, a series of huge, dark volcanic bluffs that marked the end of their grueling 52-mile desert march. As a sign of just how difficult the crossing had been, at the foot of the bluffs lay 150 dead oxen. While the men replenished the water casks, Bruff inventoried their food stocks: 1,925 pounds of bread was all that remained—the equivalent of 32 days of rations. With the mules becoming weaker with each passing day, Bruff jettisoned a wagon and distributed its mules to bolster the other teams.

While at Black Rock, Bruff explored the volcanic cliffs stacked up one on top of the other colored in pastel shades of yellow, orange, and red, purple, blue, and gray. Climbing one 450-foot hill, he found a noisy rookery of thousands of cackling ravens and crows. Here he paused to collect samples of obsidian, serpentine, and several arrowheads, mementos of his great adventure. Lighting his pipe, he sat down to sketch a series of fortress-like bluffs he named "Frémont's Castle" after his friend who had passed here in 1844.

On the other side of the dark landmass were Great Boiling Springs and the beginning of some good grass and water along the trail. So hot was the water that they were able to make coffee in it simply by placing the pot in the spring. To drink it directly, the men had to channel it into a series of basins before it was cool enough to drink. Although it was laden with minerals, no one was complaining after the waterless desert trek. Moving on the next day, they encountered more hot springs and a hot creek that the mules stubbornly refused to cross until whipped and prodded. By evening some of the Company's mule trains had become so weak they lagged miles behind. To signal the rear wagons, Bruff ordered the greasewood bushes torched. Fueled by the dryness, the flames quickly spread from tree to tree a great distance, "bringing out the hills near us, from their evening curtain."

A few days on, the rift in the company grew wider when a fight broke out among some of the younger men caught with excess baggage. After Bruff intervened, two of the most troublesome began to talk openly about quitting the Company and going their own way. "The quicker they do so, the better," he fumed.

On September 24, while riding in the late afternoon, Bruff

heard of good grass some 3 miles from the trail and decided to split the Company. The weakest teams were sent to graze, while the rest would move up the trail toward the Great Mud Basin to find good camping ground. Mounting his tired horse, Bruff rode ahead of the grazing wagons to scout for the grass. When he rejoined the other wagons in camp the next day, he was astonished to find the quirky Keller family whom he had last seen at St. Joseph. The Kellers informed him that the old silver-haired Swiss, Abbott, had died back on the Platte, his final wish fulfilled.

Even though it was late September, daytime temperatures were soaring into the 100s. The men were anxious to get to higher elevation where the temperature would moderate. But the trail refused to cooperate, twisting and turning agonizingly for miles to circumvent the many marshes. After several hours, they reached the crest of a steep hill where the trail abruptly disappeared. Looking down, Bruff gasped at the precipitous descent. In addition to being steep, the hill was more than 200 yards long and covered with loose sand and scree. As they started down, the teamsters once again double-locked the wheels, allowing the wagons to skid down to the plain below. One by one the wagons descended without a hitch and the men marveled at the good luck they had had in negotiating dangerously steep terrain. Other companies had not been so lucky, for at the bottom of the hill lay the wreckage of dozens of wagons and dead animals.

The Company had not gone very far when they were faced with yet another, more dangerous descent. Once again, the wagons descended without mishap—although in negotiating the descent, the mules were being pushed to their limit. They were now at the entrance of High Rock Canyon, where they were rewarded with a smooth trail, good grass, and just beneath the surface, fresh snowmelt, cool and pure. Here they laid over a day to rest and feed the weary animals.

As they proceeded through High Rock, the defile opened onto a wide gorge lined by immense volcanic walls. In the center of the gorge was a circular spring with a white sandy bottom and water delightfully "clear, and cool as ice." Exiting the canyon, they ascended a rugged gulch to the top of a mountain where they beheld a breathtaking panoramic view. To the southwest, they could see vast, undulating plains and shallow valleys green with grass. Twenty-five miles to the west lay the 10,000-foot Warner Range and 40 miles beyond it the lofty peaks of Sierra Nevada, already covered in snow.

On September 27, tensions that had been simmering for so long in the Company finally boiled over. After Bruff meted out penalties to several men for sleeping during guard duty "and other infractions," two of the worst offenders submitted a written letter requesting to be formally discharged from the Company. Intending to pack in on their own, they requested two mules and six days of rations. Several members objected that honoring the request would set a bad precedent and could lead to the dissolution of the Company prematurely. But Bruff countered that two mules and some rations were a small price to pay to get rid of the miscreants. Eventually everyone approved, belting out three cheers "such their joy at the riddance." Before departing, the disaffected men managed to make off with the Company's wine, which was used for medicinal purposes.

They were now moving through a lunar landscape of volcanic, grey-brown rock. Protruding from the hillsides were gigantic pockmarked boulders resembling cauliflower, which Bruff judged to be where the volcanic fires "exerted their dying powers." A few miles farther on they came to Spring Branch, an idyllic mountain spring with a pebbly bottom containing "the clearest, coolest, and sweetest water" he had ever tasted.

On and on they marched through canyons filled with aspen, sage, sand, and lava, past shattered wagons and more dead cattle. After crossing the white plain of Surprise Valley, they arrived at Goose Lake in the upper easternmost corner of present-day California.

In camp that night, alarming news had come from the Cherokees and the Horns camped nearby: word had flowed back along the trail that Lassen's ranch was a great deal farther than Bruff had calculated.

It seems that the road which leads into the Sacramento Valley, is not the same as Frémont's trail; but a great deal longer . . . that it follows the ridges of the Sierra Nevada a long way down South, instead of taking the direction we all thought it would.

He now wanted to search for Frémont's trail, but the rest of the men refused to "entertain experiments." In any case, it was already too late, since by the time they hit the Black Rock Desert they had already passed the entrance to the cutoff. The route Bruff was hoping to find was an obscure passage Frémont used during his third expedition in 1846. Not only was the route shorter and more direct than Lassen's, but easier, too, for it followed a series of beautiful valleys without any rugged or steep trails to cross, where wagons could travel easily. Bruff had drawn the maps for Frémont's report, *Geographical Memoir upon Upper California*, which showed the explorer's path leading more or less directly east from the Upper Sacramento near Lassen's ranch. In it he states that in April of 1846, he left Lassen's ranch and headed up the Sacramento River. Near Cottonwood Creek he turned east "up one of the many pretty little streams that flow into the main river around the head of the lower (Sacramento) valley," a frustrating vague description to be sure. To make matters more difficult, Frémont had approached the trail from the west, not the east, making identification of accessible valleys and landmarks from the eastern side difficult if not downright impossible. Even though Frémont said the elevation of the pass was at 4,600 feet, he probably crossed at 5,700-foot Fredonyer Pass, which, at 40 degrees latitude, is consistent with his own coordinates. By the time of the Gold Rush, the trail was being referred to as the Cherokee Cutoff after a Cherokee guide named Senora Hicks who had come over it early in 1849. Hicks would guide Major Rucker along the trail during the government's relief mission later that year. Captain Lyon who also used it to go back and forth over the Sierras in 1849–50, later described it to Bruff "as a series of fine valleys, no rugged steep hills to pass."

Sadly, it was this route that McGee was also looking for when he turned off the Humboldt Trail, drawing thousands in his wake to make the same tragic mistake. Born as it might have been of Lassen's desire to lead emigrants to his ranch, the trail was a long, meandering trek through one of the continent's highest mountains. Instead of turning west to the Sacramento Valley as many had hoped, it led south along the ridgeline of the Sierras 150 miles to Big Meadows, then turned southwest another 50 miles before reaching Lassen's ranch. Bruff had originally calculated the distance from where they were camped near the head of Lassen's Trail to the Sacramento Valley to be 60 to 70 miles. In fact it was almost 200 miles, "farther than I or anybody else ever dreampt of," he lamented. It was an enormous discrepancy, given the fact that winter was beginning, men and animals were exhausted and malnourished, and snow had begun to fall on the higher peaks. In being a little-used trail, Lassen's would also prove far more rugged than either Carson's or the Truckee.

Bruff had gambled and lost. As they and thousands of other Gold Rushers would soon learn, it was not a better route into California and those who followed McGee came to rue the day they made that decision. So many people died on Lassen's trail in 1849–50 that it would be scorned as "the death route." One pioneer later described this section of Lassen's Trail as "a mountain which could not be ascended except by some creature that had either wings or claws."

Bruff concluded finding Frémont's trail was like threading the needle's eye and would have necessitated returning to the Humboldt to find the valley leading to it. That of course was now out of the question. Had they found Fremont's elusive pass, they could have been digging in the Redding area already. Likewise if they taken Carson's or the Truckee. As it was, everyone—including Bruff—was dismayed by the added distance. But they should have been more concerned that winter was approaching. Every additional day spent lingering in the mountains ran the risk of being trapped there like the Donner party.

Departure the next morning was delayed two hours because the mules had wandered off thanks to the carelessness of the guards. As they ascended toward Lassen's Pass, they came upon an ox dying in the middle of the narrow trail. In their struggle to get up the rocky trail, teamsters in front were paying no heed, driving wagons and animals over the poor beast as he groaned in pain. Early on the morning of October 3, the Company reached Lassen's Pass. At the crest of the hill, Bruff planted the Stars and Stripes to encourage those in the rear just as he had done at South Pass. As he stood waiting for his wagons to ascend, he beheld the sorry state of his Company. Weary teamsters were lashing their tired animals up the rugged hill amid blinding clouds of dust and sand. So fatigued were the animals that single wagons were being dragged up the hill by 12 oxen. Animals too weak to draw a wagon were being led up the hill by small boys. Men, women, and children were plodding up the hill with boxes, bags, and trunks strapped to their backs to ease the burden on the animals. In the choking dust, one teamster was clutching a baby as he urged up his team. One old man, pale and weak from scurvy, rode up strapped to a mattress on a jaded horse. Behind him came a man on a mule, wrapped in a blue blanket and shivering from malaria. Another wagon carrying women and children was just nearing the summit when its tongue snapped, sending it careening back down the hill with the terrified occupants screaming. Fortunately, the renegade wagon snagged onto a dead ox lying on the trail, the beast of burden proving to be of service even in its demise.

Many of his party were now showing suppurating wounds and blotchy skins—signs of scurvy. Due to the lack of fruit along the trail, the disease was fatal unless treated. Although none of Bruff's men exhibited any signs of serious malnutrition thus far, they were down to bread and coffee. That they were low on food owed to Bruff's miscalculation of the distance from Lassen's Pass to the Sacramento Valley. He had expected to be in the settlements within a day or two of crossing Lassen's Pass and could then replenish their stocks. Instead, they were now confronted by a riot of ridges, mountains, and valleys still to cross. Other companies had run out of food entirely and were attempting to eat the local plants, which proved risky. Among the several graves they passed was one of a man who had died two days earlier:

Jno. A. Dawson,
St. Louis, Mo.
Died Oct 1st 1849,
from eating a poisonous root at the spring

Whether it was from the rigors of the ascent or the impatience of the men now that they were within sight of the Sierras, many large companies—if they had survived at all—were now breaking up into smaller ones. Others were dissolving altogether and abandoning their wagons. The Wolverine Rangers lost so many oxen ascending the summit that they dissolved the company and abandoned the wagons on the spot.

As Bruff was fording the Pitt River, he noticed a sign affixed to an oak tree indicating the distances to grass, water, the Sacramento Valley, the nearest gold diggings, and so forth. At the bottom was written:

> *Where the road leaves Pitt Riv: it passes over the hills and is very rough for 20 ms. Mr. lassen recommends keeping to the right, & going around these hills, over and longer, but smoother road . . . Beef at Lassen's is $50 a head, and Flour $50 per hundred. Plenty of provisions & clothing in Sacramento City, and cheap. Pork $35 per bbl. bought at prices the same, or higher than at Lassen's.*

While the sign indicated it had been signed by Lt. Williamson of the U.S. Army, it suggested the promotional hand of Lassen himself.

Since the Humboldt, Indians had been entirely absent from the trail. On the Plains, the natives had been generally friendly, seeking mostly to trade or beg. There had been the occasional theft of livestock, but Indians had scrupulously avoided direct confrontation with whites and had rarely been a direct threat to emigrants themselves. But on the western slope of the Warner Range, Gold Rushers were now encountering a different breed of Indian altogether: the Pitt. The Pitt, who numbered around 3,000, lived along the Pitt River in an area that stretched west from the Warner Mountains to Mount Shasta in the north and south to the end of the Cascade Range. Wrongly called "Diggers," for the deep pits they used to trap game and enemies, the Pitt River Indians bore no relation to the Basin Diggers by blood or temperament. While the Basin Diggers were known for their petty thieving, the Pitt River bands would be the most hostile that travelers encountered on the trail. Many parties were being attacked outright or losing large numbers of animals, reawakening—for once legitimately—the emigrant fear of the murderous native.

Murderous indeed. At camp, Bruff learned that one of his friends from the Corps, Captain William H. Warner, had been killed and a number of his men injured a few days earlier by the Indians. The soldiers, who had also been deflected by Lassen's circuitous route, had been exploring 6 miles north for a better route through the Sierras. The next day, Bruff was told of a camp farther up where the injured men were being treated and hastened ahead of his train to find out more about Warner.

At the surgeon's camp, Corporal Schekels related the details of Warner's encounter with the Pitt. As the column was passing through a narrow defile east of Goose Lake, a party of thirty to fifty Indians appeared on the ridge above and began firing simultaneously. One soldier at the scene said, "the arrows flew like hail." Worst hit was Warner, who took eleven iron-tipped arrows through his arms, legs, and jaw, killing him instantly. Their halfbreed guide, Bateau, took nine arrows—including one through the mouth—and was in such pain he offered to pay anyone $500 "to shoot his brains out." He died shortly after. Two other soldiers were wounded, one of whom would die before reaching Sacramento. As the soldiers were retreating, one Indian was seen on a precipice howling an angry, incomprehensible tirade.

As they made camp along the Pitt River, the men were on edge. All around the camp were signs of recent Pitt presence: moccasin prints in the dust, arrowheads, wicker fish nets, fires, roasted mussel shells. Even more disturbing were the warning signs other Gold Rushers had posted in the camp. One posted by a Mr. Collins announced that a few days earlier Indians had attempted to steal their cattle. More worrisome was the sign of the Charleston Company, a party of seventy-four, stating they had been attacked by Indians. Not far off was an emigrant grave marker, the breast of which was shot through with an arrow on which a note was attached: "this is the fatal arrow." Although the cause of the Indians' hostility was not entirely clear, with the onset of winter, the Pitt were moving down from the mountains to their permanent dwellings in the valley and were running smack into the thousands of emigrants flooding into their hunting grounds. When the men made camp that night, they slept on their arms.

In his journal, Bruff's wary attitude toward Indians was hardened by the news of Warner's death:

> *Yet no indian has attempted any hostility with my company, for the reason that we are always ready, and keep strict guard--, night and day. I believe that the company, with the exception of a few turbalent [sic] braggarts, are a good fighting party. I know many in it, who would have been pleased to have had a fight with the Indians of the plains--, the Pawnees, Sioux; &c--in which event we'd most certainly have made some horses. I could have had no objection, as its effects on the company, would have been beneficial.*

But the Company had more pressing problems than the Pitt. Since Lassen's Pass, animals and humans had begun to fail in still greater numbers. Shattered wagons, discarded clothing, dead oxen, and graves were everywhere. Some hills were almost too steep for the oxen, and even Bruff's agile mules stumbled and fell, becoming weaker with each mile gained. While water was available in the ravines, people were being advised not to let their cattle go down as they lacked the strength to climb back up. Many had ignored the warning and now hundreds of dead cattle filled the ravines. With food running perilously low, Bruff and his group had begun to shoot their draft animals for meat. To top it off, nights were in the teens and the first snowflakes had begun to drift down idly, a sign of worse times ahead.

In stark contrast to the suffering and anguish of most emigrants were the rare few who seemed to hover miraculously above the arduous conditions—if for a time. Bruff was enchanted by the young Alford couple, proprietors of a "steam-boat wagon" with a built-in stove, its exhaust pipe sticking out of the top of the canvas. Mrs. Alford had successfully given birth on the trail a month earlier. Another wagon had a hen-coop attached to the rear filled with hens and roosters. Its owner, a plucky Irishman named Pat, intended to turn a huge profit on the fowl in California. How he refrained from eating his charges along the lifeless Humboldt was a mystery. Indeed, Pat said he'd rather starve than kill so much as a single one of his precious birds.

On October 6, the Company encountered a government relief party coming up Warm Spring Valley, a sign of just how dire the emigrants' situation, especially for those in the rear, had become. In August, General Persifor F. Smith, Commander of the Pacific Army based in Sacramento, had learned from arriving Gold Rushers of the serious plight of those crossing the precipitous Carson and Truckee Passes. Early snow had left drifts four to five feet deep. As a measure of the severity of the emergency, Smith immediately appropriated $100,000 from the civil fund for the relief effort. Residents of San Francisco had donated $12,000 to the relief fund. Smith charged Major D. H. Rucker with organizing and directing the expedition. In mid-September, Rucker dispatched relief teams to the three trails. On the Truckee, Captain Charles Kilburn was delivering food and supplies to starving people and distributing mules and horses to bring in the many women, children, and sick now stuck in the rear. When he learned only one train remained on the rear of the trail, he moved to assist Rucker on Carson's. At a higher altitude, Carson's was already buried by a snowstorm that had passed two days earlier on October 10, Kilburn reported:

> *On the summits we found a fall of snow; and in many places it had drifted to four or five feet in depth. In a short report of this kind it is impossible to detail the amount of suffering relieved by my party on the two lines. The energy and generosity of the government in thus relieving the needy was openly expressed and commented on by the whole of the emigrants. After passing the two summits on our return, we found many in utmost need.*

Kilborn had found pack animals frozen in the snow and many travelers frostbitten. Although only four inches of snow had fallen on Lassen's, General Smith was even more worried for the Gold Rushers still on the Black Rock and Humboldt heading for the much longer and rougher Lassen's Trail. In mid-September, he had received a disturbing report from Milton McGee who had led the first wagons across Lassen's. In his report, McGee said, "I have just come in from the northern route and can assure you . . . that many are now entirely destitute of provisions, while others will not have a sufficiency to bring them within many days' travel of the Sacramento Valley." With winter approaching and emigrants exhausted, sick, and starving, Smith saw a perfect storm brewing.

What frustrated Smith's relief effort was that no one knew exactly how many Gold Rushers were still on the trail or precisely where they were. While travelers continued to stream into Lassen's ranch out of harm's way, as many as 8,000 were still somewhere on a 300-mile stretch of trail from Lassen's Pass all the way back to the Humboldt. Without assistance, those in the rear wouldn't reach the Sierras until late October or November when the chance of a snowstorm was extremely high. If the Donner Party had been a tragedy, what was now shaping up was a human catastrophe.

Having gotten delayed assisting the emigrants in the south, Rucker sent a civilian, John H. Peoples, to lead the rescue party on Lassen's. In early October, Peoples came up with a relief train with fresh mules, hard bread, pork, and beef. But by the time Peoples encountered Bruff on the trail, he was already quite sick with what was then known as "mountain fever" (Rocky Mountain spotted fever), a little-understood disease that had been claiming emigrant lives since Steamboat Springs. Realizing he would only hold up the relief effort if he continued, Peoples decided to return to the settlements with the Washington Company and turned over his command to another civilian, E. H. Todd.

Todd's instructions were to issue provisions only to those who were in dire need and then only sparingly. He was also ordered to:

> *admonish them of the lateness of the season and the great possibility of a snow storm and urge them to throw away everything of any weight that may not be absolutely necessary . . . See that all women and children have the means of riding to Lawson's even if you are obliged to make your own men walk.*

Todd was advising travelers to abandon their teams and hurry for their lives for the road ahead would be "the worst in all the world."

Even though he was working his way along the Pitt River and still 180 miles from Lassen's ranch, Bruff did not register Todd's sense of urgency—nor did most emigrants who stubbornly refused to abandon their wagons and all their belongings.

As they moved along the Pitt River, the Washington Company was faced with a number of minor cutoff choices. After Bruff held a Company meeting, the men opted for a rugged, hilly road that was a couple of miles shorter than one following the river. Ascending the first hill, the men beheld a magnificent sight. Spread out before them was the vast panorama of the Sierra Nevada. To the southwest were the 12,000-foot extinct volcanic peaks of Snow Butte (today called Lassen's Peak); to the northwest was Mt. Shasta, mantled in snow, and a host of smaller cones covered in dark pine spread out in the distance. From their altitude they could also glimpse their Holy Grail, the Sacramento Valley, riven by silvery rivers and streams. Buoyed by the nearness to their goal, Bruff indulged in a moment of levity in his journal:

> *Enraptur'd with a landscape! --how ridiculous! I have seen many, and some nearly as gran; besides I must look out for the train, or there will be some accidental capsizements, maybe a broken neck or leg!--No time now for the Fine Arts, we must patronize the rough ones, just now!*

As they advanced, Bruff could now see what Todd meant about the trail. It was a corrugated mass of rumpled hills that were steep, crooked, and slippery. The Company's progress was reduced to no more than 13 miles a day. As they approached a narrow defile, Peoples warned Bruff of a Digger village of several hundred warriors fully mounted with horses and mules who had attacked the relief convoy as it was passing through. But as they descended once again the Company's good luck prevailed, for they saw no Indians.

From the Missouri Nodaway Company, Bruff was able to buy some bread, sugar, and bacon at exorbitant prices. Only later did he learn the Nodaways had begged food from the relief wagon and were reselling it to emigrants. Fortunately, Major Rucker wasn't far below, leading another relief party up the mountain for those in real need.

Eleven days out of Lassen's Pass, the Company reached Feather Lake, so called because of the enormous piles of feathers deposited along the shore by frequenting fowl. They were about 75 miles from Lassen's now—no more than four of five days, according to Bruff's calculation. Peoples had nearly recovered thanks to the ministrations of Dr. Austin. Proud he had been able to assist a member of the relief team, Bruff accompanied Peoples to Rucker's tent to deliver him. Much to Bruff's annoyance (and no doubt Rucker's, too) the Major was besieged by begging emigrants behaving like a pack of hungry wolves. Only a few of them, however, needed provisions, and even those showed no gratitude for what they received. Because Rucker was unable to distinguish between starving and the greedy, he was obliged to distribute food to all of them. When Rucker, who still had no idea how far back the emigrant line extended, refused to give three men on mules anything on the grounds that they could eat their mules, the men became indignant and an altercation ensued.

Now it was Bruff's men who wanted handouts from Rucker. Bruff flatly refused, arguing that the food was destined for the starving families in the rear, especially women and children, most of whom were now stuck at Goose Lake or even farther back.

"There were some who would take a biscuit out of a woman's mouth," he wrote. Once again he was overruled and, sheepishly, he went back to beseech Rucker who gave him 31 pounds of pork and 14 pounds of crackers. The men hastened back to camp with the sacks of provisions like mice with a piece of cheese. While Bruff was busy talking with Rucker, they quickly distributed and ate all the rations. Not a scrap had been left for their Captain.

On they marched down the Feather River Valley through hills stacked thick with tall pines and cedars. Coming upon a broad, grassy plain teeming with emigrant encampments, they halted and made camp. The whole scene could have been mistaken for a happy, prosperous village: children cavorting and laughing, oblivious to the general suffering; men cutting hay and fixing wagons; clothes drying on the grass; and cows grazing, their tiny bells tinkling consolingly. With pale green willows marking the course of the stream and the pine-covered mountains in the background, the scene appeared incongruously idyllic.

The reality, of course, was quite different. Even the Company was down to six days' rations and only bread at that. To preempt theft or quarreling, Bruff decided to distribute the remaining provisions. A few days later they arrived at Deer Creek, a narrow valley filled with mammoth yellow pines 10 feet in diameter, 200 feet tall, and needle-straight. The pine cones were a foot and a half in length. But the grandeur of the trees could not redeem the extreme difficulty of the trail. It was steep, narrow, slippery, and riddled with stumps, large rocks, logs, and dead oxen. Bruff described how they labored forward:

> *Road now ran W, a short distance, then turned S.W. - very*
> *rough, and in all, about 2 ms. [miles] from Feather River, it*
> *turned short round S.S.W. and then descended S.W. a very*

steep and rugged hill; - but short, thank God! Next over the
rocky dry bed of a stream, which ran N. & S . . . Now descend
by a winding trail, a stony hill S. - a mile: 3 mules exhausted
& fell, raised them, replaced the team with better, and drove
the weak ones along.

So many oxen were now failing that wagons, in a rush to get off
the mountain, were rolling gruesomely over their legs and heads
pressing them farther into the mushy soil. Many oxen simply no
longer had the strength to ascend the hills. Despite all the kicking
and shouting of the teamsters, they had simply stopped in their
tracks, unable to go a single step farther. The Washington Company was faring little better. The long journey of attrition had
reduced the number of their wagons from thirteen to five. The one
thing that kept them going was the knowledge that they were now
very close to the Sacramento Valley.

Yet the closer they approached their destination, the worse the
trail became. Beyond Deer Creek the trail was so rugged and narrow as to be virtually impassable. At last, on the crown of a hill, the
wagons halted. They could proceed no farther. They were 32 miles
from Lassen's ranch. Exhausted and hungry, the men made camp
in the woods along Deer Creek near the encampments of several
other parties. From their encampment at 4,000 feet, they could see
the Sacramento Valley below shimmering tantalizingly in the distance like a dream.

As the men took stock of their situation, the Washington
Company was on its last legs. Several of the mules were too weak
to continue and one of the remaining wagons was on the verge of
collapse. Bruff planned to consolidate the stronger mule teams
and send three of the wagons down empty because heavy rains had
reduced the trail to muck. One person would stay behind to look

after the last wagon and effects that could not be packed in. In the evening, as they sat around the campfire Bruff told the men of his plan and all approved.

"But who would remain here? There was the rub!" Bruff wrote with mock humor.

As Captain, Bruff had capably led the Company across 2,000 miles of wilderness with a single loss of life. While most companies had broken down on the trail, some as far back as the Platte, the Washington Company had made it intact. No one could then know if Bruff's recommendation to take Lassen's Trail had been a mistake, given that relief parties had also been sent to the Carson and Truckee Trails as well. But he was now about to make two critical mistakes out of his selfless disregard for his own welfare. Relinquishing his command to a young friend, George Young, Bruff decided to remain behind and look after the wagons.

Under the circumstances, Bruff's decision to remain behind and not pack in with the other men is hard to understand. The wagons, along with the property they could not pack in, could not have been worth more than a few hundred dollars. In any case, the gold they assumed awaited them would more than make up for any loss incurred in abandoning the wagon on the mountain. Even harder to understand was his decision to lend one of the men, William Edmundston, his pack horse, effectively leaving him on the mountain with no transportation and with winter approaching.

Early on the morning of October 22, the remaining 55 men of the Company moved off for the valley. As they departed, they promised Bruff they would return in a few days, if not with a team, then at least with Bruff's horse. After Edmundston packed all his effects on the horse, he rode off right past Bruff, callously neglecting to offer him so much as flour or bread. Dr. Austin gave Bruff two hands-full of rice, to which another man added two small biscuits and some pipe tobacco. This, added to 2 pounds of Bruff's old beef and a few ounces of coffee, was the sum total of his food supply. With plenty of guns and ammunition, Bruff expected to live off the Deer Creek's abundant game. At the last minute, Josias Willis offered to remain with Bruff, which he accepted as "I believe him to be a clever fellow." Clever, Willis would prove to be.

Thus did the expedition end with no fanfare or praise for Bruff's superb leadership in bringing the men so far safely. Despite their insensitivity, he would sorely miss them:

> *Some I shall never see again, and there are a few whom I never wish to see again; But therere's* [sic] *many of that company, yes, most of them, I shall ever be happy to meet with, or travel with again. And my sincerest and best wishes accompany them, wheresoever they go.*

Little did he know, he was about to begin an entirely new and harrowing phase of his journey.

Chapter Nine

BRUFF'S CAMP

IT TOOK THE MEN THREE DAYS TO REACH LASSEN'S
ranch. Once in the valley, they scattered, some on their own, others
in pairs to mine for gold. For all practical purposes, the Washington Gold and Mining Company ceased to exist.

Back on the mountain, Bruff looked forward to a few relaxing
days, now that he had relinquished once and for all the burdens of
his command. At sunset on the first day, he and Willis made "quite
a supper" of the remaining rations. Afterward, he made entries in
his journal by the campfire while he puffed contentedly on his pipe.

When he first arrived on the mountain, he had noticed four
men in the woods felling some of the sugar pines. After talking to
them, he learned they worked for Lassen, who was paying them
$10 a day to cut pine shingles. Lassen's men, however, were far more
interested in the emigrants. Each time new wagons arrived, they
wasted no time in informing the weary travelers that the settlements were 50 miles away (they were 32) and that the route was
"the most rugged and difficult ever traveled by Christians." The
loggers would then admonish the disheartened Gold Rushers to
leave their wagons behind and pack in the rest of the way. Grateful
for the advice, most emigrants at once abandoned their wagons,

cattle, and all their effects, save what they could carry on their backs. As soon as the travelers were out of sight, Lassen's men fitted their wagons with an eyebolt and lowered them down the ravine into Mill Creek gorge. With "some mysterious assistance," according to Bruff, the wagons were then transferred from one gorge to another. Once they were safely out of sight, the loggers would claim the Indians had stolen them, thereby precluding any attempt to retrieve the pilfered wagons. Once again, vulnerable travelers were being preyed on, this time by men who had been emigrants themselves. When Bruff inquired as to the yield of the mines, the men said between one to two ounces a day ($12 to $24) but that mining "did not agree with them."

Camped as he was at the final stage of the long, arduous journey, Bruff now bore witness to the sorry state of his fellow Gold Rushers. Sixty a day were staggering into Deer Creek, including many women and children. If they had an ounce of energy remaining, they watered their animals and moved on. Others rested for a night or two before making the final descent. Whatever their station in life at the outset—lawyers, doctors, farmers, unemployed—they now all looked alike: haggard, starving, and in tatters. It was a grim pageant of the weary and wasted. Many were sick with mountain fever or scurvy. Those who had started with large companies had been reduced to small units of one or two wagons and a few tired animals.

Weary and forlorn, most had dark stories to tell. The St. Louis Company had lost all its cattle to the marauding Pitt Indians. One couple was packing in with all their goods heaped on a lone remaining ox. A scabrous-looking man had been coldly ejected from his company's wagon because he had scurvy. Several children had been burned in the face after playing with matches near gunpowder. One of Captain Warner's wounded soldiers was being carried to Sacramento for treatment. He died en route. A woman, still grieving, had buried her husband at Chimney Rock. Another was widowed on the trail and left with eight children, one of whom was sick and "ragged as a beggar." A man had buried his parents and a child on the Platte. In his journal, Bruff summed up his impression of his fellow Argonauts:

> *It is a queer sight now, to observe the straggling emigrants coming up and going in. Wagons of every kind, oxen, horses, mules, bulls, cows, and people,--men, women, & children, all packed. A few weeks travel has wrought a great change in their circumstances,--Many of them I recognized as old acquaintances as far back as Pittsburgh, and all along our western waters, and over the long travel. Large companies, fine animals, a great amount of provisions & stores, and smiling faces; were now a scattered, broken, selfish stragglers, dusty in faces and dress, and many of them, thin with hunger, as well as anxiety.*

Surprisingly, there were those who managed to slip through the jaws of defeat. A Frenchman with a son and two daughters came up in high spirits, as did a group of Wyandot Indians from the fork of the Missouri and Kansas Rivers. The daughter of the celebrated Philadelphia landscape painter William Russell Smith appeared, full of mirth. A Dutchman, tired of hauling his heavy tools up the mountain, had energy enough to destroy them on the summit. When Bruff asked why he had done so he replied, "Dey cosht me plendy of money in St. Louis, and nopoty shall have de goot of dem, py Got!" One woman claimed the journey had miraculously cured her of fits.

But at night, the merriment and chatter that had enlivened camps along the trail was noticeably absent. Instead, an eerie quiet hung over Deer Creek as emigrants were too weak, sick, or hungry to do anything but sleep.

Sleep they needed, for they were not yet at the end of the journey. The trek down was as hard as anything they had seen so far. It ran perilously along narrow ridges between glacier-cut and river-cut valleys and was riddled with deep crags. In good weather it was rough enough, but October's seasonal rains had turned the trail into a hellish slog of mud and rock. Horses and mules slipped and broke their legs; oxen with wagons in tow sometimes went crashing down into the precipitous canyons along with wagons and contents. When wagons broke down or became mired in mud, they would back up traffic for miles. Once in the settlements they would find, not an end to their suffering, but more of the same conditions that had prevailed on the trail.

A week had passed since Bruff's men had descended to Lassen's and there was still no sign of a relief wagon or his horse. Although anxious to get off the mountain, he refused to leave behind his journals and notebooks, drawings, minerals, and other artifacts of his journey until he could transport them by mule or wagon. When a member of the Company returned on a pony to fetch his personal baggage, Bruff sent a note along to Edmundston requesting his horse. He also sent a note with a passing emigrant to Peter Lassen requesting pack animals.

Since arriving at Deer Creek, Bruff had noticed oxen mysteriously disappearing on a daily basis from the campground. He suspected Lassen's men were also stealing the animals and paying Indians to herd them to the ranch. One morning Bruff and a few others campers hiked down to Mill Creek to look for the missing animals and to hunt. Although they did not find any oxen, the men managed to kill a grouse and a quail and find some delicious wild grapes along the way.

When he returned to camp, he was surprised to see five men from his Company had come up with eight mules. Camped some distance from Bruff, they did not inquire as to his well-being or offer him so much as a cup of coffee. These were the very men Bruff had hoped "never to see again." It was payback time. Now that he was no longer "Captain Bruff," he couldn't command their respect, much less their obedience. On inquiring about his horse, he got a vague, disinterested reply. Feeling rebuffed, Bruff angrily said he would not have loaned his horse had he known it would not be returned to him. One of the men shot back angrily that "I have kept my word and come back and *this* was the thanks for it!" At this Bruff roared,

> *You came for me! You came for those wagons, and their con-tents, that's what you came for!--take the plunder, and roll on; I'll not disgrace myself by further companionship with you! I shall go when it suits me!*

Once again, hubris had gotten the better of Bruff, just as it had at West Point. Even if he detested these men, under the circum-stances, he was no longer their Captain and in no position to shun them—not if he wanted to get off the mountain.

The next morning Bruff eyed the men indignantly as they loaded up the wagons. As they were loading the last of the packs on the mules, they tried to confiscate his tents on the grounds that they were Company property—until Bruff protested. As he watched them drift off down the canyon, he thought to himself, "This ends my connection with the Washington City Company, as an organized body." Looking to use one of the many unused har-nesses should he find a pack animal, he found they had all been spitefully slashed and rendered useless. Later he heard that one wagon was so overloaded it broke down on the trail below and had to be abandoned.

Bruff felt woefully betrayed. Had he not done all the planning and mapping of the expedition? And successfully borne the burden of leading the Company across the frontier? They had not sustained a single attack by Indians, not even along the Humboldt or Pitt Rivers where many emigrants lost animals or were killed. The only loss was three or four mules and even that was due to negligence of the very men who had now turned against him. Thanks to Bruff, the men had arrived at the gold fields safely and ready to make their fortunes. If Bruff was hard on some of the men, he reasoned, it was only because "there were some who could only be kept in subjection like slaves." Nor was that the end of the matter. Unbeknownst to him, several of the men later wrote to Bruff's wife informing her of "his certain death."

Although abandoned, Bruff at least had good company, food, and shelter. In addition to Willis, there was also a stalwart Missourian named William Grissom. Grissom was famous for having attended to the celebrated Chief Black Hawk in his final days. In accordance with his last wishes, Grissom had dug the great Chief's grave and buried him in a sitting posture with his cane clenched in his hands. He then picketed the grave and covered it with stones to prevent whites from digging him up. Together Bruff, Grissom, and Willis shared companionship and hunted the abundant game in the forest.

Bruff also had fashioned decent living quarters. His "Lodge in Perpetuity," as he called his makeshift abode with a hint of irony, was securely set among the tall pines and stout oaks of Deer Creek Canyon. It consisted of a rotunda-like area formed by canvas draped over a lodge pole with two tents connected to it on either side. Beneath the rotunda was space for a fire, as the temperature at night was often freezing. With no snow yet on the ground, he could survive by foraging and hunting. But the clock was ticking, for soon snow would be blanketing the ground.

That night Bruff had a nightmare, waking Willis with his nocturnal cries. They returned to sleep when they were again awakened, this time by real, blood-curdling wailing in the distance. Lighting a lantern, he and Willis rushed to the source of the commotion, where they found heavy rains had caused a rotting oak to fall on two tents, killing a father and his son and seriously wounding the other son and his friend. It was the Alford family who had been so full of joy when he first encountered them on the trail. The wife and daughters were now beside themselves with grief. Her son was barely alive with two broken legs and a broken hip. While Bruff dug two graves, Willis and Grissom sat up all night with the injured boys. As the son writhed in agony, he turned to see his dead brother on one side and his dying friend on the other. By dawn, both boys were dead.

Heavy snow the next morning made it hard for Bruff to widen the grave he had already dug for the dead man and his son. In accordance with the woman's wishes, he read the burial service from a Presbyterian prayer book. Then he arranged the bodies, the father on the right with the eldest son next to him, followed by the younger son and his friend. At the last minute the woman asked to see the faces of her husband and boys one last time. Descending into the grave and supporting himself by placing a hand on the breast of a corpse, he pulled back the sheet to expose their faces. Upon seeing them the mother cried out in anguish, "Why did He take them all at once? And not leave me one!" The woman had come so far to find a better life only to lose, at the end of her long journey, everything dear to her. As she wept, Bruff filled in the grave. Then, taking the tailboard of a wagon, he scratched an inscription followed by an epitaph:

> Their journey is ended, their toils are all past,
> Together they slept, in this false world, their last:
> They here sleep together, in one grave entombed,—
> Side by side, as they slept, on the night they were doom'd.

Bruff then gave her one of his wagons, which was stronger and lighter than hers, and helped her load it. Just before she left, Dr. Austin, who had come up at the behest of Captain Peoples to warn the travelers a snowstorm was approaching, gave sedatives to the widow's distraught daughters. The shattered widow then disappeared down the trail, not to fortune but to a grim and uncertain future.

True to his Freemason ideals of brotherhood, Bruff selflessly assisted hundreds of other needy and stricken emigrants, demonstrating an almost saintly compassion for their plight. Sometimes with the help of Willis and others, more often on his own, Bruff became a one-man humanitarian committee for the hundreds of despondent and haggard travelers still coming up the trail. At his camp, they found a warm fire, axes, fuel, cooking utensils, and even food when it was to be had. To a man whose heavy Conestoga wagon would be unable to negotiate the rough trail, he traded his lighter wagon. A man from Illinois entrusted his wagon to Bruff; another left a box of articles until he could return to reclaim them. He consoled a family whose mother died as she was ascending to Deer Creek. For those needing shelter—including two Germans and an old Frenchman who had served under Napoleon—he transformed wagons left on the hill into "apartments." To a sick man he even gave his own bed. He collected discarded clothing, boots, and shoes and distributed them to threadbare emigrants. For children arriving nearly barefoot, he fashioned moccasins out of elk skin. He allowed countless other cold and hungry travelers to warm by his fire and share his meager fare. He even tended to their weary pack animals, covering the worn-out creatures with blankets against the wetness and biting cold. And for his generosity, astonishingly, not a single person answered his own pleas for help in getting off the mountain.

Time was now of the essence, for the ferocious Sierra winter had begun to stir. More than 36 inches of precipitation would fall that year, twice the average. On the evening of November 4, snow began to fall and continued throughout the following day. When it was over, between two and three feet of snow lay on the ground. Until now hale and vigorous, Bruff was suddenly stricken with a severe case of rheumatism brought on by the cold and damp. His condition, known today as polymyositis rheumatism, is an incurable disease that causes inflammation of joints and muscles so painful as to be crippling. Even though Lassen's ranch was not far away, a descent on foot was now out of the question, with or without his personal effects. Realizing the gravity of his situation, Bruff resolved to descend on foot as soon as his rheumatism abated, even if it meant leaving his precious notes and artifacts behind. But with the November weather turning colder and more snow a certainty, a quick recovery seemed unlikely. Even the cattle were now dropping dead in the camp from cold and exhaustion.

While Bruff struggled with rheumatism, Captain Peoples and Dr. Austin were moving northeast along the trail, where they found the rear of the emigration in the upper Feather River Valley. Among those struggling were General John Wilson and his family. A lawyer and relative of the president, the 60-year-old Wilson had been unhappy with his position in President Zachary Taylor's cabinet and decided to seek his fortune in California gold. After finagling for an official position that would take him west at the government's expense, in April 1849 the curmudgeonly Wilson received an appointment as Special Agent to the California Indians. So little was known of the Shoshone and Paiutes in the region, he was given just two tasks. The first was to seek the release of a Mexican held captive by the Indians. The second was to temporarily amalgamate Mormon Deseret and California, with a view to avoiding problems on the slavery issue. President Taylor foresaw a bitter struggle over the slavery issue in Congress and hoped to avoid further conflict by allowing states to decide the issue. The previous March, Mormons had formed a provisional constitutional government with the name "State of Deseret" ("Land of the Honeybee") with Brigham Young as governor. When Wilson arrived in Salt Lake, he met with Brigham Young, who was in support of the idea. Young advised the general to get Sam Brannan's media support (he owned a San Francisco newspaper) if he hoped to convince the California legislature. The California legislature would eventually reject the proposal, however, having already passed its own state constitution that banned slavery.

Wilson was infamous for his violent, abusive temper. While living in Missouri in 1827, Wilson had nearly started a riot at a 4th of July barbecue over criticism of his preferred presidential candidate, John Adams. On the trail he had been having a running quarrel with his military escort, Captain Morris, whom he deprecated as "wholly inexperienced... wholly unfit." It seemed the cantankerous Wilson's main problem with Morris was that it wasn't the escort he had been promised. Wilson also objected to Morris's using Wilson's teamsters as night guards. In late September, Wilson finally dismissed Morris near Goose Lake and hired a seasoned guide, Joel Palmer, to take him down Lassen's Trail for $2,000. In the first range of the Sierras, the Pitt stole 22 of their mules. Near Fandango Valley, they encountered a violent snowstorm in early November, forcing Wilson to abandon half his goods and cache his enormous law library. (For years after, the surly Wilson would complain of the high cost of getting to California and demanded $10,000 in recompense from the government, which he never received.) When Peoples arrived, he gave Wilson two mules to pull his family wagon and urged him to pack lightly. Disregarding Peoples's advice, Wilson loaded up the wagon heavily and lost both mules in the storm that night, leaving the family to go in on foot.

Near sunset on the 12th, Wilson and his family stumbled into Bruff's camp for the night. It had been raining and snowing since October 30, and now the trail was a quagmire of rock and mud. Showing his usual deference to the high-ranking officer, Bruff quickly set about making lodgings for them—tents for the women and girls and a large one for the esteemed general and two of his three sons. (His third son was in the rear with Palmer looking after a man who had lost his arm.) Too weak to proceed on foot, Wilson sent his son William in to the settlements with a letter requesting help from Lassen. The letter stated that Wilson was a representative of the U.S. government and that he would reimburse Lassen for any supplies and pack animals he could render.

Young William arrived at Lassen's on November 8. Lassen gave him eight mules and provisions. As he was ascending to Deer Creek through the deep mud and snow, the mules gave out, leaving the family to trudge in 20 miles on foot. Although Bruff had asked Wilson for help in being rescued, once in the settlements, Wilson virtually forgot about him. Nor did Wilson or the government ever reimburse Lassen for his assistance. It wouldn't be the last time the two would be hoodwinked by the good general.

Meanwhile, back on the trail Peoples was struggling to assist other emigrants. With the trail under deep snow and his best mules having been killed in the snowstorm, Peoples was urging travelers—many of whom were families who had fallen to the rear—to abandon all their belongings and for the men to go in on foot while women and children rode on whatever animals remained. By the second week in November, Peoples had succeeded in moving all the stragglers forward to Deer Creek. Behind them, for 200 miles along a trail that had promised to be a shortcut to the gold fields, was a ghostly scene of wagons buried in snowdrifts, canvases of empty tents fluttering in the wind, and the rigid legs of animal carcasses poking up through the snow.

When he was finally down to his own horse, Peoples gave it to a desperate family. He then led eleven women and six children on foot from the Feather River as far as he could before another snowstorm forced them to take cover in several abandoned tents and wagons. The next day they were still unable to proceed so Peoples killed an ox and left them with enough food for 10 days while he hiked back to the settlements for more mules and provisions. As he made for Deer Creek, he descended a valley where the snow turned to slanting rain so violent they were blinded and had to camp for the night without food.

By the time Peoples reached Deer Creek, word had filtered up to Deer Creek that no shelter was available in the settlements. Emigrants decided they were better off for the moment on the mountain until the road dried up and they could descend in their wagons. Before he left, Peoples promised to send a relief team to rescue Bruff. He gave Bruff permission to use any of the government mules left along the trail but Bruff could find none strong enough to carry anything, let alone him.

Although Bruff's body was failing, he remained in good spirits. After all, he thought, with all the notes he had sent down and promises from reliable men like Peoples and Wilson, rescue appeared imminent. There were also some reliable men from his own Company who would surely come to his aid once they learned of his plight. And then there was Willis, who decided as soon as a dry spell broke, he would assemble a team and make for the settlements. There was also the sick man who had recuperated in Bruff's wagon and was now feeling well enough to travel; he assured Bruff he would send a relief team for him as soon as he reached the settlements. Any day now, Bruff thought, he would be safely off the mountain. Until then, he used the time to correct his notes and drawings and collect additional information on the emigration for Captain Peoples.

But as he waited for help to arrive, events quickly conspired against him. Two weeks of unremitting rain and snow had rendered the trail down impassable. Emigrants who had tried to descend in wagons were stumbling in on foot and leaving everything behind—wagons, pack animals, and provisions—to be plundered by Lassen's men. Wagons were buried up to their beds in mud, and dead mules stood frozen on the trail mired in mud up to their chests. Even Captain Peoples's mare had gotten stuck in the mud as he was descending. One emigrant described the harrowing descent to Lassen's ranch:

> *We pressed on in line. In the darkness, wind, and rain, on we went. The road was muddy and rocky . . . We kept on it with great difficulty. We finally turned out on wet and rocky soil to get a little rest. We sat until we became chilled through. It was dark and raining hard all the time. Then on we went, over the rocks, and in the mud and water and in the storm for an hour longer . . . We could make no fire, for the wet oak was the only timber. We suffered on through the night.*

This was essentially the condition of the trail when, in mid-November, Peoples dispatched a man named Ford to rescue Bruff. Ten miles from Deer Creek, Ford abandoned his mule—stuck upright in the mud—along with all of the provisions Peoples had sent: flour, pork, and a bottle of whiskey. He stumbled into Deer Creek exhausted, telling Bruff the trail was bad all the way to Sacramento and it was now impossible to get wagons or animals up or down it. With this dispiriting news, he handed Bruff all he managed to bring up a bottle of sour wine and a note from Peoples.

In some ways, the loss of the food was even more grievous than the mule. With so many travelers on the mountain, most of the game had been killed off or slipped off into the valleys after the heavy snow. Although wolves and grizzlies continued to prowl the area, the former was too wily to hunt and the latter too dangerous. To add to his woes, Bruff also had another mouth to feed. A few days earlier, he had observed a man named Lambkin abusing his four-year-old boy William. "His little boy he treated in the most brutal manner, suffering it to want for everything, and then beating him most unmercifully, for crying," Bruff wrote. After seeing the child left cold while Lambkin was off chatting, Bruff had exchanged some angry words with the heartless father. Lambkin, he learned, had abandoned his wife in St. Louis, then taken their son and ran off with another woman to start a new life in California. While on the trail, the woman gave birth, although she later died along the Humboldt. The child died at four months of age. When he arrived at Deer Creek, Lambkin saw an opportunity to work with the shingle men stealing wagons and provisions. He even had the audacity to steal two pack saddles from Bruff's camp one night. Bruff thought Lambkin "an inhuman wretch," as did all who had the misfortune of accompanying him across the frontier.

Lambkin had brought little William to Bruff's camp, asking

Bruff to look after the boy while he went to the settlements for provisions for a few days. Expecting Lambkin to return with bread for him and the boy, Bruff agreed to look after the child. Upon seeing Bruff, the boy cried out for bread. With nothing to offer, Bruff handed him a spool of cotton to distract him. As the starving boy played with the spool, he quietly intoned, "Mother has cotton, mother has bread, mother has cake, mother has tea." That night, Bruff made a bed for him in the wagon and little William cried himself to sleep.

On November 21, the last government relief party came up from the rear with a relief wagon filled with the women and children Peoples had left behind two weeks earlier. Once again, Bruff sent a note for help, this time asking simply for "a riding animal." Peoples assured him it would be taken care of. Bruff also sent a note with the emigrants requesting an ox and some provisions from Lassen.

By the last week of November, most who had holed up at Deer Creek had moved off to the settlements despite the condition of the trail. Winter was beginning in earnest and emigrants had become fearful of getting trapped on the mountain. Now the only remaining Gold Rushers were Bruff, the Roberts family and their teamster William Poyle, a Santa Fe trader named Seymour and his sons, and the "shingle men," still busy harvesting wood and plundering wagons. A Canadian, Poyle had arrived on the mountain on November 10 and, like Bruff, had been helping other travelers to get in ever since. Poyle was also a Freemason and resolved to stick by brother Bruff and share his fortune—or fate. Whenever Poyle killed a deer, he invariably shared the meat with Bruff, although hunting was yielding less and less.

Indeed, as November drew to a close, Poyle was having little luck finding game. So the men turned to scavenging what little food remained from abandoned wagons. It didn't take long before they exhausted the wagons around Deer Creek and had to go farther out. As Bruff was too weak to walk any distance in the deep snow, Willis went back along the trail to scavenge from the wagons. He returned distraught and empty-handed: the Pitt, it turned out, had plundered all the rear wagons and carried virtually all the contents back to their villages. What they left behind had been devoured by wolves, grizzlies, or starving emigrants. In their anger at the whites, the Pitt had exhumed a man's body and dragged it by the neck some distance before impaling it with a stake. Although sick from exposure, Willis wandered down into a hollow where he was able to scour up some discarded meat and black flour for the two of them. With conditions dire, Seymour and his son, on whom Bruff had relied for venison from time to time, decamped and moved off.

Depending on the season, Deer Creek contained a cornucopia of edible plants and animals. In addition to the deer, there were ducks and geese. Pine nuts and hazelnuts, buckeye, manzanita berries, huckleberry, wild raspberry plum, elderberry barberry, and thimbleberry grew in abundance. There were edible seeds like sage, tarweed, and clarkia, and roots of the camas, annis, and tiger lily, as well as certain grubs and worms. But it was winter now, and with snow on the ground that would only get deeper, nature's pantry was closed for the season. Had Bruff befriended the Yahi, they might have shared their winter food stocks. Time and again he had seen the pale blue smoke of their campfires curling up in the distance but had not so much as seen a single Indian. In any case, he viewed them as more of a threat than potential benefactors.

Starving, Bruff now looked to the anticipated return of Lambkin for food. His hopes were quickly dashed when one day he spotted Lambkin wandering around the hills with the shingle men. Lambkin, it turned out, had never left.

The next night, Bruff made dinner with flour scraped from an old bag. For the boy he made a cake from mildewed pinola. He tried to roast the local acorns, but they proved too bitter. Mixing them with flour and warm water, he let them stand overnight. The next morning the acorn flour had risen and, with some meat provided by the last of the passing emigrants, Bruff and the boy made it through another day. That evening, two emissaries of Captain Peoples brought Bruff a few pounds of flour, a piece of salt pork, and an apologetic note from Peoples saying it was all he could send. The two men also brought bad news: Torrential rains had inundated the Sacramento Valley and all communication with Lassen's ranch had been cut off. With food in the settlements dear and shelter at Lassen's no better than a tent, the men had decided to winter a few miles below Bruff's camp.

By the end of November the last of the rear Gold Rushers—harassed by Indians, suffering from the snow, cold, fatigue, and starvation—were now stumbling into Lassen's ranch. On November 26, in his report to General Smith, Major Rucker summed up his impressions:

> *A more pitiable sight I never beheld as they were brought into camp. There were cripples from scurvy and other diseases, women prostrated by weakness, and children who could not move a limb, or be lifted off the animals, so entirely disabled had they become.*

By comparison, Bruff's situation was somewhat better, although he had still not received so much as a tired mule. With so little assistance forthcoming, he came to the bitter realization he wasn't going to be rescued anytime soon and began preparing a possible winter in the Sierras. He cut fresh poles, reinforced the lodge canopy with wagon canvas, and laid down boards for the beds. Taking a wagon tail board, he fashioned a table and cut up more firewood. He had decent shelter and a fire, but with his nagging rheumatism he was in no condition to walk far or hunt. Food remained his abiding concern. Poyle was an ingenious cook, however, and with meat unavailable, he boiled down animal joints and bones to a nutritious, if unsavory, jelly.

That Bruff found himself marooned in the Sierras, he knew all too well, was as a result of his decision to look after the wagons. But what was Willis still doing there? Why, after traveling more than 2,000 miles to dig for gold had he remained on the mountain and endured its hardships?

The answer to that question became clearer in early December when a Prussian named Joseph Petrie arrived on foot bearing a note from Colonel Ely Davis. Davis, who had come from Missouri with Lassen in 1848, offered to send Bruff a mule that he had recently purchased from the government and any other assistance he desired. Just why the government had sold all the mules when Bruff so desperately needed one probably owed to the confusion in the settlements. Petrie, who struck Bruff as a "worthy fellow," gave him a large loaf of white bread, a piece of fresh beef, and ground coffee. After assisting other Gold Rushers, Petrie planned to return to the ranch the next day. Aware of Bruff's deteriorating condition, Poyle urged him to accompany Willis to "secure at once the succor that I so much needed, which had been so long deferred, and was now in reach . . ." Willis quickly objected, insisting he be the one to go. "Very well," said Bruff agreeably, since someone had to look after the boy, who was too small to descend on his own. In return, Willis agreed to return in three or four days to rescue Bruff. Later that day, with no reason to doubt Willis's integrity, Bruff noticed Willis frantically gathering up every article he could lay his hands on and packing them in trunks and chests and locking them. Bruff thought the behavior strange but only for its futility, for in Willis's absence the materials would surely be at the mercy of Indians and wolves. That night, as heavy snow fell, Bruff penned several more letters of help for Petrie to carry down including a note to Davis authorizing Willis to make all arrangements for his rescue.

On the morning of December 4, as Willis was shouldering his rifle to leave, Bruff pointed to a few pounds of smoked beef hanging in his lodge. "Willis," he said, "do you see that—it is all the provender for three of us till you return." "Very well, Captain," Willis replied. "I will certainly return with supplies, etc., in not more than three or four days." Petrie echoed, "Yes, Captain, I will see that he comes back and brings you what's needed."

Before leaving, Willis pinched Bruff's only pair of boots.

Unable or unwilling to see the perfidy in Willis's theft, Bruff began getting his effects in order to move down. With all of the emigrants gone, the camp now consisted of himself and his trustworthy friend Poyle. The Roberts family had decided to winter in a cabin at Mill Creek three miles below. With his rheumatism still raging, Bruff was unable to hunt and now relied entirely on Poyle. But with three feet of snow on the ground, even the hale and healthy Poyle was finding the hunt fatiguing. Increasingly, they turned to scavenging, taking care not to surprise a grizzly, wolf, or cougar in one of the abandoned wagons.

A week passed with no sign of Willis. Bruff worried if his comrade had taken ill. That very day Clough had come up from Lassen's saying that Willis and Petrie had joined a posse to search for "the shingle men" and the animals they were suspected of stealing. Clough also said that Davis and Lassen had gone to Sacramento Valley for two weeks to obtain provisions, since they had been so long cut off from the city the ranch had nearly run out of everything.

Still, Bruff clung to the hope Willis would come through.

Thick snow lay on the ground, and the temperature during the day barely registered above freezing. Day after day, Poyle returned empty-handed from the hunt, sometimes not even having seen game. Since Willis's departure, Bruff had eaten little more than boiled beef bones and tea, giving the boy the largest share of whatever food he and Poyle had. One day he made soup out of a tin of mustard found in a wagon and a half-quart of flour he got by beating an old flour sack. For the first time since being marooned on the mountain, he talked about making the descent on foot and leaving his effects behind. Poyle attempted to dissuade him, warning of a camp of hostile Indians he had seen while hunting three miles below. Moreover, Poyle pointed out, should he have a severe attack of rheumatism on the trail, he would be in far greater danger from grizzlies and wolves than from any Indians.

By mid-December, Bruff's predicament took a turn for the worse. On top of his rheumatism, malnutrition had weakened him to the point where he now had inflamed eyes and a severe cold. Most of the burnable wood had been used or gotten wet, as it was sleeting or snowing almost every day. One night he was forced to burn pine so fresh and green that he awoke at midnight nearly suffocating from the acrid smoke. The next night so much snow had fallen it dashed any hope that Willis—or anyone else—would be coming up from the settlements to rescue him.

On top of this, little William was failing. Pale and weak with sunken eyes, he had begun to bleed from the ears and nose. Many nights he cried all night long from hunger. On those nights, Bruff would take the boy by the hand and walk him to and fro inside the tent for exercise. To amuse the boy, Bruff found a three-month old terrier born on the mountain that he named "Nevada." Were it not for the boy's rapid attachment to the emaciated creature, Bruff would have made a meal of him, as the men were now down to a single meal a day.

Poyle, being younger and in better condition than Bruff, could probably endure the harsh winter at Deer Creek. But Bruff was approaching a critical stage and he knew it, estimating he could hold out two or three weeks before his body failed entirely. If there was one bright spot, he thought, it was that the deep snow made it difficult for Indians and wild animals to move about. The deep snow also acted as a refrigerator for the dead oxen—if they could only find them.

As he contemplated his grim fate, the specter of the Donner party in the Sierras just a few years earlier no doubt haunted him. His one hope remained Willis. After all, he reasoned,

Willis must surely entertain a spark of gratitude towards me—I have protected him in the Company, and I have every way been his friend, and he appeared quite attached to me—or why did he volunteer to remain here with me? Unless ill, he will assuredly come out soon!

Meanwhile, the snow continued to fall. On the morning of December 17, the men had just gotten a fire going when they heard a cracking noise. Turning around, they saw two of the tent poles buckle and snap under the weight of the snow and rushed to apply temporary supports against the immense pressure. Although they were able to shore it up, snow had fallen in through the top and sides, and they could now only use the lodge by day to make a fire. Beating the snow down with a shovel to make a path to two nearby wagons, they moved their beds into them, even though the snow had crushed the wagon's canvas ribs. Snow was now so high it reached to the beds of the wagons, making them look like giant snowdrifts. Snow hung on the evergreens in great crescents. Later Bruff captured in watercolors the image of his tent, now nearly buried under snow, which he aptly titled, "The Lodge in Adversity."

As the mighty Sierra winter closed in on them, the two men hunkered down stoically:

> *On going into our bed-chamber (wagon) the bedding was white with drift snow. We stood outside at the back of the wagon . . . took off our gum coats and laid them on the tail-board, then sat on them, and took off our leggings . . . and shoes, which we deposited in the corners, under our heads, shook the snow off as well as we could, got under cover, closed all the crevices we could with clothes, and hung the lantern up to a hook above. Poyle lay sometime reading "De Toqueville's Democracy of America," while I wrote up my notes.*

All the next day, the men fashioned snowshoes using wagons bows for the frames and canvas for the body. The Canadian Poyle had considerable experience in snow and instructed Bruff in how to use them. Once mobile, Bruff cut up Company wagon number 12 to make a sled and a fire. As he lifted his axe, he was struck by the tragic irony of his act: "How could I have entertained such an idea, when, all hands full of glee, put it on board the Steamer *Robert Fulton* at Pittsburgh!"

With a campfire again going, the men went in search of a dying ox they had seen before the snowstorm. But finding anything now was difficult, as the snow had obliterated not only the animal's tracks but all the distinguishing landmarks by which they traveled. All afternoon they slogged, weak and hungry, through snow three to six feet deep. With so much snow weighing on the trees, they had to be on guard against falling limbs. Even the enormous pine cones falling from 200 feet could be fatal. After searching for food or game as far as their bodies allowed, they returned to the lodge exhausted, distraught, and unsuccessful. The two men had reached a critical stage, for they were now expending far more energy than they were taking in. Even when they did find some stale meat to eat, it had few nutrients and left them hungry an hour later. Although loathe to do it, Bruff wondered if it was time to eat Nevada.

The next day Poyle found a small piece of dried beef and a handful of white beans behind an old trunk. Supplemented with a raven Bruff was able to shoot, it made the only meal of the day. "*Nil desperandum*!" ("Never Despair"), Bruff cried out. With each meager meal, he took renewed hope that he and Poyle would survive their ordeal.

Christmas Day was a festive affair under the circumstances. To celebrate, Poyle stewed the neck and shoulder of an ox exposed by the melting snow, along with a large tree squirrel Bruff had shot. The hearty meal and week-long thaw in the weather put the men in a pleasantly sated state. To amuse themselves, each sang a few songs and told a story as they smoked their pipes. The men were once again enjoying three meals a day.

Bruff's abiding hope remained Willis. Even though he had been gone 22 days, he still had not lost faith in him.

What can be the matter with Willis? He was aware of our limited provisions, for I called his attention to it, he knows that game has disappeared from these hills; aware than in a week after I left, a severe storm ensued, which could have no other effect on us than the most disastrous consequences; and he must think that if we have survived, the starvation we must have been subjected to, would render us too weak to attempt going

in; and surely humanity, if not friendship would prompt him
to take advantage of this favorable spell of weather. We cannot
conjecture the cause of his delay.

One afternoon, while tending to his tent, Bruff was surprised
to hear human voices coming from the rear of the trail. At first he
feared Indians, but as the voices came closer, he saw five gaunt, hag-
gard-looking men. Two of the men were lame and walking with a
staff. Even more astonishing was that the men weren't Gold Rushers. The oldest man, Elliot, who had brought along his two sons,
said he had been engaged as a teamster by the government from
Fort Leavenworth to Fort Hall in order to purchase some land in
Missouri. When he arrived at Fort Hall, Elliot was told he could
not be sent back and was urged to join a train headed to Oregon.
At Goose Lake, instead of heading north, he claimed to have mis-
takenly taken Lassen's Trail. While passing through the Pitt River
Valley, Elliot was joined by an Irishman and two Dutchmen, one
of whom was left to die with frostbite. When they left Fort Hall
they were fully provisioned, but after 30 days on the trail they were
forced to eat their mules. Since then, they had been living on carrion and moss. When they spotted Bruff's camp, they thought they
had finally arrived in the settlements. Although suspicious of these
wild-looking men and their strange, improbable story, Bruff offered
them his ox meat. The Irishman, whose feet were badly frostbitten,
said he planned to lay over on the mountain several days. Anxious
to get rid of them, Bruff urged him to leave the next morning for
the settlements, where he might get medical attention.

The next morning Bruff went over to their camp to make sure
they went off. Four of the men were strapping on their packs, planning to leave behind the frostbitten Irishman lying under a tree
with a large kettle of boiled meat at his side. Bruff was astonished

to see they had just eaten bacon, dried apples, and bread. Angered by their dishonesty, he insisted the Irishman leave with the other men. Reluctantly, he shouldered his rifle and moved off.

On December 30, having survived 48 days mostly on stale flour and rotting beef, Bruff decided to visit the Roberts family at Mill Creek. In his weakened condition, it took him half a day to reach their cabin. One of the Roberts' sons had just returned from the Davis Ranch where he had seen Willis, who seemed perfectly unconcerned about Bruff and Poyle. Even more disturbing, young Roberts said that Davis had offered Willis mules, provisions, and an ox team to rescue Bruff, but Willis had declined. Davis was so angered by Willis' callous disregard of Bruff's predicament that he ostracized Willis from the ranch. The young Roberts tried to impress upon Willis Bruff's dire condition, whereupon Willis glibly replied that Bruff "ought to come in." After nearly two months of waiting to be rescued by Willis, Bruff had finally realized Willis had betrayed him.

Fearing another major storm could send them over the edge, Bruff and Poyle decided to move down to the Roberts' cabin, where there was greater security in numbers. On the final day of 1849, a year that had begun with so much excitement and enthusiasm, Bruff packed his belongings, put them on a sled with the boy, and descended to Mill Creek. It took Bruff four hours to reach the cabin. Upon arriving, he collapsed and fainted at the door. If Bruff had any notion of going directly to the settlements, it had now become unthinkable.

Chapter Ten

THE UNTHINKABLE

ON NEW YEAR'S DAY, LITTLE WILLIAM PASSED AWAY. With the help of one of Roberts's boys, Bruff dug a grave and fashioned a headboard with an inscription as short as the boy's sad life had been:

WILLIAM,-
Infant Son of
Lambkin-
an
Unnatural
Father,
Died Jan. 1,
1850

Tragic though it was, the boy's death spurred Bruff's resolve to get off the mountain as soon as possible. Earlier that morning, Poyle and Clough had set out for the settlements to buy provisions and seek help for Bruff. For their journey, the niggardly Roberts had spared but two pints of sour flour and a few slices of venison. Setting out at night, the two men traveled by moonlight with the intent of arriving at Davis's in two days. If the compressed schedule wasn't demanding enough, immediately after leaving camp the two men were stricken with food poisoning from the spoiled bread they had eaten at dinner. Sick and weak, they traipsed through deep snow, sticky mud, and icy streams. Yet by evening of the second day, they had managed to make it to the settlements. After buying provisions, they secured a promise from Davis to send help for Bruff as soon as the trail improved. Two days later they returned to Deer Creek bearing two sacks of flour, dried apples, and fresh beef with a note for Bruff from Davis. Attached to the note was a bill for the provisions that included a charge of $30 for 10 days' lodging for Willis.

Two weeks passed with no sign of help from Davis. Again Poyle and Clough descended to the settlements. This time Davis received the men coldly, saying he had no food to spare. At Lassen's, they were able to purchase 80 pounds of flour that turned out to be sour. Supplemented with some venison Clough had shot, the meager fare would at least get them through the rest of January. But with no rescue forthcoming, Clough and Poyle realized any assistance for Bruff would now have to come from one of his far-flung friends or acquaintances in the cities. But how to reach them?

February came on clear and unseasonably mild, with the temperature a balmy 64 degrees. A chorus of croaking frogs and buzzing flies signaled the approach of spring, momentarily lifting Bruff's spirits.

If the worst of the ferocious Sierra winter was over, Bruff's predicament was not. A host of ailments continued to plague him, including a sore back and groin, hemorrhoids, a swollen abdomen, dizziness, and nausea. With milder weather, he began planning a descent as soon as the trail improved, unwilling to acknowledge he was far too weak to travel on his own. To the extent possible, he tried to exercise—listlessly chopping wood, gathering bark, fetching water—in the hope it would strengthen him for the journey.

On February 5, Poyle and Clough went into the settlements. This time, the Roberts' youngest son accompanied them to buy oxen with which to move his family off the mountain. Here at last was an opportunity for Bruff—or so it seemed. In their month together at Mill Creek, the elder Roberts had taken such a dislike to Bruff he refused to help him. Roberts believed Bruff was feigning infirmity, telling Clough he would rather "see him dead" than hunt and pack meat for him as Clough was doing. For his part, Bruff thought Roberts selfish, hypocritical, and abusive. Whatever the differences between the two, Bruff had alienated the one person who could have saved him. Not only did Roberts's plan to leave Bruff behind, but he refused to allow him to use his cabin where the bulk of his property was stored. As he was leaving, for good measure Roberts took one of the tents he had lent Bruff and attempted to persuade Clough to abandon him, which the latter flatly refused to do.

Having exhausted all options, Poyle headed for Sacramento to post Bruff's letters to colleagues in Monterey and Sacramento and to Dr. Austin and Colonel Frémont, wherever they might be. The letter went to great length to explain his reasons for remaining in the mountains and the callous treatment by his Company. "I have been too feeble to travel any distance . . ." he wrote:

> *The succor & friendly assistance I need, are -1st - Sufficient Provisions for 3 of us, for, say 2 months; means of transportation, or preferable - a team of Oxen. They could bring out the supplies, & then take in, when I can travel, my wagon, containing tents, bedding, saddles, clothing, arms,&c, camp utensils, books papers, instruments, &c, and a mineralogi-*

cal collection . . . Credit for the supplies & contingencies, and sum sufficient loaned, to purchase the team; or the loan of a sufficient [sum] to cover all. I have in view some ravines and streams a day's march in from here, which doubtless are rich, and may as soon as I can examine them, prove the realization of that hope which brought me across the continent; if so, you shall promptly be informed thereof.

It was a rambling, long-winded missive, enumerating how much he owed Davis and Lassen for flour and promising to liquidate his debt, including the cost of his rescue, as soon as he "struck it rich in the valley." Little did he know that few emigrants were finding gold—let alone getting rich—and such assurances could only have sounded empty. Having sent messages ad nauseam that had not elicited so much as a single response except Peoples's attempt months earlier that had foundered, he might have simply focused on the stark fact that he was dying on the mountain and needed help urgently.

On the morning of February 16, the Roberts family moved off for the settlements with Clough, who promised Bruff he would return.

Bruff was now entirely on his own.

His one abiding fear had always been the Indians. Now that he was alone, his concern intensified. All the months at Deer Creek he had not seen a single Indian, although from time to time could see the smoke from their campfires rising from the ridges. They were surely aware of his presence. The area was inhabited by a small tribe of 3,000 or 4,000 Yahi, a hill tribe who had inhabited the foothills between the Feather River and Deer Creek for nearly 4,000 years. Fortunately for Bruff, despite their reputation for being fierce warriors, the Yahi were a peaceable people. They did not have horses or weapons of war and were repulsed by the white and Indian practice of scalping. Indeed, that Bruff never spotted a Yahi while on Deer Creek suggested they were as much afraid of him as he was of them.

February was a lonely and trying month for Bruff. Unless prematurely wakened by the howling of wolves, he rose at dawn. Stirring the dying embers in the fire, he put on some wood to cook breakfast, which consisted of a small amount of stale bread (if he had flour) and possibly a little meat. If he was low on food, he would skip lunch and sleep longer to conserve his energy. After breakfast, he checked to make sure his tent was secure and conducted an inventory of his provisions. Late morning was used to look for firewood or hunt, although in his weakened condition he could not stray more than a half-mile from camp. The effort in doing either one was invariably so exhausting that by midday he had to return to camp to rest. Often he would fall down on his pallet breathless from merely a short hike. Other days, he was too ill with fever and headaches to do much of anything but lie in his tent. His gums were inflamed and his teeth, back, bladder, and kidneys ached. For diversion some days, he inked over his penciled notes or touched up his drawings, which always gave him pleasure. Dinner was much the same fare as breakfast. In the evening he warmed himself by the fire and wrote up the day's notes before retiring—a remarkable achievement in view of his failing condition. The days were monotonous, made worse by the anxiety and uncertainty of ever being rescued after so many fruitless requests and frustrating snafus. Increasingly, his sleep was being interrupted by Nevada's wild barking at the approach of wolves. Instinctively sensing Bruff's growing vulnerability, they were now approaching closer and closer each day to the tent. One evening, he saw two large gray wolves about 300 yards off fixing him with

Bruff's drawing of the first desert stretch they encountered after leaving the Humboldt River

The Rabbit Hole Springs

Above: High Rock Canyon Pass near the Sierra Nevada

Below: The eastern slope of the Sierra Nevada

Above: By the fall of 1849, many stragglers clogged the trails in the Sierras, abandoned by their companies.

Below: Trading with native tribes helped sustain many emigrants along their journey.

Indians of N. Valley of Feather River
(from life)

Bruff's camp as it looked in October 1849

Above: Making a snowshoe in the interior of the lodge

Below: Bruff's mountain lodge in the dead of winter

THE MIDNIGHT VISITOR

Above: Midnight visitors such as bears and wolves were common

Below: Scene on the emigrant trail, November 1849

Scene on the Emigrant Trail,
near Settlements. Nov. 1849.

Lassen's *Rancho Bosquejo*

A contemporary depiction of a prospector

Bruff's representation of a prospector's life in the Sierra Nevada

A weary explorer on the trail

Upper Station, five miles below the mouth of the Klamath River

Bruff witnessed the execution of an Australian named John Jenkins for the crime of stealing a safe from a shipping office.

an enervating stare. Approaching them with his rifle, he got off a shot that only scared them back into the woods.

True to his word, Clough returned on the 20th, cold, tired, and weak. With the wages Roberts had paid him, he was able to purchase 15 pounds of crackers and some molasses—a luxury at any time, but particularly so under these circumstances. Clough found prices for basic goods in the settlements even higher than they had been along the Missouri in April. An ox was now going for $700 and a mule anywhere between $200 and $400—which explained in part why none had been sent up.

Bad weather returned, bringing sleet, hail, and snow. One night Bruff had a dream: In late morning, a small brown dog with a slender tail and a string around its neck wandered into his tent. Upon seeing the dog, Bruff cried out to Clough, "There's some stranger about, probably some damned Indian." Looking to the southwest, Bruff saw "an old and highly esteemed friend," coming up the trail. Shaking hands with Bruff warmly, the friend asked how he had gotten along. "Bad enough," was his understated reply. "Well," said his friend, "here's a pack mule train at hand, coming up with supplies, to take you and all your effects down." When he awoke, he was in his tent covered with fresh snow.

March brought more snow to the mountain and rain in the settlements. While Clough was out hunting, Bruff heard someone whistling. Looking out from his tent, he saw a man in a white hat shouldering a gun. The man, named Withers, said three comrades were not far behind with pack animals and that they were from the settlements prospecting for gold. Although surprised they were looking for gold so far up the mountain, Bruff neglected to ask why they were prospecting so high up. He was more taken with Withers's resemblance to his savior in his dream a few days earlier and the fact that he had said "pack animals were coming." With no clear solution to his dilemma, Bruff had begun to cling to the false hopes of dreams and hidden meanings.

On March 10, Roberts returned with a team of oxen and wagons to collect his belongings. He brought nothing for Bruff, apart from a bit of infuriating news: Willis, who had promised to rescue him months ago, had just returned to Lassen's from the Feather River, where he had been prospecting for gold. After loading the wagons with valuables Roberts had plundered from the rear trail—cashmere, silks, white cotton, and so forth—he secured his cabin and started off his team without saying so much as a goodbye to Bruff.

By late March, Poyle had been gone several weeks, although Bruff still clung to the expectation he would arrive any day. As for Clough, he was forced to hunt for deer farther and farther out and had now been gone several days. A day or two Bruff could understand, but several days? He could not have been lost because Clough knew every ridge, spur, dell, and gorge for many miles and could find his way back to camp even on a dark night. There remained only two possibilities: He either met with hostile Indians or, more likely, was attacked by a grizzly. Just a week earlier Clough had expressed his desire to obtain bear meat. At the time Bruff had admonished him not to shoot one of the "Kings of the Sierra Nevada" because only a seasoned mountaineer could fell one in a single shot, and a wounded bear would certainly kill him. Ironically, as Clough took off the morning of his disappearance, he went about ten paces and turned to Bruff, saying, "Cap, I wouldn't wonder if some of these times, in my wild ramble over these ridges and hollows, that some damned grizzler or Indian would pin me!" Whatever happened to Clough, one thing was certain: Bruff was far too weak to go looking for him.

The day Clough left, Bruff ate the last piece of meat he had.

Game nearby was scarce and he was unable to venture more than a few hundred yards from camp, even less when the snow was deep. One day, he managed to take down a small, blue woodpecker only because it was near camp. With the prolonged exposure and lack of food, his condition was now spiraling out of control. Most days, his entire body was wracked with pain, especially his back, which prevented him from performing strenuous but essential activities like chopping wood or hunting. Sometimes the pain was so great that he was unable to sleep, which only made him weaker. If he couldn't hunt, he couldn't eat. At this rate, he would soon be dead, and he knew it. So full of despair was he that when a grizzly appeared just 10 feet from his door one night, Bruff was indifferent. "I was not alarmed," he wrote, "for I knew that if he was set to wind me up, I had the consolation also to know, that it would terminate much suffering." Fortunately, the bear moved off, causing him to remark, half in jest, that the bear had found him "too contemptible to kill." On March 28, he summed up his situation in the direst of terms:

> *Do not know where I am to obtain food, am perfectly perplexed how to sustain life much longer. The birds are scarce, and very shy, and I am weak and nervous . . . Surely one or both of my friends will be out to-morrow. - If not, poor Clough is lost, and I must soon follow; for I feel myself sinking, in spite of all my philosophy.*

The next morning, with nothing to eat and wracked with fever and stomach pains, Bruff shouldered his shotgun and staggered off to hunt. A flock of geese passed tantalizingly overhead, but he was too weak to raise his gun in time. Returning to camp empty-handed and exhausted, he ate the only thing he had left: salt mixed with coffee grinds. For a moment, he gazed hungrily at the pup but decided Nevada had been too faithful a guard and companion to be repaid by being eaten. Growing desperate, he broke into the Roberts' cabin and, rummaging around, found several deer leg bones. Extracting the yellowish, stringy marrow from each of them, he boiled it and drank the broth.

Each day Bruff could hear flocks of birds flying overhead—geese, pigeons, and cranes—so close, yet frustratingly out of reach. Poyle had now been gone two months and there was still no sign of Clough. He continued to speculate as to Clough's fate, ultimately concluding his friend had been "filled with arrows by Indians." As a requiem *in abstentia*, Bruff paid homage to the man whose altruism he had encountered so rarely on the trail.

> *Sacrificed in my service! Magnanimous, intrepid, and kind old man! Shall I ever forget thee? Never! Let my days be few or many, the grateful remembrance of thee will never leave my head and breast! Thou wast a MAN!*

One night, with great difficulty, he climbed onto the roof of the cabin in the hope the grizzly he had seen around camp would return. As he waited in the dark, silent forest, he suddenly heard a flute playing, followed by the laughter of a child. He listened transfixed, wondering who it was and where it could be coming from. Alas, he realized it was just the creaking of his own enfeebled mind. Dejected, he climbed down from the roof and went to sleep.

As March drew to a close, Bruff was down to extracting nutrients from the least bit of organic matter he could find around the camp or in the cabin. Laying out worm-ridden deerskins he pulled out of the cabin, he scraped off the worms and tore off tiny bits of dried meat still clinging to the inside of the skin and boiled them with two leg bones. For supper he ate more salt and coffee grinds.

April 1 came on ferociously with snow and hail. The day marked six months and ten days that he had been on the mountain—even longer than he had been on the trail. As he was heating "bone broth" prepared the previous day, he accidentally knocked over the kettle, spilling his last paltry meal to the ground. Falling to his hands and knees, he desperately gathered the bits of bones and gnawed at them like the starving man he was. With renewed resolve, he went off to hunt but once again came back exhausted and fell asleep. When he awoke, he suddenly recalled Roberts had put a deer's head in the eaves of the cabin. With the aid of a pole, he was able to pry it loose. Although it was half decayed and seething with worms and insects, he pulled out the tongue and cooked it and gave the rotting head to Nevada.

One again he took stock of his situation. The letters he had sent out had not produced so much as a single response. Nor had Davis made an appearance. Even Peoples had forgotten about him. With Clough presumed dead, Poyle had remained Bruff's one last hope. But now he had given up on Poyle, too, whom he surmised was either dead or had returned home. With the possibility of rescue now appearing hopeless, Bruff concluded his only chance to save himself was in doing what up until now had been unthinkable: descending on foot. It was a conclusion he should have reached months earlier, for he was now far weaker to undertake such an arduous journey—indeed, he was on the verge of starvation. Nor had he so much as a scrap of food for the trip, save two tallow candles and a dozen acorns that he had been preserving as specimens. Yet try he must, for he was out of options and failing fast. To prepare his rheumatic body for the journey, that night he massaged his legs several times with a mixture of camphor and cayenne to relieve the pain and went to sleep.

Reasoning he must start very soon lest he be too weak to

attempt it, the next day Bruff gathered his substantial stack of note-books and papers, a clean shirt and socks, comb, towel, soap, acorns, candles, matches, pipe and tobacco (which he had not smoked out of sympathy since he gave up on Clough), a small quilt, and ammuni-tion and rolled them all into his knapsack. Then he laid out his rifle pouch, powder horn, bowie-knife, and weapons. What he could not carry he stored in the cabin accompanied by a note directing his effects be sent to his family should he die en route.

In the morning came disappointment when he realized he was simply too weak to travel. To build his strength, he went out a mile in search of game and killed a small bluebird. When he returned, he scoured the cabin for something more to eat and found two old flour bags. Beating and scraping the bags, he extracted about two ounces of dark yellow lumps of flour mixed with hair, cotton, lint, and mouse droppings. With the small bird and scrapings he made a soup, giving the wings to the pup. Once again, he burned more calories hunting and preparing the food than the food itself had provided. Time was running out and he knew it. So, too, did the wolves, for late in the afternoon the yelping of Nevada had awak-ened him to find an immense gray wolf staring at them from 30 yards away.

The next morning Bruff resolved to move from his position, whatever the consequences. Lightening his knapsack, he set out with Nevada, now a mere skeleton, close on his heels. No sooner had he ascended the first hill in front of the cabin than he was out of breath and perspiring. After a brief rest, he continued, stopping to rest every 30 or 40 paces, expecting any moment to keel over. By midday, he was astonished to find he had reached Steep Hollow, seven miles from the cabin.

There was now no question of turning back.

Descending a steep, rugged portion of the trail, Bruff's legs gave out several times as he fell and righted himself, each time with great difficulty. When faced with an incline, he could only manage ten paces at a time before gasping for breath. Each time he stopped, little Nevada would scamper ahead and look back whining, as if to remind Bruff he could not linger too long or too often if he hoped to make it.

While resting in the afternoon, he spotted a blackbird sitting in an oak tree. Resting his gun on a branch of a tree, he shot and ate the bird before covering three more miles. As the last rays of the sun were gilding the hilltops, Bruff sank to the ground, wet with perspiration and gasping for breath. Too tired to search for water, he dissolved into sleep. With wolves howling all around him, he wondered if it would be his last night.

When he awoke the next morning, he discovered he was not only weaker from the previous day's exertion but sore and lame as well. Casting about for water, he found some in a muddy rivulet about 300 yards off. Before proceeding, he shot a tiny bluebird for breakfast. After ascending the first hill, his legs gave out and he collapsed. When he recovered, he took out one of the candles from his sack and, sprinkling it with salt and pepper, ate about a quarter of it. For Nevada he cut up some rawhide to chew on. When the pup finished, he lay down next to Bruff and emitted a deep sigh. Looking around, Bruff suddenly noticed he had stumbled into an emigrant camp several months old. Here some seeds had been spilled and tiny sprouts of cabbage, lettuce, and radishes had begun to sprout. Crawling on his hands and knees, he pulled up and ate each plant—root and all, gratefully calling it "the sweetest cold salad I had ever eaten in my life." He climbed, wet and cold, into an abandoned wagon to sleep but the howling of wolves kept him awake all night.

Dawn came on with heavy rain. Too tired to start out, he made a fire with wood from a broken wagon. At 10 o'clock he went a short distance before showers and a cold gale forced him to take shelter against an abandoned cart. He ate another piece of candle and adjusted the straps of his knapsack to alleviate the chafing on his shoulders. Bit by bit he staggered on. At sunset he found himself near a brook with a heavy rain threatening. With no firewood or shelter, he took cover under a large bush. As he was cutting a niche in the bush, he heard a group of men on the trail below. Too worn out to care if they were Indians, he rushed ahead. Seeing that they were white, he cried out that he was starving and collapsed. One of the men rushed up and gave him some bread and salt pork grease. The men said they were headed to Deer Creek to prospect for gold and had heard of Bruff's predicament from Roberts. Just then, rain began falling and the men decided to make camp for the night. Making a makeshift tent with some blankets, they invited Bruff to share their shelter, but there was only enough room for his head and shoulders. As he lay down to sleep, he spotted the gravestone of a young man who had died in September.

The next morning, as the prospectors were preparing to leave, Bruff begged them for some food from the several sacks of flour they had. "Oh, Captain! said one of the men, "you can soon get in now; you needn't be alarmed." With that breezy assurance, they shouldered their rifles and marched off, leaving Bruff with not so much as a morsel of bread. With 16 miles still to go, he was dumbfounded. How, he wondered, could they ignore his plea given his weak and emaciated appearance? Not so much as a handful of flour was offered him. "I thought how differently I would have acted toward one of them, had our positions been reversed," he seethed. Still, he was not entirely ungrateful for they had fed him the previous day and given him a small breakfast, thereby staving off starvation another day.

It rained the rest of the day and night. Soaking wet and cold, Bruff crouched under his quilt by the fire all night, shivering and listening to the howling of the wolves nearby. He described it as "the most wretched night I ever knew."

Daybreak came as a balm, clear and mild. For breakfast, he made some coffee and ate the grinds while he waited for his quilt to dry. The previous day he had heard footsteps and thought it was a wolf. On the soggy trail he saw the small tracks of a Yahi, which, in his depraved condition, caused him to consider what would have been unimaginable to him under normal circumstances:

> *Oh! if I can over take him! when will I have one hearty meal! a good broil ! I felt relieved, it gave me additional strength; to think I might soon get a broil off an indian's leg! I could not but laugh, when I thought of it, - the expressions I have heard, how people would starve to death rather than eat human flesh! Fools! how little could they form an idea of the cravings of hunger! Let them be placed in my circumstances, and see how soon they would discard such silly ideas! My mouth fairly watered, for a piece of Indian to broil!*

In a half-demented state, he stalked the Indian down the trail until he disappeared. For lunch he ate the last of his candle, giving the wick to Nevada. When he reached Dry Creek, he startled two Indian dogs and fired at them to no avail. As he was drinking his coffee, he spotted a lizard on a rock. Seizing a stick, he impaled it and roasted it over the fire. He then rolled his aching body in the small quilt and went to sleep under some manzanita bushes.

Day six began clear and cold. He was eight miles from the settlements but began to doubt he would make it. He wondered if it would have been better just to die atop the mountain than put himself through such an ordeal. Coming to an icy, fast-moving stream, he attempted to cross by hopping from rock to rock, but was too feeble for such an agile maneuver and slipped and fell in. He raced waist-deep through the water to the opposite bank, where he threw himself on a rock, trembling with cold and fatigue. But he needed to keep moving, and staggered on another three miles before collapsing in mud. Realizing he could no longer carry his knapsack, he buried it under a pyramid of stones.

After a brief rest, Bruff staggered on. A quarter-mile on, he encountered a nearly naked Yahi out hunting with bow and arrow. Bruff attempted to communicate in Spanish, but the Indian didn't understand. He then made signs that he was hungry. The Indian signed back that he had nothing and was on his way to Dry Creek to shoot birds. When the Indian was about 40 paces gone, Bruff turned around and contemplated shooting him but could not bring himself to shoot a man in the back, no matter how hungry he was.

A little farther on he stopped to rest. There being no stones or trees about, Bruff squatted on the rotting carcass of an ox while Nevada gnawed and tore at the desiccated remains. Continuing on, he reached Deer Creek, estimating he was probably 3 miles from the Davis Ranch. To spur himself on, he told himself he would soon have plenty of food to eat, a bed, and an end to his terrible suffering.

But in his debilitated condition, three miles was still quite a distance. Stopping to rest on a rock, he fell backward into the bushes as if into an easy chair and passed out. He might never have awakened had it not been for Nevada's barking. Unable to get up, he turned to see a white man coming up the trail.

It was Poyle.

His old friend was aghast at Bruff's appearance. He quickly gave him some hardtack, which Bruff devoured "like a starved wolf."

Although Poyle had traveled the length and breadth of northern California, he had not had an iota of success in finding any of the individuals to whom Bruff had written letters. (Frémont had his hands full keeping miners from helping themselves to the gold on his on his 44,000-acre ranch on the Mariposa River.) Poyle was on his way to Bruff's camp with some flour and pork and planned to assist him until he could walk in. He was about to light a fire to prepare a meal, but when Bruff learned he was only 300 yards from Davis's, he insisted on walking in with Poyle's help. The 15 minutes it took Bruff to reach the ranch were the longest of his life.

At long last, his horrifying ordeal was over.

At the Davis Ranch, Bruff met Colonel Ely who was running things in Davis's absence. After a hearty meal with the boarders, Bruff took out his pipe and announced joyfully, "Well, I'm not dead yet!" "Oh, No!" replied one of the men, "You're worth several dead men yet, Captain." Mounting his horse, Ely rode up to fetch Bruff's knapsack cached at Deer Creek. With all the bunk beds taken, Bruff and Poyle slept on the floor in front of the fire. It was the soundest night's sleep he had had in a long, long time.

Chapter Eleven

OLD PETE

IF BRUFF'S LONG NIGHTMARE HAD ENDED, HIS LONG road to recovery had only just begun. On the mountain, he had survived mostly on carrion and stale flour while his fare on the trail had consisted of little more than bacon and biscuits. That, combined with prolonged exposure, had taken its toll on him physically, if not mentally. He was so weak that he was unable to stand or sit in a chair for any length of time. Headaches and rheumatism continued to plague him. Withal, his perennial optimism and goodwill remained intact. Despite having been abandoned by some of his men, betrayed by Willis, and rebuffed by dozens of people he had assisted, he bore them no ill will. At the ranch, Mrs. Davis tended to him with maternal kindness. Laying out a snow-white tablecloth set with fine china, she served up his first meal of pancakes and molasses, rolls and fresh butter, and stewed beef with coffee and milk—which he promptly threw up. It would be a week before he could begin to hold down normal food.

While he convalesced at the ranch, Bruff passed the time chatting with the staff and gold miners, some of whom he knew from the trail. His first concern was answering the mystery of Clough's disappearance. When he heard J. J. Myers had been prospecting around Deer Creek, he inquired if he had come across any human remains, but Myers had seen nothing. Although the question would continue to haunt him, Bruff never learned what had befallen the man who had saved his life and probably gave his own in doing so. For Clough's body was never found, nor was there any record of his death.

Myers did say that he had been to Bruff's camp and that his wagon and all his property had been completely ransacked and destroyed. No sooner had Myers spoken when a black man rode past wearing Bruff's saber, with another bearing his rifle and prized mineral collection, which he recovered on the spot. A week later the few items Bruff had left in his possession—some food from Poyle, his weapons, and valuables—were stolen. One of Davis's sons wasted no time in pointing the finger at the Indians. Suspecting instead one of Davis's own sons of the theft, Bruff moved to Lassen's ranch two miles below.

Round-faced and balding, with bushy mutton chop sideburns that reached to his chin, Peter Lassen looked more like an ancient mariner than a successful California rancher. Lassen had come a long way from the little thatched house of his birth in the tiny village of Farum, Denmark. His father, Lars Neilsen, was an unemployed laborer and alcoholic who died early. His mother stoically toiled to cook food from scraps. Young Peter became known in the village as "Lars's son," a name that he grew to like and eventually adopted. He was the eldest of three children, one of whom had died next to him in bed after falling through the ice one winter on Lake Farum. At five feet two-and-a-half inches in height, Lassen was unusually short but strong, healthy, and limitlessly ambitious. Although he was conscripted in the army, he was too small to become a soldier and served instead in the civic corps. At 17, Lassen apprenticed as a blacksmith with his uncle. A few years later he became a master smith and took a job with an established forger in Copenhagen whose daughter, Regitze, he fell hopelessly in love with. Whether because of her unrequited love or the lack of work in economically-depressed Copenhagen, Lassen decided his future lay in America. He sold his tools to raise money for his passage and returned to Farum to bid farewell to his mother. Among the parting gifts she gave Peter was his father's beloved meerschaum tobacco pipe. When the wee blacksmith set sail for America in October of 1830, little could he imagine he would one day become a founding father of California.

Lassen landed in Boston where, just as he had hoped, he found work as a smith. He struggled to learn English, a language he never mastered and would forever speak with a pronounced Danish accent. With its seaside location and cold winters, Boston was too much like Copenhagen and within a few months Lassen moved west in search of the wide open spaces of his imagination. After a short stint in St. Louis, he landed in Keytesville, Missouri, a town that had been established a year earlier as the seat of Chariton County. Lassen started his own blacksmith shop, bought some land, and grew with the town. Uncomfortable in the company of women since his rejection by Regitze, he found fellowship in the town's Masonic Lodge. As they had with Bruff, Freemasonry's high-minded ideals and codes of moral conduct appealed to Lassen. Nevertheless, when the Sioux began attacking the town's citizens, he established a civic guard corps similar to the one he had served on in Denmark. On numerous occasions, the corps clashed with the marauding Sioux. The diminutive Lassen proved so effective a leader in battle he became known as "the little Captain." Even though Keytesville needed to be protected, Lassen never forgave himself for killing Indians, whom he liked and admired.

With a growing business and prominent standing in the community, Lassen may well have put down roots for good in Keytesville had not John Sutter passed through in 1838. When they met, Sutter extolled California's beauty, fine climate, and endless possibilities and invited Lassen to stay at his fort. It was enough to reawaken Lassen's wanderlust. The following spring, he joined an emigrant party consisting of a motley assortment of missionaries, mountain men, traders, and doctors bound for Oregon. The party had gotten no farther than the Blue River in Kansas when they ran out of food. For the remainder of the journey, they relied on nature's pantry, shooting and eating everything that moved from deer to dogs.

When they reached the Green River Basin, Lassen tried to find a guide to take him to California, but no one was willing to venture into what was then largely unknown territory. Disappointed, he continued on with the rest of the party to Oregon City, where he spent the winter.

In the summer, Lassen boarded the ship *Lausanne* for Bodega, California. The ship was nearly destroyed in a violent storm and later struck a rock at the mouth of the Columbia River. When they reached Bodega Bay, a contingent of Mexican soldiers, suspicious of outsiders, refused to let the ship land. As the passengers mulled their predicament, the Russian governor arrived and ordered the soldiers to leave or be shot. Although the soldiers stood down, the Mexican authorities refused to allow Lassen and his fellow passengers to stay in Bodega. So they wrote a letter to the American consul, requesting assistance in obtaining a Mexican visa. As they waited for a reply (no such consul yet existed in California), the Russian governor not only offered them a place to stay but regaled them with the music of Mozart, fine wine, and cigars.

When they learned no reply would be forthcoming, they purchased horses and set out for New Helvetia. Two weeks later Lassen arrived at Sutter's Fort, where he went to work as a blacksmith and handyman. Within a year, the industrious Dane had built a cabin on the Consumnes River 16 miles south of Sutter's Fort, tended to by an Indian woman. He built a water-powered sawmill, the first of its kind in California, and developed a reputation for his honesty and craftsmanship in making everything from saddles to furniture.

Shortly after Lassen acquired his land grant from the Mexican government, he went to work with a passion, trapping, trading, farming oats and cotton, and acquiring livestock. Early on, he saw California's potential for producing grapes and started a vineyard, becoming the first to produce wine in the region. There wasn't anything the industrious Dane couldn't do with his hands or his imagination. Within a year of settling on Deer Creek, he began laying out the site of a city on the north bank of the creek: Benton City, named after Frémont's father-in-law, Senator Thomas Hart Benton, who had sponsored his adventurous son-in-law's exploratory career.

Lassen's *Rancho Bosquejo* (Wooded Ranch) quickly became one of the finest ranches in California, consisting of several thousand acres of pasturage covered with oats, grasses, and clover, as well as huge herds of cattle, horses, mules, sheep, and hogs. Three small adobe buildings made up the ranch houses nestled among the alders and sycamores on the banks of Deer Creek. One housed a small store that did a lively business in flour, groceries, and whiskey.

Because Lassen's ranch was the northernmost settlement in California, trappers and traders passing through often stayed there. When Frémont came down to California from Oregon in March 1846, he stopped at the ranch and was deeply impressed with what he found:

*In the afternoon, about half a mile above its mouth, we camped
on Deer Creek, another of those beautiful tributaries of the
Sacramento . . . Mr. Lassen, a native of Germany, had established a rancho here, which he has stocked, and is gradually
bringing into cultivation. Wheat, as generally throughout the
country, gives large returns: cotton planted in the way of exper-
iment, was not injured by frost and succeeded well; and he has
lately planted a vineyard, for which the Sacramento Valley is
considered to be singularly well adapted . . .*

The two men became friends, and Lassen invited Frémont to
stay at the ranch as long as he liked. Using the ranch as his base,
Frémont and Kit Carson explored the northern Sierras, trying to
connect the region on his maps with the area he had just come
from. As he was exploring the Cascades, Lieutenant Archibald
Gillespie arrived in search of Frémont. Gillespie claimed to be a
friend of Frémont's and wished to get family letters to him. Lassen
warned of hostile Indians in the area, but Gillespie was adamant.
Since he was unfamiliar with the area, Lassen offered to guide
him to the colonel, evidence of how well the Dane had come to
know the area. Riding 200 miles over seven days, they caught up to
Frémont camped near Klamath Lake on May 9.

In camp that night, Carson was awakened by the sound of an
axe striking the skull of one of Frémont's men. Before he could
rouse the others, Klamath Indians had killed three men, including one of Frémont's Delaware guides, and wounded one. Frémont
and Lassen began firing, killing the chief. In the chief's quiver were
forty arrows with six-inch poisoned iron tips. To avenge the deaths
of his men, Frémont, accompanied by Lassen, continued around
the lakeshore, wantonly killing every Indian he saw and sacking
an Indian village. What part Lassen played in the bloodbath is

unknown though, given his partiality toward natives, he was likely horrified by the carnage. Frémont later asked Gillespie not to mention the incident when he returned to Washington.

On May 24, they arrived back at the ranch to learn Mexican Governor Castro had issued a proclamation ordering all noncitizens out of California and prohibiting any new ones from entering. The next day Frémont moved south to Bear Valley to avoid entrapment by Castro's men, eventually ending up at Sutter's Fort. When he learned of the Bear Flag revolt, he rushed to Sonoma to assume command. Whether Lassen broke his oath of fealty to Mexico and participated in the revolt is unclear, although some believe he joined Frémont in the fight against Mexico.

Meanwhile, U.S. Commodore John Sloat, who was aware the U.S. was now at war with Mexico in the south, was stationed off the coast of California. Upon hearing the Bear Flaggers had taken Sonoma, he rushed ashore and planted the U.S. flag over the Customs House in Monterey. But when Sloat learned the Bear Flaggers had not acted on orders from Washington, he reluctantly resigned, putting Commodore Robert Stockton in command.

Every bit as brash and daring as Frémont, Stockton wasted no time promoting Frémont to major and putting him in command of the California Battalion. Together they fought the Mexican garrison in Los Angeles before Mexico capitulated. Stockton rewarded Frémont with the governorship of California and in July 1847 returned overland to Washington. Among the men of Stockton's large party was Peter Lassen.

When Lassen and his small group of settlers returned from Missouri on the eve of the Gold Rush, it looked as if his timing could not have been better. But, as he was soon to learn, it could not have been worse, for he would lose everything he had worked so hard to build. As Gold Rushers flooded into the valley, they began over-running his ranch and helping themselves to his livestock.

Then General Wilson arrived at Lassen's in November 1849. With the Gold Rush in full swing, Wilson saw the enormous potential of Lassen's ranch and the city the Dane planned to build. Feigning concern for the Dane's problems at the ranch, the disingenuous Wilson advised the 49-year-old Lassen he should take on a younger man to manage the ranch and to keep travelers from stealing his livestock. He also proposed he and his guide Joel Palmer purchase a portion of the ranch, in return for which Wilson would use his considerable influence to sell lots in the city of Benton. A man given to speaking in hyperbole, if not outright falsehoods, Wilson, who had been involved in land speculation in Missouri, claimed to have purchased a half-interest in 15,000,000 acres of land.

To Lassen, who wanted more time to prospect for gold himself, Wilson's idea sounded like a plan. The unsuspecting Dane seems to have known and trusted Wilson from his Missouri days when the latter lived in neighboring Howard County and was editor for the *Missouri Intelligencer* and a (seemingly) respectable district circuit attorney. Yet, given his poor command of English, it is unlikely Lassen knew what—or with whom—he was getting into. Before the month was out, Lassen had sold Wilson and Palmer each a third of his interest in the ranch for $15,000 each. According to the terms of the agreement, Wilson and Palmer were required to pay $3,000 in cash within a year and the balance in five years. During that time, Palmer would manage the ranch while Wilson sold lots in Benton City. Wilson and Palmer also convinced Lassen to give them each a share in his store—its contents valued at $1,100—in return for which they would double the inventory with supplies they would purchase in Sacramento.

In mid-December, Wilson and Palmer took a steamer for Sacramento on the pretext of procuring their share of the goods and requested Lassen meet them there with wagons to transport the supplies back to the ranch. But when Lassen arrived in Sacramento, he found neither Palmer nor Wilson. Unbeknownst to Lassen, Wilson had taken a steamer straightaway to San Francisco to assume his job as Indian Agent. Suspecting nothing amiss, Lassen proceeded to purchase $4,500 worth of food and supplies. By now, heavy rains had inundated the Sacramento and its tributaries, making return overland impossible. From the same supplier, Lassen purchased a steamer, the *Lady Washington*, paying cash for all but $3,000 of the total bill, which he covered with notes from Wilson and Palmer. Returning to the ranch, he stocked up the store that, conveniently, was now being run by Wilson's son, William. By April, Wilson would be boasting in letters home of the financial success of his ranch that he claimed was 100,000 acres.

When he first met Bruff in April, Lassen expressed his anger at the lack of compassion shown by his men for his predicament, apologizing and saying that had he not been in Sacramento the entire time dealing with the ship and supplies, he would certainly have rescued him. Bruff hit it off with the kindly Dane immediately, not least because Lassen was a fellow Freemason. Much as Clough had been to Bruff on the mountain, in the gold fields Lassen would become a trusted companion whom he referred to affectionately as "Old Pete." With all of the rooms at the small ranch occupied, Bruff slept on the floor in front of the fireplace.

On April 20, feeling well enough to travel, Bruff joined Lassen and his men, who were leading a large team of oxen up the mountain to collect shingles and the abandoned goods and wagons of the Gold Rushers. When Bruff arrived at the Roberts' cabin, he discovered most of his effects had been stolen. His old camp at Deer

Creek was littered with broken boxes, trunks, torn-up canvas, and trash. The Company's feather beds and pillows had been slashed and the camp was ankle-deep in feathers. Appalled by the wanton destruction, Bruff glumly gathered what little that remained of use: some cooking utensils and a couple of old saddles.

But the plunder at the Roberts' cabin and Deer Creek was dwarfed by an even more disturbing discovery. As he was descending the trail, Bravo, his horse, tried to throw him. When Bruff dismounted to inspect the position of the saddle, Bravo broke free and ran off with a snort. Momentarily stranded, he walked to the Roberts' cabin to wait for the shingle wagons to come up. There he saw something he had missed earlier: little William's grave had been dug up and the headboard had been insensitively re-inserted upside down. As Bruff was righting the headboard, he noticed a hole where Billy's head should have been. Instinctively, he walked down the trail, where he found the boy's skull 50 yards away and returned it to its resting place.

Even though he was still weak, Bruff stayed a week on the mountain helping to repair and load the wagons to pay for his room and board at Lassen's. While he was leading some wagons down the mountain, one of Wilson's sons came up the trail to tell Bruff that four men from his Company had stopped at the ranch on their way to the Trinity River mines and heard that Bruff was still trapped on the mountain. They were about to mount a rescue mission when they learned that he was in fact safe. Late though it was, their concern was reassuring to Bruff that many of the men, having bolted for the gold fields upon arrival, had simply been unaware of his plight at Deer Creek.

In taking up with Lassen, Bruff had not only found a good friend but one who was well-positioned to profit from the sudden spurt of growth in California. When Lassen learned of Bruff's

mapmaking skills, he hired him—at two ounces of gold per day—
to lay out the plans for nearby Benton City. Grand Master Sashel
Woods had already established California's first Masonic Lodge in
October 1849 in the soon-to-be city. Bruff had met Woods at the
Washington Lodge, where Woods had given him valuable information about the trail, having made the overland journey twice
before. Lassen became a Junior Warden of the Lodge and Bruff a
senior member.

While Bruff was surveying the site, a young man came staggering down the hill. Drawing a deep sigh, the man asked Bruff where
he was. When Bruff informed him, the man, a German immi-
grant named Nicholas Loux, burst into a flood of tears. In broken
English, he related how he had left his wife and children in New
York to join the Gold Rush. Having gotten a late start with two
other men, by the time they reached Lassen's Pass it was snowed
in and they were unable to proceed. Forced to winter near Goose
Lake, the men survived mostly on carrion. Maidu Indians generously gave them small fish and ducks from their precious stock
out of the belief that whites and Indians were sons of the same
Great Ancestor. When the spring thaw arrived, one of the men
attempted to raft down the Feather River and drowned. Nicholas
and his remaining partner subsequently set out on foot for Lassen's. By the time they reached the Roberts' cabin, his partner was
too weak to go on.

Upon hearing this, Lassen immediately mounted a rescue for
Loux's friend the following day. They found him three miles below
the cabin lying dead on his back, apparently having been dragged
some distance by a wolf. Superstitious about touching the dead,
Nicholas left his body exposed for the wolves to eat. So similar was
the story to Bruff's own that it was stark reminder of just how fortunate he had been.

When he finished the survey, Bruff returned to Lassen's to rest. While poking around the Lassen ranch, Bruff was shocked to find all the Company's property piled in a loft. The entire lot had been pledged as collateral for a $75 loan from Lassen. In seven months no one had ever returned to reclaim the property or settle the debt. Since the wagon and provisions were the whole reason Bruff had gotten marooned at Deer Creek in the first place, the whole ordeal that had nearly killed him had been for naught.

Although keen to begin prospecting for gold, he was still too weak, suffering daily from debilitating bouts of rheumatism and indigestion. Most days he was unable to keep down solid food, making him all the more susceptible to illness. It wasn't long before he came down with typhoid fever.

While laid up with fever, Bruff learned another reason why many of his cries for help on the mountain had gone unanswered. One of the prospectors he had encountered as he was descending Lassen's Trail in April had passed by the ranch and told him that after the quarrel with his men at Deer Creek, they had spread a rumor that Bruff had robbed the Roberts' cabin. Believing the malicious story to be true, neither Willis nor Roberts ever delivered Bruff's messages, leaving him to think his rescue was imminent.

Despite his infirmities and the malicious betrayal by so many, Bruff was nonetheless in good spirits and his interest in the grand adventure remained undiminished. He reveled in meeting the sundry people passing through the ranch, each unique as the stories they told. With Dr. Drinker, the great-great-grandson of the first resident of Philadelphia, he found kindred company, for Bruff was a member of the Oldest Inhabitants Association of Washington. Together they amused themselves with target practice with their rifles. He particularly delighted in meeting some of the rare female emigrants, who were outnumbered thirty to one by men in the emigration. Occasionally, members of his old Company would, upon hearing of Bruff's presence at the Lassen ranch, stop by to pay their respects to their former Captain.

But of all his encounters, those he most valued were with his spiritual kith and kin: military officers. On June 8, Captain Chadwick pulled into Lassen's landing on the steamer *Lawrence*. Chadwick was on his way to the Sierras to recover Warner's remains and punish the Paiutes for his death and the continued slaughter and plunder of emigrants. Indeed, not ten days after Chadwick's arrival, two men from an emigrant party rode in on exhausted mules to tell of their own sorrowful encounter with the Pitt. They had departed Ohio early in 1850, but with insufficient provisions and arms. By the time they got to the Pitt River, they were out of food and on the verge of starvation. The Pitt wasted no time in attacking the vulnerable party, killing several men and stealing what few pack animals they had left.

As the Pitt were in a remote part of the Sierras, the military had been waiting for the snows to melt before mounting an expedition. Wishing to learn about the conditions of Lassen's trail, Chadwick invited Bruff aboard the steamer for the night. When Captain Lyon arrived to command the expedition, Bruff briefed Lyon and his men on the route and conditions over the Sierras using his detailed notebooks. (Lyon, however, would not take Lassen's Trail to the Feather River but the easier and elusive Frémont route by way of Redding—the very one Bruff had failed to find.)

Pleasant though these encounters were, Bruff did not come all the way to California to socialize but to claim his fortune in gold. As he waited for his health to improve, he spent a good deal of time gathering information about the gold diggings from the miners passing through the ranch. What he learned was as deflating as anything he had seen or encountered along the trail.

Chapter Twelve

THE GREAT CALIFORNIA LOTTERY

BRUFF HAD BORNE WITNESS TO THE THRONGS OF
Gold Rushers in Pittsburgh and St. Joseph and along the trail. But
neither he nor anyone else could have any idea of the vast number
of people who poured into California in 1849. In addition to the
35,000 emigrants who traveled the Oregon Trail, nearly 10,000
more had come up from the Santa Fe route, not to mention the
6,000 Sonoran Mexicans who had arrived the previous year or
the 1,500 miners who were the very first to respond to President
Polk's announcement. But great as the overland emigration had
been, even more had come by sea. By December 1849, nearly 700
vessels had entered the San Francisco Harbor, delivering 40,000
Americans and foreigners. Overnight California's population had
increased tenfold, and there was little infrastructure to accommodate the flood of people.

Mining camps sprang up like mushrooms, with peculiar names
like Bogus Thunder, Gomorrah, Skunk Gulch, Gospel Swamp,
and Hangtown (later Placerville) where a lynching took place in

1849. Although some threw up shacks, most miners continued to live in their wagons or tents—which were better than the brush lean-tos those who had abandoned their wagons were living in. Some even lived in the open air without so much as a tent or a blanket for shelter.

Conditions in the camps were appalling. Shacks, wagons, and tents were crowded together with virtually no sanitation. Not surprisingly, their old nemesis on the trail, cholera, reappeared as did other diseases like typhoid and the greatest killer of all, dysentery. The few doctors to be found in the camps were, like everyone else, too busy participating in the crazed and chaotic search for gold—a quest that was proving, despite all the hoopla, frustratingly futile.

Until Lassen's Trail had diverted him unexpectedly to the south, Bruff had planned to mine along the Trinity River—the northernmost of the gold fields called the "Redding Diggings." Gold was discovered in one of its tributaries, Clear Creek, near Lassen's ranch, in 1848 (and possibly as early as 1844) and on the Trinity shortly thereafter. Although the river was now overrun with miners, he had heard the water was high due to the Sierra snowmelt and little gold had been found. Most others passing through the ranch reported finding little, if any, gold and were still in search of their big strike. How could this be, they wondered, when they had been led to believe the Sacramento Valley contained a virtual mother lode of gold?

The nuggets that Marshall had plucked with such ease from the American River were the product of geological activity beneath the earth that had begun 200 million years earlier. As tectonic plates collided, super-heated molten rock bubbled up, most of it cooling long before it reached the surface. As the liquid rock cooled, gold and other minerals became trapped in veins lodged in a huge mass of granite bedrock underneath present-day California and Nevada.

About four million years ago, the entire mass was uplifted, forming the Sierra Nevada Mountains, whose fissures were filled with gold-laden quartz veins. Over eons of time, melting water dislodged some of the gold from these veins, depositing it in the form of dust and nuggets in creeks and riverbeds. Along the western slope of the Sierras, there were ten such rivers and their forks in a swath of land 250 miles long and 50 miles wide, stretching from the Mariposa River in the south to the Feather River in the north.

By the time 49ers arrived, most of the easy gold in the form of flakes and nuggets on the surfaces of streambeds had been picked clean by the 6,000 miners who came in 1848. Of the early miners, the Reverend Walter Colton, the Alcalde of Monterey, said they were "running over the country and picking it [gold] out of the earth, just as a thousand hogs let loose in a forest would root up the ground nuts." Early comers may have taken as much as $10 million from the surface. As one 49er lamented, "In short, most of the cream had been taken off." Just as emigrants had failed to appreciate the hardships of the overland crossing, they had vastly underestimated the difficulty of finding and mining gold. The 65,000 men who went into the gold fields in 1850 now faced a hurdle as great as the overland journey itself: teasing gold from the earth. And to this, they brought Yankee ingenuity and a passion that only gold can inspire.

There was still plenty of gold, but what remained lay deep in streambeds and in quartz veins in the rocks. Because of its greater weight, miners could find flakes and nuggets by river mining: digging six to ten feet into the riverbeds. This did not require a large capital investment and could be pursued with a pickaxe, shovels, and pans.

And so they dug. At first they dug a few feet down, then deeper and deeper into the riverbed. Called "coyote holes," some diggings were hundreds of feet deep, with miners laboring in cramped, dark quarters to fill buckets with sediment that were hoisted by another to the surface and then washed to extract the gold. It was filthy, backbreaking work and hardly what emigrants had imagined they would be doing when they had set out for California with such enthusiasm.

As gold became harder to find, miners devised new methods of sifting the sediment in greater amounts by a process called washing. Isaac Humphrey, who had previous experience in mining, devised a mechanism called a "cradle" that vastly increased the amount of sediment one could sift. It consisted of a wooden cradle four to six feet in length with wooden strips or cleats at the bottom to catch the gold. Using some of ~~some of~~ Sutter's Indian ranch help to shovel dirt into his cradle, Humphrey washed $16,000 of gold in just five weeks.

Frequent interruptions in the washing to clean the gold from the cleats led to the development of an even larger contraption, the long tom. An enlarged version of Humphrey's cradle, it was eight by fifteen feet in length, its upper end attached to a flume that provided constant running water to wash gravel. Miners soon learned that by placing mercury at the bottom, the device could capture every fleck of gold. At the end of the day, miners heated the mercury to vapor and distilled the gold from it. Once cooled, the mercury returned to its original form and could be used the next day. Highly toxic, the mercury poisoned streams, many of which are still contaminated to this day.

Eventually, miners found that even more sediment could be washed using a sluice, which was a series of several long wooden boxes that allowed water to run directly into the boxes to wash away the sediment dumped into the sluice. Gold nuggets and bits were then trapped in the bars at the bottom. They also built dams and races to divert the river and lay bare the bed. This required filling sacks of sand and building stone walls, filling the cracks usually with earth, dirt, and brush.

There were also many bizarre and grandiose experiments. One old Georgia miner, with experience recovering treasure from the bottom of the Mississippi, combed riverbeds in a submarine suit. Others employed diving bells to explore river bottoms.

The results of all these efforts varied widely from miner to miner. A few men got rich, such as the two men working the Yuba River in November 1850 who culled $5,000 in a single week, or the company of miners who made $15,000 in three weeks on the American River. Such miners usually doubled their income by selling their stake in the claim for thousands of dollars before heading home. The unlucky went into debt, such as the German who spent a grueling 17 weeks damming the Yuba River at Foster's Bar at a cost of about $8,000, only to find nothing. More common was the experience of William Swain of the Wolverine Rangers, who made enough each day to pay for food and provisions and keep going in the hope he would strike it rich and could go home.

Fueling the feverish quest for gold were stories of fabulous finds that circulated like a contagious fever from camp to camp. One prospector related to Bruff he had heard of a man who had extracted 60 pounds of gold in a single day on the Feather at a place called Rich Bar. It was rumored that two men took out $22,000 in gold from the Middle Fork of the Feather. Several others had accumulated "all the fortunes they desired" in no time and packed up and returned home.

Yet, for all the head-spinning stories of fantastic gold strikes, most had only disappointment and frustration to show for their efforts. More common was the experience of a party of prospectors Bruff had met. Beginning in December and packing in on mules, they had explored the American River from its mouth to its head-waters, all along the Truckee River up to Truckee Lake and along the Yuba and Feather Rivers. For all their efforts, they and their six comrades had accumulated a sum total of nothing. Even Poyle, who had gone off gold hunting when he got Bruff safely to Lassen's in April, had yet to find any gold after three solid months of prospecting. One never knew when he would be among the lucky few to strike gold, and it was largely this flimsy hope that kept men at it despite the high cost and hardship.

In the end, many failed to turn up any gold whatsoever. For one thing, there were legions of gold seekers—for every man who prospected in 1848, there were now 15. And when they arrived, they found most rivers and streams had already been claimed, a claim being essentially anywhere a miner or his tools were. Another factor was that no matter which tools or methods were used, finding gold was often a matter of luck. Indeed, so much did luck play in the equation that the gold hunt came to be called the "Great California Lottery."

Since 49ers had come expecting to get rich quick, the disappointment was devastating for many. For those who came later and were unwilling, or simply too weary from the long journey, to do the elaborate digging and sifting were often so disappointed they went home—if there was even someone or something to return home to. As one miner wrote:

> If there had been a vessel lying upon the Feather River bound for New Orleans, there was not one of us who would not rather have stepped on board than to have gone one step farther in search of gold, for our prospects are truly gloomy . . . Almost every man we meet who has been in the mines is wishing himself out of this country . . .

One man who had arrived in the gold fields on April 1 was on a steamship home a month later. Some committed suicide, including two members of the Washington Company who had found nothing after panning on the Trinity. Some ended up in an insane asylum in San Francisco. Others went to work in the burgeoning cities of Sacramento and San Francisco to fill the acute shortage of skilled workers in virtually every trade from carpenters and masons to seamstress and farmers. Still others refused to admit defeat, especially after the hardship and expense they had endured getting there, not to mention the abject shame in returning empty-handed. As news of new strikes periodically surfaced, it only served to convince the unlucky that gold was just around the corner. And so they dug, dammed, and blasted, refusing to give up on their dream.

Miners who stayed with it eventually learned most of the gold turned out to be embedded in quartz veins buried deep in the earth. Extracting this gold required even more sophisticated techniques and extensive labor. The methods were as effective as they were costly. To get at the gold, mines were built with tunnels and timber supports and a device to crush the quartz. This required capital, which usually came from investors in major cities. With few miners finding gold on their own, it wasn't long before emigrants ended up working for a large operation for daily wages. Given the high cost of provisions in the valley, most were not much better off than they had been at home.

Another thing that miners deduced was that the gold was being washed down by erosion of quartz veins in the mountains' fissures. Over time, they noticed that gold became coarser as they ascended streams, giving rise to the belief that farther up lay a single massive source of the precious metal thought to be a mother lode beyond anyone's wildest dreams. In late June, Bruff and Lassen had begun to hear of a body of water in the mountains believed to lie between the Feather and Yuba Rivers called "Gold Lake" said to be "laden with nuggets of the purest gold." The fantastic rumor had been circulating for several months, and miners had perished searching the High Sierras for it. The Indians, too, believed in a lake lined with gold and infested with demons.

Bruff laughingly dismissed any notion of such a lake. But when Lassen organized a prospecting party, he immediately signed on in the hope he might find in the hills "a rich gold place, if not a gold lake." For Lassen it wasn't a question whether such a lake existed, only where it was to be found. In addition to Lassen and Bruff, the Gold Lake party consisted of several Americans, another Dane, and two Russians, one of whom spoke not a word of English. One of the Americans was Bruff's shooting companion, Dr. Drinker, who agreed to become partners with Bruff in the venture—a common practice among miners—and share in any gold found. Such was their rosy expectation they would soon all be fabulously rich.

Lassen's party wasn't the only one in search of Gold Lake. The rumor had touched off something of a mini-Gold Rush that summer. Hundreds of men were scouring the hills and gorges between the Feather and Yuba Rivers in search of it.

By June, Lassen realized he had been swindled by Wilson and Palmer. Attempting to string the gullible Dane along, Wilson sent him a letter expressing his pleasure at the purchase of the boat and encouraging Lassen to sow extensive vegetable gardens in Benton City. Meanwhile, Palmer had already sold his share in Lassen's ranch to a newly arrived emigrant from Maine, Colonel Charles L. Wilson (unrelated to the general), and absconded to Oregon. To add insult to injury, Wilson's son, William, had sold virtually all the supplies Lassen had brought up from Sacramento as well as his cattle, and Lassen never saw a penny of the profits. The final blow struck when Charles Wilson, who was bringing up the *Lady Washington* from Sacramento, hit a snag and sank the ship.

Looking to reverse his losses, Lassen turned to Gold Lake. On a sultry afternoon on July 14, he and a large company of Indians and pack animals started up the trail toward Big Meadows where he maintained a depot. After outfitting at Big Meadows, Lassen and several men set out with some of the French half-breed Oregonian Indians—Fox and Battis—he employed at the depot.

Still nursing a mild case of typhoid, Bruff planned to follow four days later with several other men. In the meantime, he ran Lassen's store. While sleeping one night at the ranch, Bruff dreamed he was home in a room containing kegs of gunpowder with loose grains of powder on the floor. Having carelessly thrown a burning match down, he suddenly became alarmed, ordering his wife and children to bolt from the house to save their lives.

Three days later, feeling well enough to travel, he set out for Big Meadows. Strangely enough, while sleeping in camp, he was suddenly awakened by a sensation of heat. Assuming it was the effect of the sun's rising, he rose up to see the pine straw around him ablaze. His knapsack containing his salt pork and beef jerky as well as some implements were being consumed by the fire. The rifles and powder horns, all charged, were propped up against a pine tree with flames licking up all around. Rousing the party, Bruff frantically pulled the weapons from the fire and salvaged what he could of the food. In his first quest for gold, Bruff had narrowly averted yet another freak accident presaged in the strange dream five nights earlier.

On the ride out, one of the Indian women traveling with Bruff had to dismount in order to give birth. Emerging calmly from the bushes a half-hour later, the mother mounted with the infant wrapped in a gray rag, although it did not survive the ride. On July

25, they caught up with Lassen's party, which was prospecting on a western branch of the Feather River, where it was reported much gold had been taken. The next day they panned for gold in a northern branch of the Feather farther up but found merely "a streak." As the party reconnoitered for Gold Lake, they panned for gold in streams and rivers all along the way but found nothing. Lassen's men were learning the same painful truth that other emigrants had: Finding gold was as much a function of luck as anything else.

Up the trail they rode through grassy meadows, over hills thick with pine and oak, and along ridges still encrusted with winter snow. Bruff was still too feeble to ride in the saddle, as evidenced by his entry for July 27:

> *When we reached the hills . . . we had an ardious [sic] time getting up. - Our course we had to scramble and drag our animals up by the reins. I grew very weak, with severe pains . . . [It was] as much as I could do to keep in the saddle, during the last 2 hours. I was so ill and weak. It was about 5 p.m. when with the greatest difficulty, I dismounted here unsaddle[d] my horse, and threw me on the ground, upon the smoking horse-blanket, and laid two full hours in a feverish lethargy, and exhausted.*

All throughout the expedition, Bruff would struggle with his health, racked with fever, chills, nausea, and mind-numbing headaches. In his weakened condition, several boils had developed on his legs, making the rough ride all the more painful. At their altitude, nights dipped below freezing, which only added to his suffering. Like other sick gold miners, he self-medicated, ingesting copious amounts of opium, quinine, rhubarb "to correct bad blood," cream of tartar, and blue mass (which contained dangerously high amounts of mercury). Apart from the fact that he was now holding down food, he was little better than when he had descended from Deer Creek in April. He did not even feel well enough to smoke his beloved pipe.

One afternoon, Bruff was awakened from a "feverish sleep" by an outcry of Lassen's Indians. On rising he saw six mounted Indians that looked like Pitt coming into camp. One of them dismounted and gave a long speech accompanied by angry gesticulations in a language no one understood. One of his comrades, who spoke a mixture of Spanish and English, then came forward and said they, the whites, were good but that Lassen's Indians were not. On inquiring into the reason for their hostility, Bruff learned that while out hunting for gold three miles to the east, the half-breeds had robbed one of the Pitt of some dried salmon and his bow and arrows. To placate the aggrieved Indians, Bruff offered some dried salmon, which seemed to have settled the matter.

Before sunset, however, a much larger party of Indians entered the camp solemnly in single file. Their faces were daubed in black and large black streaks were on their arms and breasts. Realizing they were war symbols, Bruff pulled out his weapons and set them within easy reach. Two of the Indians embarked on angry tirades, although no one could understand what they were saying. Then an old dark chief spoke. Once again the tone was angry. Bruff deduced the Indians had come to seek redress for the robbery, failing which they would kill all of Lassen's Indians. Since some salmon had been earlier offered as restitution, this time Bruff instructed them to hand over the bow and arrows. At this, the aggrieved chief exclaimed, "Bueno!" and the Indians departed. Once again Bruff had defused a tense situation and probably saved the lives of Lassen's Indians.

Shortly after the incident, Captain Lyon passed through Big Meadows on his way down to the settlements. Lyon had been to the site of Warner's murder but had found only some quadruped bones that they deduced were the remains of a mule. Other bones they recovered had been so mutilated by wild animals as to make them unidentifiable as human remains. Lyon and his men were too sick with typhoid to make camp and conduct an extended search and were returning to the settlements. Before leaving he managed to locate General Wilson's law library cached in the Fandango Valley. On opening it, however, Lyon found that nearly everything had been destroyed by the elements. Given the scarcity of legal texts in the new territory of California, Lyon salvaged about 50 volumes he thought would be valuable for the fledgling territory.

On August 12, several of Lassen's men came down to Big Meadows on their way to the settlements for more provisions. That Lassen had found nothing at Cow Creek or around Snow Butte only convinced him they were narrowing down the area where the lake was to be found. Any day now, Lassen expected to stumble upon it, and then each man would reap their mule-load of gold. He decided the best way to cover ground was to break up into two groups. Four men would go with Lassen to prospect in the Shasta region—a risky venture, for it was Pitt country—and a second group would explore the promising Feather River Valley and its tributaries. Too sick to travel, Bruff languished at Big Meadows, passing the time reading, playing monte, and shooting his rifle.

A week later, two men came up from Rich Bar on the Feather claiming diggers there, including J. J. Myers, were taking an astonishing $100 to $1,500 of gold a day and that shares in the claim were selling for $10,000 each. Three men had made $2,000 each a day over three days. The very area where Lassen and his men had unsuccessfully prospected days earlier was now miraculously yielding 60 pounds of gold a day!

And so the tales of riches ran. Stories of fabulous gold strikes sent men scrambling from one stream to another in a fevered—and usually fruitless—search for the elusive metal. Even though he, too, hoped to find his fortune, Bruff wisely saw through the rumors:

Thus the gold-stories run.-- One, whose veracity you can rely on, tells you that a few only, are doing remarkably well, numbers are making about 1 oz. per day, and hundreds are not earning their salt. (the most likely) Whilst another, whose veracity you have no right to question, informs you that hundreds are very rapidly accumulating fortunes, - none making less than $100 per day, etc.

As if to confirm his suspicions, that very afternoon four men came through Big Meadows from the same locale with nothing to show for their efforts except malaria and a near scrape with the Pitt Indians. With so few finding gold and fewer still striking it rich, Bruff nonetheless refused to return home to his wife, now a "California widow," and children. Even after three months of fruitless searching in ravines and creeks, he was convinced he would find "rich deposits" to compensate him for the enormous expenditure of time and money—not to mention physical suffering—since leaving Washington. After all the fanfare surrounding his departure, to return without gold would be a shameful defeat, even for the eternally stoic Bruff.

One day he ventured out to prospect on his own. Near the Feather River, he discovered a white quartz vein, but it contained no gold. Four miles farther up the trail, he surveyed several dry gulches that had not so much as a flake of gold dust. In a tributary of the North Fork of the Feather he found some promising sandbars. All proved empty. After examining several more hollows, Bruff at last spotted a vein of white quartz ten feet wide that had been shattered by the frost. Here he found several specks of gold and two small nuggets the size of buckshot. All told, the gold could not have been worth more than $20.

On August 20, the party that had gone to the settlements came up with food, supplies, and mail for Bruff, the first letters from home he had received since leaving the Missouri more than a year ago. Accompanying the group was none other than James Marshall. Since the day Marshall had first stumbled upon the nuggets shimmering in the American River, bad luck continued to haunt him, as even he had found little gold.

Later that day, Poyle came by and related his misadventures in the diggings around Redding. While miners explored for gold, Wintun Indians had swept off cattle, horses, and provisions at every opportunity. Day and night the Wintun fired arrows at the miners, forcing them to work with their rifles by their side and sleep in log defenses. Even though several men had been killed, the miners stubbornly refused to form a reprisal party lest it detract from their mining activities. Bruff attributed the cause of the conflict to whites. Whatever the reason, the fact was that digging had become dangerous in some areas.

Indeed, the next day, two men rode in from the northern mines with a wounded man, Frank Pickering, spitting blood. While Pickering was serving as night guard, the Pitt had fired a volley of fifteen arrows at him, hitting him with three. The next day he passed away and was buried beneath a large pine. At the burial Bruff gave the eulogy and penciled an epitaph on a makeshift headboard—although no one was quite certain where Pickering was from. To keep wolves from unearthing the body, he piled rocks on the grave. By now he had lost count of the number of people he had buried.

Miners were now chafing for revenge. The day after Pickering's death, several of the men who had brought him in were headed back toward the Pitt Valley to search for Gold Lake when they came upon two Indians, an old man and a boy, hunting squirrels. Taking the two Indians prisoner, they held a consultation as to whether they should kill them on the spot to avenge Pickering's death. Perhaps thinking the reprisal would only escalate tensions, saner heads prevailed and the two Indians were given a hearty meal ... and their liberty.

Dangerous though gold mining was in some areas, Bruff wasn't getting any richer lazing around Big Meadows. Now that he was ready to join Lassen, he no idea where Old Pete was.

While he waited for Lassen to return to base camp for more provisions, he and Poyle formed a small party to explore the white quartz vein Bruff had discovered a day's ride out on a tributary of the North Fork of the Feather. To get there, they traversed rugged ridges, forded creeks, and ascended and descended hills so steep they had to lead their horses by foot. All along the way, they prospected in every dry gulch they came upon, leaving no stone unturned. On the second day out they located the quartz vein, eight or ten feet wide and broken in blocks by the frost. Poking around the loose gravel, Bruff found a few specks of gold and two pear-shaped gold nodules "as large as robin shot."

During the ascent, Poyle came down with chills and vomiting, and the other two men had contracted mountain fever. Too sick to continue and still with no word of Lassen's whereabouts, they returned the next day to Big Meadows. Taking a roundabout route, they prospected in several dry, pebbly brooks and mountain rills, to no avail. One pleasurable moment came when Bruff encountered his old friend from the previous winter, Seymour (author of the *Emigrants' Guide*), who was prospecting with his son along the Feather. Starting in Yuba City some 30 miles west, they had prospected all the way up the Feather and found not so much as a speck of gold.

On September 11, several men rode into Big Meadows with word that Lassen was camped in a meadow about eight miles south of the Feather. He was starving and the animals were exhausted. In their determination to find Gold Lake, they had traveled 40 miles north of Mt. Shasta and from there 200 miles to the east and south. All along their route they had been harassed by the Pitt Indians, who nearly captured one of the men had it not been for the spectacular performance of his mule, which was so terrified by the howling devils chasing it that it leaped 40 feet clear across a deep stream.

With winter approaching, Lassen decided to step up his search. To cover more ground, he increased the size of the party to twenty-three men and broke them up into five distinct search parties. Believing he was on the verge of the momentous discovery, he sent word to base camp for Bruff to bring 20 more days of rations from the settlements.

On his way into the settlements to purchase the provisions, Bruff ran into a young man named Gibbs from Boston. Gibbs, who had accompanied his uncle, told Bruff they had found a large hidden freshwater lake—none other than the fabled Gold Lake—east of the Pitt River, nestled high in the mountains and surrounded by three buttes. The lake was deeply set and could only be seen from the crest of a high ridge. So laden with gold was it that Gibbs and his uncle culled $5,000 in the form of walnut-sized nuggets in a few hours. Gibbs's uncle, a government surveyor, had gone back to Boston to procure a quartz-crushing machine. When Bruff asked to see the location on a map, Gibbs said unfortunately, his uncle had lost the map while crossing the Isthmus of Panama. When asked to be guided there, Gibbs claimed he could not recall the route that had led him to the mythical place but that surely with the information he provided the many squads of men combing the area would be able to find it. The only part of this fantastic tale that Bruff felt bore any resemblance to reality was that a few of the men had been wounded by Indians.

That miners failed to see the many contradictions in Gibbs's far-fetched tale shows just how gullible and desperate they were. Few bothered to wonder why Gibbs, who related his story to everyone he encountered, shared what most would consider a precious secret, or why his uncle—if he indeed had one—was buying a crushing machine when gold could be harvested right from the surface. Bruff concluded Gibbs was in league with the traders, "mining the miners," just as Sam Brannan and so many others had done:

> [Every hollow the prospectors saw, must contain the lake; Every one or 2 buttes must be the 3 buttes; and of course any of these features, with hostile Indians to complete them, formed the exact country they sought; regardless of the character of the earth or rocks! It was amusing, and I've often laughed out, when I thought how easy it was to start such excitement.

As the men were packing, one of them even had his own story about Gold Lake. The individual knew a man who had started out from the States with five comrades. When they reached Lassen's Trail below Goose Lake, they took a cut-off in the form of a diagonal beeline for the settlements. Near the headwaters of the Yuba River, to their astonishment, they found, deeply basined and ringed with high mountains, a lake filled with gold pebbles. They managed to take $30,000 of gold before all of the man's comrades were murdered by the Indians. Conveniently, he alone escaped along with all the gold. Caching $20,000 of it, he took the rest with him, traveling by night and following the Yuba until he reached Yuba City.

As the man was relating his story, Bruff overheard whisperings and intrigues among the men as to who should go and who should stay behind. In anticipation of soon becoming fabulously rich, the men had begun to maneuver as to who should be the first to benefit from their fabulous discovery. Repulsed by their greedy behavior, Bruff would have taken off on his own, had it not been for his friend Lassen. As the men were scheming, a thunderstorm passed, leaving the mountains white with snow. Time was running out.

Bruff's contribution to the expedition was 50 pounds of flour, 10 pounds of sugar, some saleratus (a precursor to baking soda) for making bread, and two pounds of coffee. The contribution entitled him to an equal share in the Gold Lake harvest—or any other gold find. Having taken ill, Dr. Drinker returned to the settlements, leaving Bruff with no partner until Lassen's agent invited him to partner with Old Pete.

On the afternoon of the 14th, the party of seventeen set out from Big Meadows for the Pitt River Valley. By nightfall they reached Lassen's camp of six men. All night long it rained, and Bruff had gotten so wet he sat against a tree shivering under two wet blankets "like Ajax, defying the lightning." At 2 a.m., the men were so cold they made a fire and gathered round. It was an inauspicious start to the great gold hunt.

On and up they rode toward the valley, all the while on the lookout for hostile Pitt. They covered about 15 miles a day, fording cold streams and ascending and descending steep hills. Most of the time they were being watched by the Paiute and Pitt Indians, who peered at them from behind bushes or ridges, discreetly avoiding direct contact. Unable to see them, the men relied on the keen sensitivity of their horses and mules to know if Indians were nearby. Upon hearing a sound, usually inaudible to the men, the animals would invariably snort, prick their ears, and look in the direction of the sound. When that happened, the men would instantly dismount and lie on the ground and listen attentively. Occasionally, they would see a tribe's smoke signals warning others in the tribe of the approach of strangers, which kept the men constantly on their guard against attack.

All along the Pitt River they explored before turning east over a barren plain covered with volcanic rock and riven with deep canyons. For nine days they searched mostly in the rain and drizzle, sometimes passing over old ground. Obsessed with finding the lake, most were oblivious to the beauty of the Sierras, but Bruff took in the majestic scenery with the rapt wonder of a child. On the sixth day out, the skies began to clear and he beheld the graceful volcanic cone of Mt. Shasta appearing as if floating on a cloud. After crossing Fall Creek, a tributary of the Pitt, Bruff climbed a promontory to behold a stunning sight:

> *To the S.W. extended Pitt River Valley and plains; green and dry grass, marsh, pools and streams of water, in all the beautiful colors of a rich landscape. Then the hills rising from the level plain as if from the bosom of a calm sea, growing darker, bolder, and loftier, in all the tints of green, grey & blue, til they reached the majestic snow-crowned Tschastes. - A short distance, apparently, to the E. of the old sage, rises the dark form of the Snow Buttes, with patches of snow about their tops, and light floculent [sic] clouds passing by them, sometimes seeming to cut them in half. Pitt river, in the warm sun, looked like a silver thread.*

The next day they turned southeast toward Honey Lake. As Bruff was approaching a grassy-lined stream to browse his horse, he spotted a naked Indian squatting on the opposite bank motioning with his hands for the men to scram. One of Bruff's messmates in the rear shouted to him, "Shoot the damned son of a gun!" Even though they all wanted to avenge Pickering's death, Bruff felt he needed a reasonable pretext to do so and refused to kill an innocent Indian in cold blood.

After nine days they had ridden over a hundred miles over difficult terrain, mostly in the rain. Yet the lack of success only hardened Lassen's resolve. After nine days of traveling, Lassen convened a council to determine their next course of action. The group decided to ride a day east, after which they would then determine their next move. After breakfast, Bruff decided to make a side visit to a curious white cone-shaped peak two miles in the distance. Accompanied by one of his messmates, Isadore Merowitz, they hiked west on foot. The air was so pure that they were deceived by the peak's distance, which turned out to be six miles away. When they arrived at the base of the volcanic peak, they doffed their overcoats and scampered up over huge masses of angular volcanic rock. Out of breath, they paused for a moment to rest. As they were about to move on, something struck the ground on which Bruff was about to step. As they looked around for the object, an arrow struck the ground near Merowitz. Wheeling around, Merowitz shot blindly to his right before the men beat a hasty retreat to the bottom of the hill. Once at the bottom, Bruff called to Merowitz not to continue running, for it might embolden the Indians to pursue them. If either of them were injured, Bruff cautioned, it would lead to both their deaths and possibly those of the men back at camp. Slowly and stealthily they crept back to camp, arriving safely to tell their story around the campfire that night, much to the men's great amusement. Old Pete said they might "tank their Got" they weren't killed.

October 1 began with frost and controversy about which course to take. Bruff chimed in that it was all the same to him, as each mile produced new scenery; such had his faith diminished in finding any gold whatsoever. Turning southeast, they entered Snowstorm Canyon, a picturesque defile about 60 feet wide with sheer walls rising to 25 feet. All along the right wall for nearly 30 miles were petroglyphs characteristic of the Great Basin Indians, which Bruff studied with great interest.

On October 4, Bruff and Lassen arrived at the shores of present-day Honey Lake, about 40 miles directly east of Big Meadows. Nestled in the heart of tall dark mountains, the placid lake looked like liquid silver. As they approached the shoreline, they saw black smoke ahead: Indians had burned the grass to prevent the men from ascending the valley. For several miles along the trail, flames licked up and crackled. As they made their way through the inferno, Bruff and Lassen readied their rifles but could see no Indians, obscured as they were by the thick clouds of smoke. Turning off the trail, they led their horses down an embankment and made camp among some large willow trees. They slept with their rifles by their sides. As they were finishing their breakfast of jerky and tea the next morning, a couple of Indians dressed in rabbit skins and white deer moccasins blithely entered the camp. Ignoring Bruff and his messmates, they went straight to the fire and warmed their hands. To appease them, Lassen offered them a handful of jerky. As they ate, Bruff sat down to sketch the wild-looking pair.

On and on they rode in sunshine and rain, sometimes snow, through dark canyons, across high stony tablelands, and over steep granite-studded ridges. The trail was rough and the men were on their guard day and night against Indian attack. On October 8, the men were snacking on some jerky when an Indian appeared from the willows. Approaching Bruff and Lassen, he began to sign while Lassen interpreted. According to the Indian, in a day's march in the direction they were going they would find gold in abundance and miners at work there. Lassen asked him to guide them to the place but the Indian refused. Grateful for the information, Lassen gave the old man a tattered shirt and a piece of bread. Moving up the valley, they panned for gold at a natural dam but found nothing. Snow and cold were rapidly closing the door on the fruitless expedition. One night Bruff went to sleep with a headache and fever and dreamed that his family and friends—indeed, the whole world—had abandoned him "because I had not found a gold mine."

The next day they panned for gold in a branch of the Feather. Digging a hole and extracting the soil, they washed it but found not so much as an iota of gold dust. Ill all day, Bruff took some laudanum and rhubarb. The next day they essayed the soil on the north branch of the Middle Fork of the Feather—nothing.

At long last, Bruff had seen the elephant. It was time to return home.

Had such a lake existed or was it merely a figment of miners' imagination? Perhaps a bit of both. For a few days later one of the men in the Gold Lake party told Bruff that while at Honey Lake, he had asked an old Indian if he knew of such a place. Unable to speak English, the Indian took a piece of saddle leather, and sprinkling sand over it, proceed to draw a map of the region. With astonishing ingenuity, the Indian heaped up sand to form buttes and ranges. With a straw, he then drew streams, lakes, and even trails. After adjusting the entire layout to correspond with the cardinal points, he explained where the lake was to be found. Pointing to the sun, he indicated the number of days' travel to each of the landmarks he had fashioned, from Mary's River to the Carson and finally to Pyramid Lake, and explained that whites with guns were traveling along the trails. The Indian then pointed at a lake with a deep basin surrounded by three buttes where gold was plentiful. Ten months earlier, whites had tried to mine at the lake but clashed with Indians there. Several of Lassen's men went in search of the lake and found the Indian's sand map correct in distance and direction. But when they arrived at the lake, they were repelled by Paiutes and were never able to determine if it contained gold.

On October 17, Bruff ate breakfast and set out for the Sacramento Valley 67 miles below. The next day he passed for the last time the site of his winter ordeal that would forever be known as "Bruff's Camp." Five days later, he limped into the Lassen ranch, his horse Bravo barely able to support him. Soon the mountains would be covered in snow, putting prospecting on hold until spring for most miners.

For his part, Lassen refused to give up on the lake and decided not to return to his ranch. Instead he and nine others would winter in the Feather River Valley and continue their search.

According to Bruff:

Old Pete expressed a strange desire, to return at this season, to one of the Feather River valleys we passed through, to prospect, and pass the winter. He seems to entertain a great repugnance to returning to the old ranch.

Perhaps Lassen wished to avoid the scorn being heaped on him by emigrants for apparently having deceived them about the trail. Also, his dealings with Wilson and his associates had left him little to return to. To prepare for the long winter, Lassen dispatched several men to the settlements for enough food to last six months.

In his failure to find gold, Bruff could take solace in the sad fact that he was not alone. Relatively few miners found the gold they had traveled so far to find, and fewer still became rich. Many had spent their life savings to get to California and for all their time and hardship had little or nothing to show for it. It was a tragic ending to a journey that had begun with much excitement and promise.

Even as more gold seekers streamed in, thanks to continuing sensational reports of big strikes by the Californian and eastern papers, others had also seen their elephant and were heading home either because they were rich or more likely because they failed to find anything but hardship and high prices. Like Bruff, most Gold Rushers were heading home within a season or two of their arrival, usually with nothing to show for their efforts. William Swain, who had been on the trail a few days from Bruff and prospected for more than a year, was back in New York by late 1850 with about $500 in gold dust, less what it had cost him to travel there and back. Emigrant Sarah Royce summed up the frustration of most miners:

> *Discontent: for most of them had come to California with the hope of becoming easily and rapidly rich; and so, when they had to toil for days before finding gold, and, when they had found it, had to work hard in order to wash out their "ounce a day," and then discovered that the necessaries of life were so scarce it took much of their proceeds to pay their way, they murmured, and some of them cursed the country, calling it a "God forsaken land," while a large number bitterly condemned their own folly in having left comfortable homes and moderate business chances, for so many hardships and uncertainties.*

Alonzo Delano, who traveled far and wide through the Sierras seeking gold, offered this sad assessment:

Wherever we turned, we met with disappointed and dis-heartened men, and the trails and mountains were alive with those whose hopes had been blasted, whose fortunes had been wrecked, and who now, with empty pockets and weary limbs, were searching for new diggings, or for employment — hoping to get enough to live on, if nothing more. Some succeeded, but hundreds, after months and years of toil, still found themselves pining for their homes, in misery and want, and with a dimmed eye and broken hopes.

It is difficult to know precisely how much gold was taken in 1849. Estimates range from $10 million to $40 million. Even allowing for the highest figure, that came to about $100 per man per month, hardly the riches promised by the government and the eastern newspapers, and a small return given the hardships and cost of provisions. Between 1849 and 1857, a total of $500 million of gold had been mined in California. That more than 100,000 miners were in on the competition during those 10 years works out to less than $500 per man per year. In the sky-high prices of Gold Rush California, simply feeding yourself could cost that much.

Perhaps the saddest irony was that as they hurried across Nevada, gold seekers passed by far more gold there than would ever be mined in California.

Chapter Thirteen

THE JOURNEY HOME

FOR SEVERAL DAYS BRUFF WAS LAID UP AT LASSEN'S, nursing a mild case of cholera. He passed the time transcribing his notes and putting the finishing touches on several sketches from the Gold Lake hunt. In his absence, Lassen had put brother Bruff in charge of the ranch. No sooner had he arrived when he was drawn into a simmering conflict between whites and Indians.

The previous year one of Davis's sons had killed an Indian for refusing to restrain his brother, whom he wished to chastise for some perceived slight. The defiant Indian had absconded 10 miles down the valley to the safety of an Indian village, vowing one day to avenge the murder of his brother. One of the workers at the ranch had recently spotted the aggrieved Indian, who had come to see relatives and friends in a nearby village. When the Davis boy heard of this, he went to the village, took the Indian captive, and tied him to a tree. Taking a green leather thong, Davis whipped the Indian savagely until he was nearly unconscious. Later, the Indian recovered and managed to free himself. As he was escaping, one of the ranch hands fired upon him and he staggered off, wounded, into the brush.

The next day Bruff had an Indian guide take him to see the

wounded Indian, who was hiding in a copse of willows on an island in the middle of Deer Creek. After traveling a half-mile along the creek bank, they crossed to the island and followed a narrow trail through thick brush, crawling on hands and knees through a briar patch. They found the Indian in a small clearing, slumped over under a blanket in great pain as several grief-stricken women stood by helplessly. Examining the boy's back, Bruff found several deep scars and some buckshot wounds below the shoulder blades.

Unable to treat him in the bush, Bruff had his guide accompany him back to the ranch, where he gave him some vials of laudanum for the pain and a pewter teaspoon with instructions on how to administer it. When Lassen came in unexpectedly, Bruff related the incident to him. Upon hearing of the cruel treatment of the Indian, Lassen wept, saying he knew the boy to be harmless. "Captain Bruff," he said, "that's his reward for speaking in defense of his murdered brother."

Yet another problem had arisen in his absence—Lassen had been robbed. Earlier that week Bruff had been looking for some tools in Lassen's trunk when he noticed that it had been broken into. Not knowing what it contained, he was unable to determine what, if anything, had been taken. When the two checked the trunk, Lassen found all his gold had been pinched—and for the second time.

Whenever Bruff left the house, he always locked the padlock on the door and turned it over with the key still in it. He suddenly recalled that Nicholas Loux, the German emigrant whose friend Lassen had tried to rescue at Deer Creek, lived 300 yards from the camp in a tent belonging to Lassen. Since the German could see from his tent whenever Bruff left the ranch, he concluded Loux had committed the theft. After Bruff conferred with some of Lassen's men, they devised a plan to exact a confession from him to recover the property.

In the morning they sent one of Lassen's men to arrest Loux and bring him to the ranch where 15 men—the impromptu judge and jury—were gathered. On a bluff, Bruff accused the German of the theft, adding Loux had even been seen with the gold. Unless he produced it immediately, he would be hanged within a half-hour. Pointing to a clock on the wall, Bruff advised Loux to note the exact time.

> We all looked very grave and solemn, and I told the accused that I thought it exceedingly foolish for a man to be hanged like a dog, rather than give up stolen property. - That we all regretted the awful necessity, but could pursue no other course here; and were compelled to be judge, jurors, and execution-ers . . . We told the accused also, that the enormity of the crime was magnified by base ingratitude towards his benefactor; and we watched his countenance, which was down-cast; for he could not look one of us in the face; and he stammered, and told contradictory accounts of his visit to the room.

Loux, however, remained silent. One of the men then took down a rawhide lasso off the wall and, holding it close to the German, proceeded to grease the noose. Others in the jury began to discuss how to tie it to a tree loud enough so that Loux could hear them. Still, he said nothing. Leaning toward him, Bruff asked the accused if he wanted to make a statement of farewell for his wife and children back in New York. Clearing the table, Bruff handed Loux a pencil and paper and said he would forward the message after the execution. At this point, Nicholas produced some fake tears, mumbling he could only write in German. This Bruff flatly rejected. Wishing to maintain the momentum of the contrived drama, Bruff wrote a letter that diplomatically skirted around an outright confession. After Bruff read it aloud, the German signed his name. Then a member of the jury shouted, "Don't be a damned fool! But go, and get the damned gold, and save your damned neck!" It was at this point that Loux became convinced the men were serious about lynching him. Visibly shaken, he asked if he could go to his tent and fetch a document he wished sent to his wife. When he reached his tent, Loux broke down and confessed to the theft. The gold, he said, was hidden nearby in a buckskin bag under a bush. When they found the bag, they counted $1,400 in gold coins—more or less what Lassen thought he had.

Even though Loux had confessed, the men weren't going to let him go unpunished. From among the men gathered, a "judge" was appointed as well as "lawyers" for California and the defense. After a short deliberation, the jury decreed that, in view of the man's feverish condition, that punishment be lenient. In keeping with informal Gold Rush justice, Loux was stripped naked, tied to a large oak tree and given 20 lashes on his back. He was also ordered to leave the ranch before daylight.

A few days later, Bruff began to prepare for the long trip home. He returned his horse Bravo to his owner; the animal was so worn out from the Gold Lake hunt that it could not be used for several months. His wagon and a few saddles he sold for $26. He then bade a hearty farewell to Old Pete, who headed off to winter in the Sierras to find Gold Lake.

On November 17, Bruff and several of his companions from the Gold Lake party set out by wagon for Sacramento City. Looking back toward the High Sierras, which had been his home for nearly a year, he took a last look at the towering peaks shrouded in dark clouds and feared for Lassen's well-being. If anyone knew the harshness of a Sierra winter, it was certainly Bruff.

In Placer City, he ran into Roberts and his family. Having just sold his house there for $8,000 in cash, the inveterate hoarder was moving the great pile of junk he had accumulated while at Deer Creek. Even as Bruff and other 49ers were leaving the gold fields by the thousands, thousands more were anxiously streaming in. Long trains of wagons, pack animals, and pedestrians passed by blithely unaware of the challenges and disappointments that lay ahead.

In Sacramento, Bruff was astonished by the hustle and bustle of the city. Once a sleepy village of 2,000, Sacramento had more than tripled in size since Marshall's discovery. The harbor was teeming with brigs, schooners, and steamers coming and going. While chatting on the waterfront with a shop owner he had known on the trail, who should pass by but his old friend, Dr. Austin. Austin told Bruff that both Col. Ely and Seymour, who had traveled for a time with the Washington Company along the Platte, had passed away. Austin handed him a letter dated October 9 from his wife that had been carried out by Frémont who, since his return to California, had been confined to his house with a case of neuralgia. Austin said that several men of the Washington Company had returned home dejected, having found no gold. Others in the Company who had not found gold had taken jobs in Sacramento.

Accompanied by Dr. Austin, Bruff went on a tour of the city, which had been laid out by Captain Warner. Everywhere was the convulsive activity behind the quest for gold: ships pulling into port, boxes piled high in the open air, auctioneers hawking cattle and mules to the newly arrived Argonauts. Candidates for municipal office were out pressing the flesh, for while Bruff was combing the Sierras for Gold Lake, California had become the Union's thirty-first state. In town, houses had been so hastily thrown up the partition walls were made of canvas and often came crashing down. A mile out from the city was a suburb of white tents of various sizes and shapes set up among the stout oak trees. In the back part of town, they came upon the ever-present dark side of the Gold Rush: an enormous graveyard of nearly 2,000 persons who had died the previous year, 900 of whom had succumbed two months earlier to a cholera epidemic in the city.

While in Sacramento, Bruff was approached by Messrs. McNairn and Young, who offered Bruff $10,000 in cash—an astounding sum for the time—for his sketches of the overland trail. The two entrepreneurs were hoping to make a "panorama" of the trail and countryside. Hugely popular for the time, panoramas were a state-of-the art form of entertainment and education that depicted scenes on wide, all-encompassing canvases. For the many people unable to travel to far-away places, panoramas brought the scene to life with stunning effect. Wisely, Bruff declined to part with his drawings, choosing instead to return home destitute but with a trove of a different kind.

On January 14, Bruff bid farewell to Dr. Austin, who had been such a trustworthy friend and companion on the trail. He boarded the steamer *New World* for San Francisco, where he planned to connect with a ship bound for Panama. When he reached the city, one last gold adventure beckoned. While walking down Montgomery Street, where two years earlier Sam Brannan had sounded the clarion call of California gold, Bruff ran into General Wilson. Shortly after arriving in San Francisco, the ill-tempered Wilson had found his office in disarray and abruptly resigned as Indian Agent. He then set up a lucrative law practice that charged clients exorbitant fees, as well as a vegetable garden and a "wash yard" or city laundry.

Having swindled Lassen out of most of his ranch, Wilson saw

an easy mark in Bruff. It is doubtful Bruff had knowledge of Lassen's unfortunate experience with Wilson, as he made no mention of it in his journal. Lassen seems not to have confided in Bruff about his misguided dealings with Wilson and Palmer, perhaps too ashamed to reveal he had been hoodwinked by the two scoundrels. But Bruff seemed to have forgotten how, after he generously assisted Wilson and his family at Deer Creek, Wilson had failed to live up to his promise to send a rescue party.

The wily general had recently embarked on a new venture: the Pacific Mining Company. Seeing in the unsuspecting Bruff another potential shareholder in his company, Wilson invited him to dine with him and his family at the St. Francis Hotel. Over dinner, Wilson plied Bruff with fabulous stories of a place called the Gold Bluffs where gold could be found in amounts that staggered the imagination.

Located on the northern California coast south of the Klamath River, the Gold Bluffs were the latest craze sweeping the region. And as always, a dramatic "discovery myth" lay behind the gold. In the fall of 1849, several miners working on the Trinity River were finding the high cost of provisions was eating into their profits. Having heard of Trinidad Harbor and believing the Trinity had been named after it, they came to the conclusion that it emptied into Trinidad Bay and could thus be used to bring in provisions at a far lower cost. It seemed like a practical idea but for one major flaw: the Trinity actually flowed into the Klamath, which emptied into the sea another 50 miles north of Trinidad.

On November 5, two parties set out from the northern mines to find Trinity Bay. One went by land, the other by sea. Led by Josiah Gregg, an explorer who had discovered the mouth of the Klamath River, the land party started from Rich Bar on the Trinity River with a dozen horses and mules and provisions for ten days. Along the way, they encountered a party of Indians who warned them not to follow the Trinity but to head due west. Ignoring their advice, the party continued along the river, which zigzagged wildly as it flowed north. On the eighth day, they ran out of provisions but were able to subsist on deer and smoked salmon. At the mouth of an unexplored river, Gregg wished to stop and take coordinates. An altercation ensued and the party took off, leaving Gregg behind. When Gregg caught up with his men on the bank of a river, he flew into such a rage that they named it "Mad River." When they reached the thick redwood forest, the party's pace was slowed to two miles a day and they did not reach the mouth of the Klamath until December 20, thirty-five days longer than they had planned. Unsure as to how to return, they followed the mountain above the coastline, but heavy snow and deep gulches slowed their pace. Low on ammunition, they were unable to live off the game and began to starve. Gregg, who was subsisting on acorns and herbs, had become so weak he fell from his horse and died.

The following spring, the party returned by steamer to the mouth of the Klamath to explore further. Following the coastline south, about 30 miles above Trinidad they came to some high cliffs rising straight out of the sea. At the foot of the cliffs they suddenly beheld, stretched out before them, a beach shimmering with gold. But because they had run out of food, they had only enough time to gather a few handfuls of sand containing the precious metal. When the sand was essayed in San Francisco, it was found to be 50 percent gold.

Just as the newspapers had exaggerated out of all proportion the amount of gold to be found in the Sierras, they were now reporting on the absurd quantities of gold to be found at the Bluffs. A reporter for the *Alta California* whimsically wrote "the gold is mixed with black sand, the proportion of from ten cents to ten dollars the pound . . . in spring the entire beach is covered with bright and yellow gold." Two types of sand contained the gold: the black, which was far richer in gold, and the gray, which was in greater abundance. Unlike the Sierra gold fields, where gold could be had only by back-breaking digging, the gold at Gold Bluffs required no digging whatsoever. One had only to bend over and scoop up a handful of sand to reap one's fortune.

By the fall of 1850, hundreds of enthusiastic gold seekers were descending on the Bluffs above Trinidad by land and sea. General Wilson, who had visited there in 1850, returned to Sacramento claiming the beach was literally strewn with gold. "Thousands of men cannot exhaust this gold in a thousand years," he told Bruff. The company secretary, John Collins, had also traveled there and found the beach below the Bluffs "covered with gold" for 15 miles. Having measured a sample of sand, Collins estimated it was so rich that it would yield no less than $43,000,000 in gold to each member of the company! Collins told one reporter he had met a man who had accumulated 50,000 pounds or 50 tons—he could not remember which—of the gold-laden sand. Having secured claims to parts of the Bluffs, on January 10 Collins put company stock on sale by public advertisement at $100 a share. Little did anyone know that, as Revenue Collector of the port of San Francisco, Collins had been forced to retire under a cloud. He was later sued by the government for nearly $1.5 million in missing revenue. The unscrupulous Collins also had ordered the seizure of foreign vessels, principally French, and then sold the ships' cargo, pocketing some $800,000. Another principal in the company was a General James Wilson (unrelated to John) who had been involved in a land claim fraud in California.

Despite Bruff's skepticism of gold stories, especially after his Gold Lake experience where he found virtually nothing, he too was swept up in the mania and signed on. He was nonetheless skeptical as evidenced by his remark, "And a company formed, called the Pacific Mining Company, to work it, - *or* more correctly, to sell shares." What could have induced him to risk another $100 chasing the phantom gold? Was it that the existence of gold had been confirmed by a military officer, a type for whom Bruff held an almost religious devotion? Or was it refusal to concede defeat after all he had been through? Or was it simply merely for the adventure of it all? We can only suppose it was a bit of each, for he was strangely silent as to his motives.

Two days after dining with Wilson, the company boarded the steamer *Chesapeake,* bound for Trinidad. While on board, Bruff met a member of his old Company and one from the Gold Lake hunt eager to try their luck in Trinidad. At sunrise three days later, after a rough ride over deep swells, the *Chesapeake* drifted into Trinidad Bay and dropped anchor in a cove. George Lemon, a member of the company, was on hand to greet Bruff and invited him to stay at his ranch.

Wasting little time, Generals John and James Wilson, whom Bruff slavishly referred to as "the two greatest men of the party," mounted their pack mules, already loaded with bedding and provisions. Bruff fell in with the rank and file who would make the 30-mile trek to Gold Bluffs on foot. Whatever the outcome, at least the journey would be less taxing physically than Gold Lake had been.

Or so Bruff thought. After hiking a couple of miles along the high cliffs overlooking the Pacific, they came upon a series of deep gulches conveying brooks flowing to the sea. For six miles they crossed icy streams and ascended and descended muddy hills and brushy hollows. Descending to the shoreline, they slogged through heavy sand for several miles before re-ascending the high cliffs. After 22 miles traipsing up and down, Bruff began to suc-cumb to the hardship of the journey. This time he was stricken "with the most severe paroxysm of hemorrhoids, I had ever expe-rienced, causing me frequently to prostrate myself, in agony, on the ground."

Even though Bruff was a shareholder, the company callously left him behind. But one member of the company, John Lewis, refused to abandon him in such feeble condition. Limping along, by dusk the two had reached a cove at the base of a high promontory, with no provisions. A cold wind was blowing a fine mist from the surf onto them. Taking shelter in a niche in a cliff, Bruff threw his wet body down on the sand in pain and fatigue. Lewis found a wooden plank and, chipping it up, managed to get a small fire going. As the rain began to fall, the men reclined against one another in front of the fire, "alternately dozing, and gathering fuel, smoking our pipes and soliloquizing, we passed the wretched night." At daybreak, his sense of humor still intact, Bruff asked Lewis if he did not think, "according to sound architectural principles that their apartment was not well ventilated."

In late morning, the two set out from their grotto toward the cliff above. Once on top they found several two-foot circular springs and slaked their thirst with fresh water. After another mile, they once again descended to the beach and slogged three miles through the heavy sand. As they were passing a deserted Indian village, Lewis told Bruff that the previous summer Indians from the village had attacked a party of miners, wounding two. As the tribe had been known to kill whites before, the miners attacked the village, killing several Indians before the rest fled and, fortu-nately, never returned.

After a few miles they reached a body of fresh water overlook-ing the ocean: Redwood Lake. On the other side of the lake were several men operating a ferry, which they hailed. As the raft came up, to his surprise Bruff noticed one of the ferrymen had been a member of his Company, Thomas Williams, still looking for his first gold strike. Although low on provisions, Williams made the weary pair some tough flapjacks and re-boiled coffee, their first meal since the previous day. Williams informed them that General Wilson had passed through that morning and was about two hours ahead.

In the morning they pushed on for the Gold Bluffs. Once again the trail took them high above the ocean and down to the beach. After several exhausting miles they reached a damp, wooded ravine with several of the company's cabins huddled on the opposite side. They had reached the Gold Bluffs. Wilson and Collins were there to greet them and show them where they might camp under the stars.

After breakfast Bruff and Lewis walked a half-mile to the upper portion of the Bluffs. Here the Bluffs were towering sandstone cliffs crowned with large pines and firs. On the summit, the company had built a log cabin, a cook house, and a small dugout for sleeping quarters. From the cliff, Bruff could see the *Chesapeake*, moored about a half-mile from shore, which had come up with food and supplies for the company. Once it was offloaded, it would return to San Francisco for more supplies, pack animals, and passengers. The claim stake was so large it had been divided into three areas called "stations," each of which they planned to mine.

No sooner had Bruff began sleeping on the cool, damp ground than his rheumatism resurfaced, so painful he was unable to sleep. As the other men shuttled back and forth in row boats to offload *Chesapeake*, he lay feebly about camp sketching the bluffs, the Klamath Indians, and the dazzling, gigantic coastal redwoods. So large were the redwoods that one mammoth tree over 400 feet in height was felled to form a bridge across Mad River over which they led entire mule teams and wagons.

One afternoon Bruff ventured down to the beach to inspect the sand. As he sifted through the detritus, to his chagrin he found "many bones of whales . . . and numerous skate-fish, star-fish &c.- but no TREASURE." Farther up the shoreline he ran into a pale, beleaguered-looking Wilson. A short distance below the upper station Wilson had narrowly missed being buried by an avalanche when a section of the cliffs collapsed, sending a torrent of mud, rocks, and trees crashing into the sea. Bruff could commiserate: the same terrifying thing had happened to him moments earlier.

For two weeks the company lay in provisions and built more cabins, preparing for an ambitious excavation of the bluffs. But when the men attempted to mine the sand, they were unable to separate the gray sand from the black, which was believed to contain fine particles of gold. Then, as the heavy seas rolled in, they watched with dismay as the patches of black sand were swept away, and with them the company's dreams. For a time the miners waited, hoping that the seas would bring the sands back. Eventually, everyone got tired of waiting and by early February, the Gold Bluffs excitement died as quickly as it had flared up. Embarrassed, perhaps, by his credulity in having been taken in by Wilson and Collins, Bruff made no mention of the company's abject collapse.

On February 11, he returned to Trinidad with Wilson and Collins. In Trinidad they learned that the *Chesapeake* had started from San Francisco when it sprang a leak and was forced to throw all the mules overboard to lighten its load. With the mining venture now stillborn, Wilson disposed of the damaged ship for $2,000. He had purchased it for $20,000.

Was there gold at the bluffs? It turned out the cliffs did contain some gold, which was dislodged by the pounding of the surf. But the actual amount was minimal and difficult to extract from the unstable soil. Once again, a small truth had gotten exaggerated out of all proportion and led the gullible in search of a mirage.

In March, Bruff returned to San Francisco. Having seen more than one elephant on his journey, he curtailed his search for gold once and for all. For two months, he lingered in the city with no other purpose than to extend the grand adventure. And boomtown San Francisco provided the perfect venue.

Like everything else in California, San Francisco had been transformed overnight by the discovery of gold. Until an Englishman named William Richardson built his trading tent on the bay in 1835, the area's only building had been the Spanish Mission of Delores. The population of Yerba Buena, as it was then called, doubled when Sam Brannan led his group of 240 Mormons from the East Coast in 1846. After Brannan announced the discovery of gold, it was virtually empty for a time. When ships bearing Gold Rushers began arriving, they had to pass through the Golden Gate strait—presciently named by Frémont in 1846—and the city took off. By 1851, the population hit 30,000 and never looked back.

Unable to keep up with the number of people arriving each day, some of the hundreds of ships that had been left to rot in the mudflats were pulled ashore and converted to hotels, warehouses, and saloons. One became the city's first prison. To make more room, mudflats were reclaimed and hills leveled. Shoddy wood-frame structures were haplessly thrown up along with houses of canvas and rubber. In the surrounding hills, a suburb of tents appeared amid dwarf oak and sagebrush. Men lived six, ten, or more to a room and contagion was rife. A small single room at the Parker House rented for $1,800 a month. Better rooms went for $2,400. Because most buildings in the city were made of wood, fires quickly became conflagrations that consumed entire city blocks.

At midnight on May 3, Bruff was awakened in his hotel room by a fire alarm. Racing to a building on Montgomery Street where his notebooks and papers were stored, he frantically rescued them from the flames. The fire raged for ten hours and consumed 18 blocks. Some miners who arrived too late were left to sift through the ashes in search of their gold. Such was the energy of the city that within days rebuilding had begun, although a few impatient merchants had resumed operations right over the smoking embers.

Bruff found the city unlike anything back east. Here was a mixing of races unparalleled in the world: pig-tailed Mongols, turbaned Ottomans, Indians clad in deerskins, dark-skinned Hindus, black Africans, French, British, Chinese, Australians. Hardly a people or nationality was not represented in the rush for gold.

The influx of wealth had spawned an anything-goes atmosphere. Far from the disapproving eyes of family, church, and community, men with money to spend were free to indulge in activities that would be frowned upon at home. To cater to the demand, a profusion of saloons, gambling parlors, and bawdy houses sprang up, all "mining the miners." In saloons and gambling halls flooded with light and music, décolleté women sat at bars fraternizing with men or selling cigars from trays displayed below ample bosoms. Those who had struck it rich spent like drunken sailors. Prostitutes charged an ounce of gold to sit with a miner for the evening, or $200 to $400 for an entire night. Among women of easy virtue, French women were in greatest demand because of their perceived "charm of novelty." Some made enough in a month to return home and live comfortably. One prostitute reported making $50,000 in a single year. At the roulette wheel or monte table, stakes usually ran 50 cents to $5, although they could run as high as $1,000. Two bull-fighting arenas were added to the two already existing at the Delores Mission, sometimes featuring contests between bulls and bears.

Many newcomers from the east were often shocked by the level of debauchery in the city. As one miner described it:

The quantity of ardent spirits daily consumed is almost fright-ful. It is peddled out in every gambling room, on the wharves, at almost every corner, and, in some streets, in almost every house. Many of the taverns are of the lowest possible descrip-tion—filthy dens of vice and crime, disease and wretchedness.

If San Francisco had all the rawness of a frontier town, it also had a sophisticated side equal to any of the big cities of the east. It boasted seven daily newspapers, bi-weekly mail service, ten first-class hotels, a circus, museums, and two theaters. It had a variety of fine restaurants—French, Italian, Chinese, Polynesian, Chilean, Peruvian, Mexican—that reflected the great diversity of its popula-tion. Bruff partook of the full spectrum of the city's high and low life, for his March 20 entry read: "Circus, French Theater, Gam-bling, Drinking, and Preaching."

Not surprisingly, crime flourished in the raucous atmosphere. Thieves lurked in alleys waiting to bludgeon the unsuspecting passerby with a sandbag to the head. Some of them were from a British convict class from Sydney whose neighborhood was known as "Sydney Town." With little by way of government protection, citizens soon took justice into their own hands.

On June 9, 1851, Sam Brannan organized the city's Vigilance Committee to stem the growing wave of crime. In the wee hours of the following morning, Bruff was awakened by the tolling of a bell of the Monumental Engine Company at a nearby plaza. Making his way to the site, he found an angry mob assembled to witness the trial and hanging of a man by Brannan's Committee. The man, an Australian named John Jenkins, had snatched a safe from a shipping office. Jenkins had fled by boat, but his pursuers caught up with him and he threw the safe into the bay. On his way to the gallows, Jenkins was casually smoking a cigar and drinking brandy, his final request. When a minister offered the condemned spiritual consolation, he politely declined. While the noose was being placed around his neck, executioners searched his pockets and found $200 in gold. When Jenkins was asked if he had any friends to whom he wished to leave it, he replied it should be scattered among the mob. At 2 a.m. the loose end of the rope was thrown over a beam and several men drew sharply on it, hoisting Jenkins up to his demise. To set an example, he was left hanging until dawn. Within a month, three more of Jenkins's associates would be hanged for other offenses.

Shortly after the incident, Bruff began preparing to leave for Washington via Panama. There was no thought of returning overland. Even if he had the means, he had seen the frontier and was all too familiar with its hardships. With so many Argonauts anxious to quit El Dorado by sea—nearly 1,000 a week were departing—fares to Panama had skyrocketed to $300 for cabins and $125 for steerage. At those prices one would expect first-class accommodations, but most ships were squalid and infested with insects and rodents. Many of the ships had been abandoned two years earlier and had been hastily refitted to take advantage of the exodus. Food was often spoiled. Some ships ran out of food and water en route and had to be aided by passing ships.

With his maritime knowledge, Bruff was able to identify a decent steamer, the *California*, which had brought some of the very first gold seekers to California. The ship was commanded by his friend, Lieutenant Budd of the U.S. Navy. Several members of the Company came down to the wharf to see the good Captain off. On June 16, under clear skies, the ship set out for Panama. Its cargo included $1.2 million in gold. In good weather, steamers made the voyage to Panama City in 14 days, but during inclement weather it could take as long as 50. Bruff complained of the food, but otherwise the *California* encountered no mishap and arrived safely in Panama City on July 2.

Because Panama had no harbor, swarms of boats came up alongside to offload the passengers and baggage. Natives descended on the dock like a swarm of flies, shouting in English and Spanish as they fought with one another to shoulder a bag. In town, Bruff booked a room in the American Hotel. After settling in, he descended to the lobby to find a dozen natives all clamoring to be paid for bringing up his baggage. After considerable time spent determining to whom he was actually indebted and for how much, he doled out $2.50 and set out on a tour of the city. The streets were teeming with travelers, not only those wishing to go home but thousands of new emigrants anxiously headed for El Dorado. It was a derelict town, although Bruff found several interesting old buildings to sketch, including the town's Grand Cathedral.

As no ship had yet arrived on the other side of the isthmus at Chagres, Bruff was forced to lay over for a couple of days. Early on, American emigrants had found Panamanians lazy and incapable of providing the level of services they demanded, so they responded in a typically American way—they took over Panama. Panamanians didn't seem to mind, for on July 4 the entire city celebrated American Independence Day. A native band played "Hail Columbia" and Yankee Doodle" to everyone's satisfaction as drunken locals cheered "*Viva los Americanos!*"

At 10 a.m., a parade composed of native and American military officers assembled in the plaza. One of the officers, Captain Rogers, recognized Bruff in the crowd and invited him to march along. Bruff had last seen Rogers with the relief party on Lassen's

Trail. In the evening, the American consul invited him and the other Americans to the residence to partake in the celebrations and observe the fireworks display.

The next morning he set out on the last dangerous leg of his return: the overland journey to Chagres. To get to Chagres, Bruff had to go overland 25 miles through dense jungle to Cruces. From there he would take a small dugout, called *bungo*, down the crooked Chagres River 45 miles to Chagres. All along the route, brigands lay in wait for passing travelers and their gold. Americans had established a lynch law to deal with them, but it had little effect in deterring robbing or murder. In late morning, Bruff set out by mule well after the other passengers had left and accompanied only by the transit agent. The trail was once paved with large stones by the Spanish conquistador Francisco Pizzaro. But having been neglected over the years, it was now an obstacle course of large, upturned stones and ankle-breaking potholes. At length they came upon an old muleteer reclining beneath a tree. He informed them that 2 miles up at the entrance to a defile were three well-armed American brigands. Being alone, the muleteer had been waiting for stragglers to come up. As there were now three, Bruff determined their chances were now equal and they proceeded. On reaching the gorge, Bruff found it narrow, deep, and choked with foliage. After a half-mile they emerged from the gorge with no sign of the bandits. Others had not been so lucky. One party was robbed of $120,000 in gold on this leg of the trail.

After a brief but heavy downpour, they entered another gorge with a rough corduroy road made of logs and stones thrown willy-nilly in the mud. At dusk Bruff was approaching a defile when he saw several men on a cliff crouching by a fire. He called to them in Spanish if it was possible to pass to Cruces in the darkness. "No possible, God damn, you no can go Cruces esta night!" came the angry reply. Ignoring their warning, Bruff spurred his mule forward toward the gorge. In the gorge, it was already dark and Bruff took comfort that if there were robbers they could not see him. By 8 o'clock, he spotted the lights of Cruces. Just then a leopard's cry rang out in the jungle, causing his frightened mule to race uncontrollably down the hill toward the city.

At the American Hotel, Bruff met several acquaintances from the trail returning home—all with no gold. For fifty cents he was given a cot in a dormitory loft filled with more than 100 men. His baggage was still in the rear. Word was that a band of thirty well-armed brigands were on the road waiting for it, but by afternoon the baggage had come up.

For $5 he boarded a bungo, commanded by a Long Islander named Williams, down the Chagres River to Chagres. The river was no less safe than the trail, and stories were rife of organized bands attacking and robbing passing boats. Unexpectedly, one of the passengers produced several bottles of ale, kegs of claret, crackers, cheese, and tobacco. What could be more pleasurable, Bruff thought, than to drift downstream leisurely sipping on ale while admiring the luxuriant foliage on the banks as monkeys, macaws, and parrots clattered in the jungle? In the afternoon they reached Palenka, where a very small steamboat had come up from Chagres filled with women and children headed to California to join their husbands and fathers.

At dawn they reached Chagres, where Bruff encountered many old faces from the trail, some of whom had been robbed of their gold in the jungle. It was a sad and tragic ending for those who had invested so much time and effort in the quest for gold, only to lose it all on the last stage of their journey home.

In the wish to profit from the Gold Rushers, Americans had taken over Chagres and established bars, hotels, and restaurants with names like Davy Crockett and Jack of Clubs. Hotels, restaurants, even groceries all had roulette tables, and men who lingered too long in the town could soon lose their fortunes. In the afternoon Bruff bought a first-class ticket on the *Brother Jonathan*, bound for New York. When at last he arrived in New York, all his baggage had been stolen, save for his prized journals and drawings.

On July 20, 1851, Bruff departed Baltimore train station for Washington, DC. He had been gone two years and three months. During all that time, he had managed to avert disease, Indian attack, accident, starvation, even desertion in the High Sierras. Even though he had failed to realize his fortune, he had arrived with something as valuable to him as any gold: an account of his grand adventure and sketches of the American frontier. His final journal entry was bittersweet, mixing the elation of arriving home safely with disappointment in his failure to find fortune.

> *Never before did I so devoutly appreciate the heart-born ballad, "Home! Sweet home!" of my departed friend John Howard Payne, and none the less that I had "seen the elephant," and emphatically realized the meaning of the ancient myth - traveling in search of THE GOLDEN FLEECE!*

It would be Bruff's last and greatest adventure, its every moment now captured forever in his meticulously written record and copious drawings. His story would serve for him and for posterity as a reminder of the 49ers' great migration westward that year, not as the romantic adventure it was hoped to be, but one alloyed with moments of great beauty and tragic sorrow: the breathtaking panoramas of the American West, the shattered wagons and rotting carcasses, disease and death, Indians friendly and hostile, verdant prairies and parched deserts, trail friendships made and lost, and, unique among emigrants, Bruff's terrifying ordeal in the High Sierra winter. All would be forever etched in America's history and its ethos.

Bruff returned to his wife and two daughters—and to the Freemasons, becoming a Knight Templar in Washington Commandery Number One. In the lower front room of his large three-story brick residence on Capitol Hill, he created a museum containing all the artifacts he had collected during his travels: West Indian arrowheads, marine shells, obsidian from the Humboldt, stone axes from the Sierra, agate from the Platte, and other curios.

After several months knocking about in menial government jobs, Bruff received an appointment as draftsman in the Office of the Architect of the U.S. Treasury. There he was given a great deal of artistic freedom to design the ornamentation of the Treasury Headquarters' south and west wings and other Treasury buildings around the country. In 1853, he submitted the manuscript of his journey to Harper Publishers, which requested substantial revisions. With little time to spare, Bruff engaged an editor at the *New York Sun*, Dr. Richard Locke, a descendant of the British philosopher John Locke, to assist him. Locke was notorious for creating the "Moon Hoax," a story serially published in the paper alleging the discovery of lunar inhabitants, which had greatly boosted the *Sun*'s circulation. Although Locke did an excellent job revising Bruff's journal, the manuscript languished and was not published until 1909.

After a change in leadership in the Treasury, Bruff moved to the Treasury Register's office in 1869. The following month, he received a reappointment as draftsman in the Treasury's Architect Office where he served faithfully for the next 20 years.

After sixty years of government service, Joseph Goldsborough Bruff died quietly on April 14, 1889, shortly before 8 p.m., at his home on Capitol Hill. He was 84. The federal lodge of Masons handled his funeral arrangements. After a funeral conducted at the house by a Presbyterian minister and attended by many of his fellow Freemasons and representatives of the Oldest Inhabitants Association, he was interred near the Masonic Monument in the Congressional Cemetery. Today a plain small marker inscribed "Jos. Goldsborough Bruff, Died 1889" identifies the last resting place of the artist and adventurer.

To his final days, Bruff continued to refer to himself as "Captain."

THE CALIFORNIA GOLD RUSH PROVED TO BE A SALU-
brious event for the young United States of America. At a critical
moment in the nation's expansion, it hastened the opening of the
West and the building of the Continental Railroad. It spurred the
settlement and growth—indeed the very statehood—of California. It had pressured the nation to confront the issue of slavery in
the territories sooner than it might otherwise have. By the time the
madness ended in 1855, it had injected some $500 million into the
national economy. Of course, all of this would have come to pass
in the fullness of time; admittedly, gold discoveries rarely unfold in
an orderly manner.

For individual 49ers, however, the rush to fortune was a mixed
blessing at best. It was an event in which there were as many win-
ners as losers. In the quest for fortune, families were separated,
sometimes irreparably, and Argonauts endured hardships on the
trail unimaginable at home: extremes of weather, intense boredom,
fatigue, accident, Indian attack, disease, and death. Those who cir-
cumvented most of these dangers by traveling by ship would eventually confront them in the mining camps. In El Dorado, they

toiled mightily to tease gold from the earth while living in squalor, coping with homesickness, poor diet, and physical ailment, all the while gouged by predatory merchants. For every person who found enough gold to justify the journey, just as many failed to find so much as a single nugget and returned, if they returned at all, destitute and dispirited. Those who stayed usually did so because they either had nothing to return to or lacked the means to return. In a speech to the Society of California Pioneers in 1869, the historian John Hittell, himself a 49er, spoke for many when he declared, "none of the great battles of the late war broke so many heartstrings and caused such widespread pain as did the California migration."

Hittell was referring, of course, to gold seekers, but he might well have been speaking of the Native Americans. As the Sioux, Crow, and other tribes watched with consternation the tidal wave of whites wash over the Plains, little did they know that they were witnessing the beginning of the end. Soon they would be locked with whites in a death struggle for their homelands. By the end of the century, they would be decimated, impoverished, defeated, exiles in their own land.

More directly in the path of gold seekers were the peaceable Yahi of Deer Creek. As miners and settlers poured into the Sierras, the Yahi were simply in the way. One by one they were shot, hanged, or starved to death. At one point, a small group of frightened Yahi approached the settlers and submitted their bows and arrows in a gesture of peace. But when they saw one of the settlers hinging a rope to a tree, they absconded. Of the 3,000 Yahi living at Deer Creek when Bruff arrived, only 16 remained by 1871. With no other option, they went into hiding. They hunted only with bow and arrow and limited their cooking fires to small plumes of smoke. They collected acorns in summer, hopefully enough to tide them through the winter. To avoid being detected by whites when they traveled, they covered their tracks in the sand and waded up streams, even hopping from boulder to boulder to leave no trace of their movement. So effective were their stratagems that by 1870 many Californians believed the Yahi had died off. By 1884, with their best hunters having died off, they turned to raiding food stores and herds of the settlers. As white civilization continued to expand into the rugged foothills of the Sierras in the 1890s, the remaining half-dozen or so Yahi retreated into a narrow ledge 500 feet above the canyon. By 1908, only one remained. A team of surveyors from the local power company looking to build a dam on Deer Creek spotted a solitary Indian standing on a rock. Three years later Ishi turned up at a Sacramento slaughterhouse, emaciated and starving, the last wild Indian in North America.

To the *dramatis personae* in Bruff's story, the gold discovery brought mostly misfortune.

Peter Lassen has been described as "a singularly unfortunate man." In a lawsuit Lassen later brought against Wilson and Palmer, he claimed to have lost $100,000 in his dealings with them. The purchase of the steamer and supplies had put Lassen deeply in debt. By July 1852, he was forced to sell his interest in the ranch and his claim against Wilson for $25,000. A month later Wilson brought suit against Lassen claiming the sale was illegal. A year later, a court ruled in favor of Lassen. Thus had the two swindlers wrested from Lassen all the Danish pioneer had worked so hard to build. What Wilson and Palmer had not taken was stolen by emigrants, many of whom had benefitted from Lassen's hospitality in staying at the ranch.

A few years after the disaster on Lassen's Trail, it was abandoned as a feasible route to the gold fields for one much shorter called the Nobles Trail. Whether Lassen had intentionally misled emigrants into taking his trail will never be known for certain. If he had, he certainly had not anticipated the disastrous outcome. Whether justified or not, he endured opprobrium that he deceived emigrants into taking his trail that terrible winter of 1849. In any case, many Gold Rushers had threatened to kill him for his presumed duplicity, and Lassen eventually retreated to remote Honey Lake for his safety. Even though he never found Gold Lake, or much gold at all in the Sierras, Lassen refused to abandon his dream of a rich mineral strike. He prospected the entire Feather River valley, covering more territory than any other prospector. While some had made incredible gold discoveries there, Lassen found nothing. In 1854, while prospecting around Honey Lake, he found a modest amount of gold whose deposits were quickly exhausted. When another mining fever took hold in 1858, this time over silver in the Black Rock Range, Lassen went scrambling in search of it. The following year, while prospecting with two other men, he was killed under mysterious circumstances by Indians, or white men masquerading as Indians, meeting death near the very trail he had forged.

Whatever money General John Wilson made from swindling or his law practice seems not to have been enough. In 1853, he sent a letter to President Millard Fillmore seeking to be posted as Ambassador to China. "I need some office of the kind to support my family," he groused. Washington never responded to the letter. What he did for the next 20 years is unknown. Perhaps he had come to believe in his own grandiose tales. In a letter written to a friend in April 1852, he said:

All the amazing stories of the richness of our mineral resources that have ever reached you, no odds, how much they seem to be exaggerated, are as far below the truth as the hill you live on is below the Sierra mountains. The truth is, there is no known, or by man conceivable, limit. There is gold everywhere & in

every place. It is one of the prominent and abundant materials
of which our earth our rocks and our seashore are composed . . .
The intelligent man who has passed over these mountains . . .
has found it at almost every step he has taken; as I have done . . .

In 1877, Wilson died in San Francisco at the age of 87, having found no gold whatsoever.

For a time, John Frémont struck it rich. The 44,000-acre ranch he and his wife purchased on the Mariposa River turned out to be laden with gold, and he felt blessed by the Manifest Destiny he had so vigorously espoused. Yet it wasn't long before a hoard of gold seekers and squatters overran his ranch and began helping themselves to the gold. Frémont spent a decade in court fighting the squatters over rights to the land as well as the gold. By then the gold had run out. Eventually, he lost control of the ranch and squandered what gold he had earned on a misguided railroad venture. The Pathfinder of the Rockies died in New York nearly penniless in 1890.

One would have thought that at least men like John Sutter and James Marshall, having been in on gold's ground floor, had gotten rich. Shortly after gold was found at his mill, Sutter's Mormon and Indian employees quit working and headed off to hunt for gold. With no labor to work the mills and rancho, New Helvetia ground to a halt. Sutter had planned to form a gold mining company, but his ranch was quickly overrun with gold seekers and squatters who stole his property and destroyed his livestock. As Sutter watched all he had built become unraveled, he took to heavy drinking. When U.S. courts denied title to his 50,000-acre Mexican land grant, his ruin was nearly complete. When he whipped a soldier who had come to work for him for stealing, the soldier burned down the last thing he had left—his home. By 1852, he was bankrupt. In 1865, he moved east, eventually settling in Pennsylvania. He continued to seek redress from Congress for his loss of New Helvetia. While on a visit to Washington awaiting passage of a bill to provide him compensation for his land, he collapsed and died of a kidney ailment.

As for the man who started it all, James Marshall, bad luck hounded him to his grave. The sawmill he built cut logs for three years before miners diverted the American River and the mill stopped running. After a vineyard he invested in failed, Marshall returned to gold prospecting. Shouldering nothing more than his 40-pound backpack, he traipsed the Sierra hills living only on rice. In the late 1850s, he went into a gold partnership in a mine that yielded nothing and left him nearly bankrupt. For the rest of his life he drifted around California performing odd jobs, cleaning wells, sawing wood, and making gardens in return for board and his clothes. Even in old age he continued to search for gold. He died, forgotten and destitute, in a small cabin in 1885.

Although Joseph Goldsborough Bruff had also died destitute, he had fared well by comparison. After many near disasters on the trail, after nearly starving to death, he returned home safely to his family and righted his ship. He had produced one of the best and most detailed accounts of the "Great Migration," as he called it, and hundreds of sketches and watercolors of the American frontier of which he was justifiably proud. His Sierra ordeal had not permanently damaged his health and he lived to a ripe age. As a man who hovered on the margins of greatness but did not achieve it, he might have been gratified to know that like Lassen, Marshall, Sutter, and Frémont he would one day be commemorated in a memorial for the greatest of his accomplishments on the trail that year. In June 1984, the California Historical Association erected a stone marker at the site of Bruff's camp on Deer Creek. It has a bronze plaque that reads:

J.G. Bruff, leader of the Washington Gold Mining Company, camped at this site October 22, 1849 to December 31, 1849. While here guarding company goods, at what he called 'his Mt. Lodge in prosperity,' he aided, fed, and cheered many weary, hungry, and sick Emigrants struggling to the gold fields.

SELECTED BIBLIOGRAPHY

Bancroft, Hubert Howe. *History of California.* Vol . 6. San Francisco: The History Company, 1888.

Brands, H. W. *The Age of Gold.* New York: Random House, 2002.

Bruff, Joseph Goldsborough. *The Journals, Drawings, and Other Papers of J. Goldsborough Bruff,* ed. by Georgia Willis Read and Ruth Gaines. New York, Columbia University Press, 1949.

Cook, Sherburne F. *The Conflict between the California Indian and White Civilization, III The American Invasion, 1848–1870.* University of California Publications in Ibero-Americana, 23. Berkeley: University of California Press, 1943.

Frémont, John Charles. *The Exploring Expedition to the Rocky Mountains, Oregon and California in the Years 1843–44.* Washington, D.C.: U.S. Army Corps of Engineers, 1845.

Holliday, J .S. *The World Rushed In: The California Gold Rush Experience.* New York: Simon and Schuster, 1981.

James, H. L. *Bruff's Wake: J. Goldsborough Bruff and the California Gold Rush, 1849–1851.* Independence, Missouri, Oregon-California Trails Association, 2011.

Johnston, Ken. *Legendary Truths: Peter Lassen and His Gold Rush Trail in Fact and Fable.* Greybull, WY: Pronghorn Press, 2012.

Lasalle, Michael. *Emigrants on the Overland Trail. The Wagon Trains of 1848.*

Meldahl, Keith Heyer. *Hard Road West: History and Geology along the Gold Rush Trail.* Chicago: University of Chicago Press, 2008.

Parkman, Francis. *The Oregon Trail.* Doubleday and Company, Garden City, NY, 1946.

INDEX